ACKNOWLEDGMENTS

My heartfelt thanks to Sam Pack and my dearest friend, Frances Turella, without whom I could never have made the trek with the "Cattle Drive of 95." To my children, who have always supported me in all my endeavors, and whose love has been my strength and stability in all things. To Drs Carl Shrader and Jeffrey De Lotto, my professors at *Texas Wesleyan University*, who taught me the true power of words. To my editor, Dr. Fred Tarpley, and my publisher, Jim Ainsworth, who have placed their bets on this old gray mare. And to all my fans through the years who have always made me believe I could do anything I attempted. I salute you all.

DEDICATION

For Sandy Louan Manning, who has been my primary motivator, critic, and fan since the very beginning. . . .

FOREWORD

By Mike Cochran

Before dawn on a simmering July morning in 1995, Annie Golightly, giddy with anticipation, rode a horse called Gus along the storied North Platte River and down the quiet streets of an eastern Nebraska town called Henry. Their ultimate destination: Miles City, Montana, the culmination of a historic journey across Midwestern America with nearly 300 Longhorns and 109 head of horses in tow. Their immediate destination: Wyoming, the fulfillment of a little girl's lifelong dream.

At sunrise that July morning, the raven-haired rider and her sleek white mount crossed the state line and were greeted by a sign: "Wyoming, Like No Place On Earth." Wyoming! For Annie Milford Smith Golightly, nothing struck closer to home or heart.

As you'll discover via her scruffy eloquence, a blend of blunt candor and mischievous subtlety, Annie's a dreamer -- one who dreams, sings, paints, lives, and loves in Technicolor.

And her personal adventures and misadventures are every bit as compelling as the Great American Cattle Drive of 1995 she chronicles in *Dreams and a White Horse.*

"When I was a child," she writes of growing up on an East Texas farm, "going to town on Saturday nights and seeing the picture show was second only to Christmas. The Lone Ranger, Roy Rogers, Gene Autry, the Cisco Kid and Lash LaRue roamed the canyons and foothills of Wyoming, chasing the bandits and Indians and all the bad guys."

Wyoming, she rhapsodized, was magical, a world away from the cotton fields surrounding the home where she grew up near Commerce, a small town northeast of Dallas known originally as Cow Hill. "Expressing the feeling I had crossing into Wyoming is difficult," she writes. "It was the land of beautiful horses and mountains that reached to the sky, and those exciting creatures who carried six-guns, rode the fastest horses alive on saddles that sparkled with silver conchos, swung wide loops, and always got their man before riding off into a Wyoming sunset."

It was a place of emotional escape, she said, first as a child and later as a survivor: a once-divorced, twice-widowed mother raising five children as a guitar-picking and singing bartender, barrel racer, cow roper, professional entertainer, nightclub owner, songwriter, artist, and realtor. "It was a place I could escape to when life was boring or unbearable, and pretend that I, too, was riding with the wind blowing in my face, hair blowing free, my pony's belly low with his feet flying, gaining on and passing those cowboys who rode with me."

Wyoming, she said, simply, "made me feel giddy and young and very much alive."

Countless North Texans fortunate enough to hear her perform experienced similar emotions. Said the late Jim Trinkle, a columnist at the *Fort Worth Star-Telegram*: "There is a happy, vibrant quality to songs as Annie sings them. Audiences...are moved by her personal magnetism, and by subtle phrasing that changes from joyous to thoughtful to whimsical to solemn, almost in the same breath." The same might be said about her writing.

Tall and lean with jet black hair, dark eyes, brown skin and chiseled cheekbones, Annie's Indian heritage is inescapable. "My father was Cherokee and my mother German and I grew up wearing a vest and jeans and boots and smokin' cigars and ridin' a horse to school. Back then, they thought that was kind of strange... I guess I've been called kookie all my life." A Milford at birth, she became a Smith by marriage and a Golightly by whim: "It's a beautiful name, it's Injun, and, hell, nobody could remember Ann Smith. Even me."

On the flip side, her brother, Dale Milford, was decidedly more conventional and became a U.S. Congressman. Says Annie: "He was a real gentleman. I don't know how the hell he got mixed up in politics!"

◆ ◆ ◆ ◆

For nearly 30 years, North Texans called Annie the "Singing Savage," and they called her often. "With a song in her heart," a Fort Worth reporter once observed, "she fled an East Texas cotton farm to perform for the likes of Tom T. Hall, Rex Allen and Rosemary Clooney. She sang for Lyndon Johnson and Jimmy Carter and the presidents of Panama and Argentina. For Arnold Palmer and Nelson Rockefeller, Gene Autry and Roy Rogers, Slim Pickens and Chuck Connors, Gov. John Connally and wife Nellie.

"And for you and me."

When she first heard about the cattle drive, Annie was a 63-year-old honor student working on her Bachelor of Arts degree in English and creative writing at Texas Wesleyan University in Fort Worth.

Why, one might ask, would she defy cattle-drive sponsors and drovers -- and Father Time – to join 30 cowboys on a trek that in her own words exposed her to rain, sleet, hail, high winds, a tornado, extreme heat and cold—not to mention dissension, homesickness, boredom, frustration, disappointments, and misunderstandings? What's more, she was the only woman and the oldest person on the six-month, roughly seventeen hundred-mile excursion from Texas to Montana.

Declaring it her "destiny," Annie knew she was going the moment they informed her that they weren't taking women, but that she could join them from time to time and entertain at rodeos along the way.

"I can't tell you why but it was always a dream of mine to ride a horse across the Northwest," Annie told the Hood County News in Granbury, Texas. "I wanted to go all the way and write a book about it. They told me they weren't taking any women and that's when I knew without a doubt I was gonna go."

Once on the trail, and writing periodically for *Texas Longhorn Magazine,* Annie elaborated on her motivations: "I am going because for 63 years I have loved cowboys. Nothing gives me the exhilarating feeling like the sight of a big silver-belly, black, or brown Stetson with that old cow-track crease, coming at me across the street, arena, in the rear view mirror in a truck, on a horse or upon a fence—giving shade to a cowboy."

Also, she added, she was going because she "loves the wide open spaces, the smell and sound of creaking leather, the clop clop and shuffle of God's four-legged creatures, and the sense of freedom that being out in the elements -- without the need of telephone, calendar, or watch -- lends to her civilized and disciplined life."

And, finally, she said:

"I am going because my children and friends and fans ... believe me to be a bit crazy and a whole lot eccentric, which is fuel for my energy, hopes and self-esteem."

So hop atop old Gus and come along with Annie for a ride and a read you'll never regret ...or forget.

◆ ◆ ◆ ◆

Mike Cochran is retired from the Associated Press and the Fort Worth Star-Telegram. He spent almost four decades roaming Texas, uncovering its unusual stories, interviewing offbeat characters, and reporting on the state's darkest crimes and deepest secrets. The result has not only been thousands of articles, but at least four—soon to be five—books. Thrice nominated for the Pulitzer Prize, he is a Distinguished Alum of the University of North Texas, winner of six Headliner awards, Texas Institute of Letters Stanley Walker Journalism Award (twice), and is a member of the Texas Intercollegiate Hall of Fame.

INTRODUCTION

Join me on a journey, topside a white horse, following almost three hundred head of Texas' legendary longhorn cattle for approximately eighteen hundred miles. A trip back in time, over parts of the cattle trails carved out of the wilderness and the vast prairies—trails blazed by Charles Goodnight, Oliver Loving, and John Chisum, along with the young cowboys, outlaws, desperados, and ne'er-do-wells who carved out the history of the American West. This is a story experienced in 1995, by a group of thirty young cowboys from across six states and one sixty-four-year-old woman, who blazed the trail 109 years after those nineteenth century cowboys, battling miles of asphalt, automobiles, trucks, trains, masses of people and the worst and wettest year since weather reporting began.

This is an epic tale about a woman with a vagabond heart and a fifty-nine-year-old dream, searching for her place in the sun, riding a white horse named Gus, who carried her with grace, dignity, and loyalty through rain, mud, tornado, sleet, bitter cold, wind, glorious sunshine, and glory, in the realization of that dream.

You will meet the unforgettable people along the trail who supported, hugged, fed, entertained and prayed for the riders. See the raw beauty, feel Mother Nature's wrath, bask in the splendor and vastness of the mountains, prairies, rivers, and creatures along the trail, while sucking up the sounds of nature, smelling the wildflowers, tasting clean, spring water, and witnessing a dream fulfilled.

The interpretation of character in this book is my own entirely, and my intentions were never to influence those of the reader. Many events and fellow riders are absent due to lack of detail, clarity, and for brevity's sake. Several of the cowboys and members of the drive I never knew well, or had only scant relationship with. That is not to say they were minor participants; just that I was never directly involved with them.

Central among those you will meet are:

Bud McCasland, 49, Texas, drive foreman, former executive with Southwestern Bell, father of a son, and daughter.
Walt Secrest, 62, Montana, chuck wagon driver, married, brings five longhorns to the drive.
Will Miltimore, 56, Oklahoma, cowboy, father and husband.
Jim Donaldson, 29, Oklahoma, cowboy, welder and corral builder and wild hog hunter, also brought three longhorns for the drive.
Claude Voiles, 47, Wyoming cowboy, single, cowboy, has one son and a daughter.
Jim Hook, 44, father of Jodie, 23 (also on the drive), Texas cowboy and husband to Colleen.
Dick Kennedy, 49, Nebraska cowboy, cattleman, and husband to Diane.
JW Beeson, 44, Oklahoma, single cowboy, poet, singer, saddle maker, and father of one son.
Charles (Ace) Wright, 55, Montana, father of two daughters, rancher, trucker, and salesman.
Gloria Shaefer, Texas, independent sponsor of the drive, widow, and frequent rider on the trail.
Jamie Nail, 24, cowboy, heir to the famous Nail ranch, Albany, Texas.
Skip Nelson, photographer, father to two sons and two daughters, native of St. Paul, Minnesota.
Derk Hansen, artist/painter, partner to Skip, from St. Paul, Minnesota.

By the time I reached my teens, I knew what I wanted to be. I believed that I would make a great bum. Well, some call bums Gypsies or vagabonds or nomads. Names are multifaceted and subjective. Bums are like that. I wanted to ride around the country, down dirt roads, wandering, meeting people; maybe finding work in some little café in some little town, to buy food and horse feed. If I failed to get that job, I could build fences or drive a tractor, or fry cook in some Toddle House for awhile, then move on. I could sing for my supper, paint pictures of wild creatures and two-legged crazies, while being responsible for no one but myself and my horse; fishing in rivers and sleeping on the earth under the stars. Well, that didn't exactly work out. . . .

Annie Golightly

Dreams and a White Horse

Annie Golightly

1

FORT WORTH, TEXAS – MARCH 5, 1995

The day was cold. The kind of cold that seeps through your clothes like water seeps through cracks where nothing else can go. The air was thick with icy moisture that bit through exposed skin leaving chills covering my body, in spite of my goose down jacket. The sky was gray and clouds hung low overhead, attempting to put a damper on the crowd gathered there for the special occasion. It was only minutes before the beginning of the Great American Cattle Drive at Mule Alley in the stockyards in North Fort Worth, Texas. It was 7 a.m., the fifth of March, 1995.

We were headed for Montana with nearly 300 head of Texas longhorns. This monumental undertaking was the offspring of Texas-born Bud McCasland, who dreamed of driving a herd along parts of five of the old nineteenth century cattle trails.

I learned of the drive in July, 1994 when I was asked to join in the drive and perform in the ranch rodeos at each state celebration along the way, as well as the championship rodeo in Montana to climax the drive. I needed no persuasion to make the decision to go. I was currently working on my Bachelor of Arts degree at Texas Wesleyan University, and would be graduating in December of 1994. The cattle drive was scheduled to leave March 1995. Perfect.

"You bet I will sing, but I want to go, to work as a drover. I want to be there each and every day and I will write a book about the drive." Jamie McClain, a big handsome cowboy who had approached me about singing, smiled and hugged me and declined by telling me they were taking no working women on the drive. I am sure that he took one look at my sixty-three-year-old carcass and thought of old Captain Gus McCrae, being hauled back to Texas in that wagon to fulfill the promise made by his friend, Captain Woodrow Call, to bury McCrae on Texas soil (*Lonesome Dove.*) But I knew even then that absolutely nothing would stop me from going on that cattle drive. Every electrical circuit in my body was switched on. I was in good health, unencumbered, tired of the entertainment business that I had been in for almost three decades, but still enthusiastic about living. And here was an opportunity to realize that fifty-five-year-old dream of riding a horse across the Northwest. I knew that I would do everything in my power to help make the cattle drive a success and my dream a reality. I immediately began making plans to change Bud McCasland's mind about taking no working women on the drive.

It would be months before I was told for sure that I could go. Bud McCasland was evasive each time I asked him. But out of the blue one day he said, "Of course, you are going. I am making the decision, and whatever the investors have to say about it, I will have the last word." I didn't quite understand, but I certainly did not question. I was too excited. I had been ready to sell my soul to hell to go on that cattle drive. Jamie McClain, trail boss, came out of his office and hugged me; the same cowboy who had told me at the rodeo that they were taking no women on the drive.

"Annie, you'll never have to sleep on the ground, and you will have laundry facilities, your own locker and shower, and privacy. You will be one of us," Jamie said.

I would wait for a convenient time to doubt my ability to make the drive. I didn't quite know how it would happen; that part would come later. I was sure that I was ready at that moment. However, no amount of planning, imagining, or dreaming could have prepared me for the experience that awaited me. During the next six months, we rode approximately eighteen hundred miles.

We drove 262 head of longhorn steers and 109 head of horses from Fort Worth, Texas, to Miles city, Montana, for the first time in almost 120 years.

The appointed drovers, wranglers, and those who would drive the trucks, vans, and equipment, had gathered in the stockyards. They came from Custer's Battlefield, Montana to Cheyenne, Wyoming; from the prairies, ranches, and cities in Texas to the red sands of Oklahoma and the wheat fields of Kansas and Nebraska. They were the echoes and images and reincarnations of a breed of man whose tracks are still clear and distinct, the men whose grit and stamina carved the West one hundred and fifty years ago and left a legacy second to none - the American Cowboy. They were turning back the pages of time and bringing history to thousands who would otherwise never experience the thrill of seeing a herd of longhorns driven over sixteen hundred miles through the asphalt jungle, down county roads, through small towns for all to see and feel and re-live the Western History of America. Thirty cowboys and me.

The working horses and Texas longhorn steers were well-behaved and rather unconcerned. Country ponies brought to town to join the drive for a day or two were excited and fractious. Children carrying huge balloons peeked through the iron bar fence surrounding the holding pens, in awe of the longhorns. The older generation stood quietly by, some possibly picturing the months that lay ahead for us, and some feeling pangs of envy but also doubt that we would ever make it to Montana. Wagons were parked amid portable smokers as the smell of barbecue drifted among the hundreds gathered there. Many of the locals and cooking fanciers from out of town had gathered to compete in a barbecue cook-off during all the festivities for our leaving. New boots waded through the wet and sometimes muddy grass. Gala western outfits wrapped around women brought bright colors into the murky morning. As I gazed at the celebration, I remembered so many years from the past to another time and event. . . .

◆ ◆ ◆ ◆

It was 1936, and I was five years old and caught up in all the sights and sounds of carnival and circus and sideshows at the Texas Centennial in Dallas Texas.

The elephants caught my eye first. But the beautiful dapple-gray horses prancing around the ring absolutely enveloped my small being. I was there with the acrobats performing feats on those magnificent animals. I could smell the horses, and I still love that smell today. Clowns were everywhere, and I saw and heard a calliope for the first time. I was caught up in such excitement, I never wanted to move. I just sat on my Uncle Mack's shoulder in dumbstruck wonder. Mack was my uncle because he was married to my daddy's sister, Ethel, whose name a cousin had pronounced Lettie, and that name had remained.

I called them Mack, Lettie, and my paternal grandmother, Ma. In the spring of 1932, when our mother died, my brother, Dale, and I went to live with them in the old clapboard house that my grandfather Milford had built in 1876 to replace a dirt-bottom log cabin. I was eighteen months old and the youngest of three. For reasons I never knew, my sister, Frances, went to live with Aunt Kate and Uncle Cecil. My uncle Mack became my best friend, and the love of my life.

Sitting on a horse in Mule Alley, waiting to depart on a new adventure, I felt like that child again. *Mack, how I wish you could be here now. You would love all this. Your little girl is embarking on the adventure of her life, and I can't even share it with you.*

◆ ◆ ◆ ◆

I became aware of how my new saddle creaked, and Gus, my White Horse, felt tense under me until I realized it wasn't Gus but me who was drawn up in a knot, partly from cold but mostly from pure excitement. I patted him on his neck, more to reassure myself than him. It felt good just to touch him. I named him Gus because he had a perfect mustache – just like Captain Gus McCrae.

I looked across again at the hordes of people, wagons, animals, bands, balloons, and the activity and realized that it was all really happening. *This is now. This ain't no circus or carnival or centennial. This is now and here I am, going to Montana for real!* I felt pangs of doubt, excitement, anticipation, and bravado. This furnished adrenaline for the hours of sweet agony that I was to experience on the way to the first camp. Many of my close friends were there to wish me well. My son, Kenny, my granddaughter, Amy, and my old buddy Red Wilkins were there. We hugged and laughed, and Red gave me a pair of doeskin gloves, which I wore every day of the drive. My big beautiful son gathered me up in those long arms, looked down at me, and said, "Mama, I love you so much, and I am so damned proud of you and the things you have accomplished in your life. I think you are the greatest woman in the world, and the craziest female living for going on this drive, but you do your thing so well."

My son had come along, the delightful "end gate," after four girls who doted on him. I, the tomboy, who thought I could never have anything but boys, finally had one. In a fog, after his delivery, I remember the doctor saying, "Annie, you finally got one with a tallywhacker!"

Kenny defied the age-old pattern of the youngest child being spoiled, and he grew up to become a gentle, altruistic giant. He was three when his father was killed with two friends in a one-car accident. His life has been spent in a house of women who cheered him on football and baseball fields and basketball courts. He is a hard-working, idealistic leader, dreamer, laugher, and thinker who drives the speed limit, returns books and records, loves his best girl, his family, friends, the Sunday paper, two pillows, sports, and Garfield. He is heavy into jazz music, community, charities, public service, Ford trucks, and his cat, Frisco. He is also my best friend. He stood there beside me, holding my hand, proud to be a part of our send-off in the stockyards of Fort Worth, Texas.

The Great American Cattle Drive was my kind of thing, my

destiny. I felt compelled to make that trip. I was making plans before I ever inquired about the possibility or improbability of my going. It was like looking down at the last two or three pieces of a puzzle that I had been working on all my life. I was mother, grandmother, great grandmother, and had been branded "living legend" in the Metroplex. I had buried two husbands, raised five awesome kids alone, survived a flood that destroyed my home, overcome a business venture which cost me a quarter of a million dollars, and then lost everything that was left in a fire.

Now, new horizons awaited me. I never thought for a moment that something or somebody would stop my going. I had no thought of age, health, or anything else that might get in my way.

I once wrote a song that began, "I believe in fairy tales, I throw coins in wishing wells, I believe if you believe, your dreams will all come true." I believe that without dreams, we become sterile and innocuous. Dreams are manna to purge lethargy from the soul, foundations for accomplishments and fulfillments, and the spices in the blah soups of life. Every minute of my childhood was spent in some fantasy land cooked up in my mind. The cattle drive was a fantasy becoming a reality, and once again, the moment brought back memories of real adventure in my chaotic childhood carved out of ordinary days. . . .

◆ ◆ ◆ ◆

Carl Thomas' old dish-faced horse, Rusty, behaved as if he consumed a steady diet of loco weed. I rode the school bus to Carl's house, saddled Rusty, and beat the bus to school seven miles away. By the time Lettie found out, the school year was half over, and Rusty had only reared and fallen backwards with me on concrete once or twice.

"Thet crazy horse of Carl's izza gonna kill Little Mack one of these days for sure," John Hardin, our neighbor and close friend, used to say. Robert West ran the horse and mule barn in the small town of Ladonia, six miles north of us. He would take me out to his pasture and catch his half-Shetland pony for me to ride. Robert was just one of my "heroes," as was Cecil Haynes, who would let me keep his little mare, Tootsie, for weeks at a time and ride her. She was small and fast and wore a bridle without blinders on it.

On wash days, Lettie would put me on Rhody, one of Mack's mules, and the mule would wander around the yard and by the side of the country road, grazing, without bridle or rope, her two-year-old passenger topside and content and out from underfoot. Lettie and Ma would build a fire under the huge black wash pot, draw water out of the well, and fill the tubs for washing, with little thought for me, knowing I was safe on Rhody. Those days were spent loving God's hairy four-legged creatures and the joy of riding. Rhody had become a beautiful white horse I called Gus, and it was 1995.

2

HEAD 'EM UP AND MOVE 'EM OUT

The holding pens were opened, the longhorns herded out, and we paraded past hundreds of well-wishers standing and waving along narrow Exchange Avenue, turned up North Main Street, and headed out Marine Creek Parkway, winding through the country toward Coburn farms and our first camp. A cold, dreary, fine mist was falling. I was wrestling with my new stirrup straps, which were not yet trained, and still pointed south while my knees were pointed north. My hat was not yet "set" to my head, and the stiff chaps felt awkward and heavy against my legs. But no amount of pain and discomfort could dampen my soaring spirits. I was a kid again, riding with the cowboys at the Saturday movies – only this time for real! I was on my very own white steed, headed for the mountains and canyons of my dreams. The lump in my throat was as big as a Texas grapefruit, and with hot tears running down my cheeks mingling with the cold raindrops, I wanted so much to see Mack's face out there in the crowd. I wanted my husband too. I wanted to share the moment with the two men I had loved most in my life, and for them to see me, and be proud.

Hey! Maybe they can! I shook myself, sat taller in my saddle, and rode on in the rain. Even the litter along the highway seemed to be trying to drape a pall on my soul. I couldn't help noticing and being amazed at the tons of glass, cans, tires, furniture, and all manner of trash littering the shoulders of the road. It was foreboding and foreign in contrast to the creaking of saddle leather, the rattling of wagon wheels, and the rhythmic beat of steel horseshoes on asphalt. I resented all that trash of uncaring humanity. It was a blemish on my dream. It was like finding graffiti on a beautiful wall.

Inside me was a never-before-experienced fear of being thrown or falling off my horse and making a fool of myself in front of those cowboys and the people we passed along the way. The years had dimmed the confidence topside a horse. Doubts were creeping up, and for the first time, I wondered about whether I could hold up to the months ahead and if my health would continue to be as good as it was then. I remembered joking with a friend and saying that I just might end up being brought back to Texas in a wagon like Gus McCrae, to be buried in Texas soil. Doubts are just a few of the liabilities that come with growing older. The slippery asphalt tied my gut in a nervous knot. I had not ridden Gus long enough to really know him and to trust his ability to stand up on hazardous trails. The trust in a good horse is more important than his breed or conformation. Suddenly, I had a picture of one unforgettable horse that I had ridden in the past. . . .

◆ ◆ ◆ ◆

I rode Roy Savage's black gelding, Midnite, in barrel races and play days in the early sixties. Roy had a dairy up the road from Kenneth and me when we lived in the country, and the gelding was his roping horse. Midnite was big and powerful and agile as a cat. I trusted him completely. He would bank so far going around the barrels that my boot would drag a furrow in the sand. I would "lean" on him with no fear of his falling. What a glorious feeling that was. It would be only days before I felt that same trust with Gus.

◆ ◆ ◆ ◆

My fears were intensified when the first of three horses went down within a few feet of me. Dancer Davis was riding on my left, and suddenly his skittish horse went over backward and slammed on his side, throwing Davis free. Moments later, Walker Lawrence's palomino lost his balance when his hind feet slipped. The horse tried in vain to regain his foothold but ended up skinning hide and hair to the bone on his hocks and knees. Walker, a Texan and the youngest member of the crew, was bruised and later complained with sore back and shoulder. When the third horse went down, it almost took Gus with him. By this time, I was so scared, that I retired to the shoulder of the highway. I felt safer, even though it was harder to travel in the mud and glass and debris. A cowboy rode up from the herd to tell us that several of the outriders had also fallen on the wet pavement. In spite of it all, I was light-headed and giddy with excitement.

In camp, there was confusion again. The huge trailer where we were to store our tents, sleeping bags, clothes, duffle bags, and toiletries was without partitions, shelves, or racks. There were none of the private lockers that had been promised. Everything was in a jumbled pile, with all of us digging, stomping, or crawling over and under the mass of equipment looking for our belongings. Sometime during my unbridled life, I acquired a liking for a certain amount of organization. Unannounced visitors to my house might find clutter; however, my closets and cabinets were and are always organized and neat. I have a place for everything. It was quite possibly not the taste of interior decorators, but it was in order.

While searching for my gear, I met Gloria Shaefer. Her short, plump frame looked out of character in cowboy clothes. She was plowing around in all the debris, too. Gloria was one of the private investors for the drive. The tack trailer produced a different type of confusion. Racks had been built for saddles and hangers for bridles and halters. The problem was too many racks for the amount of space and not enough room to hang saddles and not enough hooks for the bridles and halters.

Mack would never put up with this mess. His barn had a special stall for the harness used on the draft animals. By the time I could climb on a box and stand on tiptoes and reach that harness, I knew which collar, bridle, and set of hames fit which horse. I learned to harness and drive those horses long before I started to school, and I was quick to remind the men who sometimes worked for Mack to keep the tack room neat. There was a box on the wall for the curry comb and brush. That box was also where Mack hid his whiskey from Lettie. He was adamant about the harness always being put in its proper place and hung straight, and he was always thankful when I brought him his bottle the morning after a drunk.

I chuckled with contentment as I shook myself back to the present, and my thoughts drifted back over the days of preparation for the magical first day of the Great American Cattle Drive. . . .

◆ ◆ ◆ ◆

Even before Bud McCasland gave me the okay to go on the drive, I had begun calling on friends for financial help. I didn't have to go far. Sam Pack, close friend and the owner of two Ford dealerships in the Fort Worth-Dallas Metroplex, and another friend who wished to remain anonymous, furnished the money for two horses, a laptop computer, printer, tack, and my other needs for six months on the trail. Bobby Platt, owner and operator of Sammie's Barbecue in Fort Worth, where I had performed many times, gave me an Omar tent; my pint-sized buddy, Margaret Bean, bought my bedroll; and Jim Taylor, at Luskey's Western Wear Store, gave me a great discount on my tack. Without those friends and their generosity, I could not have gone on the cattle drive.

First, I began looking for horses. I found Gus quickly. Big, white, and easy on the eyes, he stood peering over a pasture fence as I drove by. When I stopped, he came over and touched my outstretched hand with his velvet muzzle. I was hooked on that sweet, friendly horse.

I'll bet the guy who owns this horse won't sell him for any price, but I am sure as heck gonna find out. The sign said "Charlie Tidwell's Racing Stables." Charlie used Gus for ponying young race horses. With crossed fingers and a silent prayer, I drove up the paved road to a neat white barn with paddocks and stalls. The beautiful hairy thief who had stolen my heart confirmed my suspicions that he was great when I saddled and rode him. I did not quibble over Charlie's price.

Red, on the other hand, was not so easy to find. I drove some two thousand miles and rode many horses, mostly in mud, before finding the red dun horse that I liked upon sight. Line-backed, with not a white hair on him, Red's conformation was flawless. In contrast to Gus's childlike friendliness and desire to please, Red was all business and performed under saddle like a champion who was bred to "cow." From the moment those two horses were put together, they were inseparable friends. Red was the aggressor, even though Gus outweighed him by three hundred pounds. They were both healthy, sound as a dollar, and without any bad habits.

Early on a Monday morning, I went to the cattle drive offices to see if there was anything I could do to help with preparations. Bud was always on the phone. He seldom was without his hat and a jaw filled with tobacco. His shirt and jeans were always starched and neat. He was friendly and sometimes a bit vague. His girlfriend was usually on the other phone, talking in a voice cold enough to chill an Eskimo. There was no warmth in those offices, no camaraderie, no electricity in the air or the feeling of a team working to make something unbelievably great happen, to write a new page in history. I baked bread and coffee cakes and brought them with me two mornings in the hope of providing that something that I missed. Days later, I saw them still sitting on a small table, some eaten and the rest left uncovered and stale. My offers to help were ignored or patronizingly turned down.

I would have mopped the office each day if it had put me closer to being a part of the preparation. My offers to help were ignored or brushed off. Nothing was needed; everything was being taken care of. On one rare occasion when I had an audience with Bud I ventured, "Bud, I have entertained people who have so much money they help others and look for write-offs and such. I will be glad to talk to and introduce you to some of these people if the drive needs sponsors or investors. Also, I have had a great rapport with the media because of my years as an entertainer, and I would be available to make contact with them or do any public relations that might be needed." In a patronizing voice, he assured me that no money was needed and that meeting the press was all being handled by him and Susan, his girlfriend. I had the feeling, even then, that no "outsiders" were wanted in the operation of the drive, that he and Susan wanted no help other than in the physical aspect of the drive. My enthusiasm was dampened, and wanting to give all to whatever I was involved in, I couldn't help feeling lonely and apart from the preparations.

To me, the "doing" is the icing on any project cake. I was the principal instigator of annual parties for the old folks at Christmas for many years. When we had our Christmas party at my little club In Fort Worth, we raised the money and later had Christmas for the elderly, complete with music, turkey and dressing, gifts, and a tree. The work, preparations, and the hours spent cooking turkeys and the trimmings were among the happiest of my life. I handled the money, bought the gifts, did the bulk of the cooking, sang, and delegated a lot of the work to the willing help of my fans and customers. People only need a little gouge in the ribs, and they jump through their butts to give to others. One year, when the economy was not the best, I raffled off my Lincoln automobile to raise money. We *really* had great gifts and food that year. It was partially selfish on my part. I will always believe I got much more out of those occasions than the elderly did. I wanted that for this cattle drive.

Applicants were interviewed for the twenty-five positions of drovers, wranglers, and equipment drivers. These cowboys were to come from the six states covered during the drive. Those states were Texas, Oklahoma, Kansas, Nebraska, Wyoming, and Montana. I met Ace Wright in Bud's office. Ace was a tall, rugged-looking man in high-topped boots, red bandana, and wide-brimmed Stetson. He was from Bozeman, Montana, and had been hired as a drover. He came to Fort Worth to help with preparations for the drive and to take care of the longhorns gathered and kept in a pasture at Blue Mound, just north of Fort Worth. I liked him and his straightforward manner. He was personable, teased me about my ostrich boots, implying that I was rich, and gave me a tape of a radio interview about his being chosen to go on the cattle drive. It profiled a fifty-five-year-old man who was educated, practical, a realist and adventurer, and possibly a bit of a cynic about women.

He was divorced and had two daughters living in Dallas and Houston whom he visited frequently. My relationship with Ace never changed throughout the drive. In typical cowboy fashion, he was most often distant, but on rare occasions, he would be the first to say good morning. He never bantered with nor teased me again.

I met Walt Secrest in Bud's office. He was an older man (only months younger than I) with a shaggy mustache, piercing black eyes, big strong hands, and a tall, slumped figure. The epitome of cowboy, he spoke quietly and almost humbly, but something about his demeanor told me that he was neither quiet nor humble. Walt brought five longhorns for the drive with him from his ranch in Hardin, Montana, where he lived with his wife, Maurine (Renny). He also brought a chuck wagon on a flatbed trailer, a ten-horse Black Shire hitch, big, powerful draft horses, descendants of the war horses in England in the Middle Ages. He would be driving our chuck wagon on the drive, and his wagon would be carried along as a "spare".

Walt and Renny ran a tourist-western store at Custer's Battlefield, Montana, and two ranches where they raised horses and longhorn and Angus cattle. He told the cattle drive reporter that he built wagons and furnished horses for Hollywood movies, including those used in *Lonesome Dove.* Walt also worked as pickup man in rodeos for thirty years. At sixty-two, an age when most retire, he was excited about embarking on a new adventure. He exuded power and control. *I'll bet he is one tough hombre and used to giving orders and being obeyed. He looks like he could sit a saddle deep and handle horses easily. I can't wait to see him drive those big black horses.* My intuition proved to be well founded. Walt Secrest was to alter the outcome of the drive, probably more than any other single man or event, with the exception of Bud.

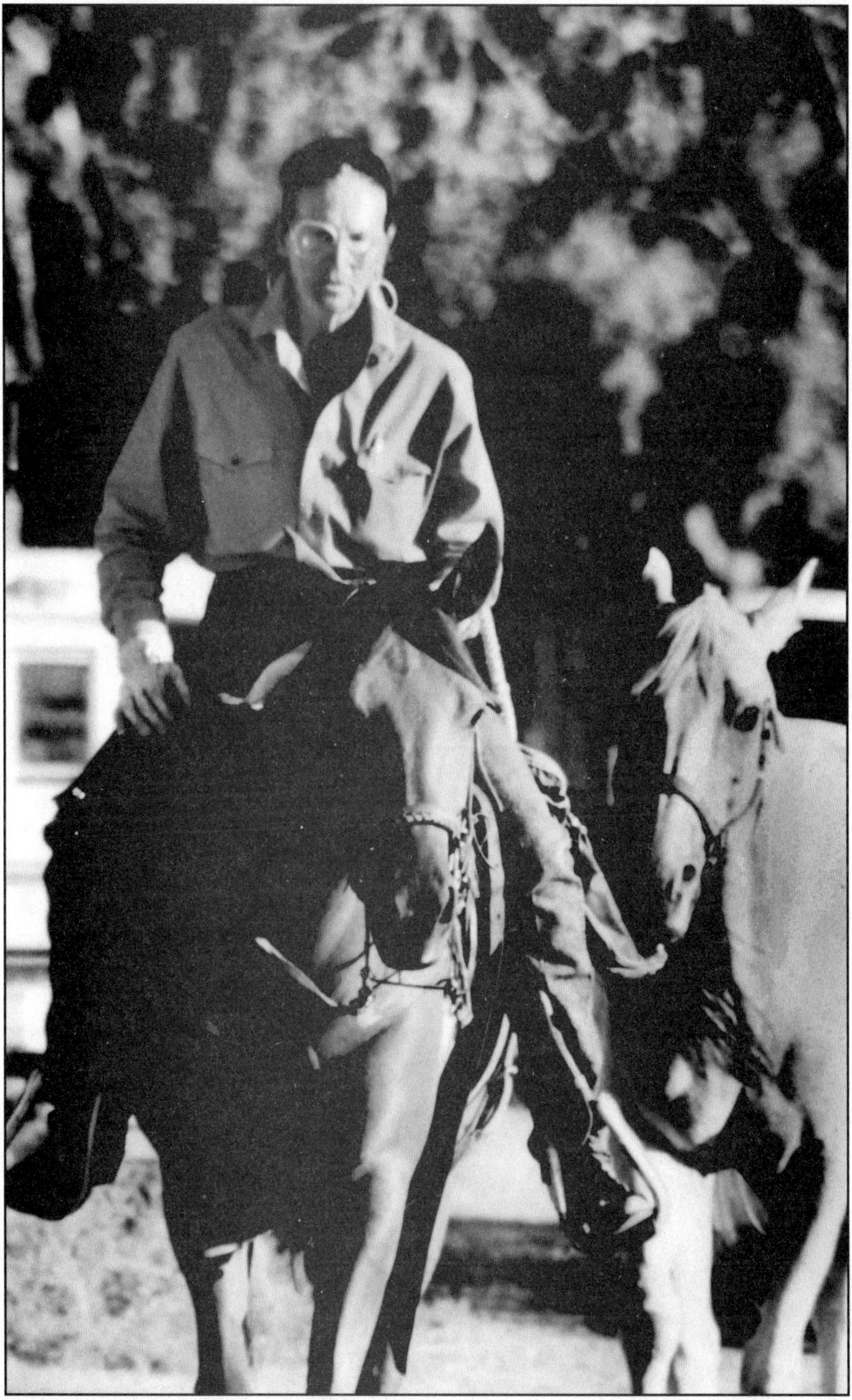

3

YESTERDAY'S MEMORIES, TODAY'S ANXIETIES AND DISAPPOINTMENTS

At no time in my life have I been tagged as being conventional in action, deed, or emotion. If reactions to my so-called antics were put before life's panel, I would be branded as different. However, some of life's realities were too tough to change, even for me. I stopped praying to God or Mother Nature or whoever was in charge, to turn me into a boy when I was nine. Ma hated girls, and besides I looked more like a boy than I did a girl. My legs were too long, my feet were too big, and I seemed to be all elbows, skinned knees, and bones.

The first fifteen years of my life were spent alternately sitting in a dentist's chair or puking in an old porcelain slop jar through rotten tonsils and a spastic stomach. When I was eleven, some old quack doctor in Greenville cut out the tonsils, and some of the retching ceased. I was always anemic, and Lettie gave me dark, thick, liquid iron from a tablespoon and it slowly turned my teeth yellow and crumbly. I had more fillings than bricks had mortar and survived the terror and pain of eternities spent in a dentist's chamber of horror. What teeth I had left when I became a teenager were either kicked out by roping calves that I was trying to tie in competition, or knocked out by my first matrimonial partner.

I spent a huge hunk of my childhood in bed with a fever, while

Lettie poked spoons of chill tonic, castor oil (poorly disguised with orange juice) down my throat. Gagging and puking it up did not work. She mixed up another dose. I remember, tears cascading down my face, I once screamed at her in a fit of anger, "When I grow up and have kids and one is sick and dying and the doctor says that only castor oil will save him, I'm gonna just kiss and hug him and tell him goodbye. I ain't *never* gonna give my kids none of that god-awful stuff." She was unimpressed.

When Dale, my brother, snuck behind the barn and smoked a hand-rolled cigarette, he burned the barn down. Lettie gave him a dose of castor oil as punishment. In later years, I told Dale and my sister that I knew why we were so damned healthy and hardy, because we survived all the "cures" during our childhood.

I believed that if I was a boy, I could spend all my time with Mack in the field or going to the blacksmith shop or the gin. Boys were not afraid of being lost from their mamas in town on Saturday night or wetting the bed. They didn't have to wear dresses, or hideous long, white stockings, or suffer the agony of tangles being combed out of long hair. If I were a boy, I would never have to worry about growing up to become as pretty as my sister or those girls I saw in the picture show.

I finally gave up on ever being a boy, or pretty either. I discovered that I could do the things that boys did, except pee while standing, and I could draw much more attention than that of just being a girl. And attention was a combination of adrenaline and aphrodisiac for me.

"Don't clap for or laugh at Little Mack; she will kill herself," Mack used to say. I graduated from riding the plow horses in harness to racing up and down the black dirt roads, bareback on Snip, the most headstrong and "craziest" of Mack's string of work horses. I met my buddies, Bobby Jack Mabry and Edward Woods, who lived just across the field from us, and we would head for muddy Willow Oak Creek to swim, giving no thought to the cottonmouths and other snakes that lived there. Once a month, I rode Snip through the country, selling *Grit,* a unique little newspaper published in Williamsport, Pennsylvania. I sold it for a nickel a copy. I rode in my first rodeo when I was two and experienced the thrill of cheers, recognition, and "stardom." I loved it. It is still, to this day, bread and good wine for my soul.

When I was three, Lettie gave birth to a wiggly little thing they named Sidney, after the doctor who delivered him. Sidney was born in the west room of the old clapboard house, the only biological child of Mack and Lettie. My older cousin, Phillip, who had come with his mother, my Aunt Cora, for the birth caught me peeking through the key hole of the door and scooped me up in his arms, carrying me from the excitement.

"Phillip, there's a little kitten in there, I kin hear him crying." I was adamant and crying also. I knew what I had heard. I never found that kitten, but that tiny red wiggly thing I finally found in bed with Lettie grew up to be my best friend and "baby brother." Sidney would always be first in Lettie's heart, but I knew that Mack's first love had been me. I constantly competed with Sidney for Mack's attention, but I never resented his being Mack's only child, nor have I ever felt anything for him but love.

Sidney and I were the daredevils of our small community. Because we were rebels, and because Dale was so sensible and genteel, Sidney and I were always closer than my brother and I. Sidney accepted me just the way I was. I could never fit into the mold Dale had cast in his mind of a pretty, docile, dependent, and feminine baby sister that he could protect and watch over. The gap between my brother and me widened as we grew into adulthood, and it never narrowed again until the autumn of our lives.

It has always been amazing to me that two people with the same blood flowing through their veins can see the world as something vastly different. Dale Milford was methodical, perceptive, tolerant, philosophical, and dull as a stump. He took on life with purpose, traveling at the same speed each day. He lived in a world of grays, browns, and tans. He excelled in all things within his realm of thinking. He was the youngest man ever in civil service because he graduated from high school at the age of fifteen and immediately moved to Fort Worth and civil service. He had begun school at Sweatbox, Texas, (its proper name was Hope.)

When he wanted to go to school at the age of four, Ma thought it silly, but his teacher suggested Ma let him attend. "He will probably get tired and want to go home," she told Ma. He never got tired and continued his education and graduated from Commerce High School. He was the weatherman on WFAA Channel 8, Dallas, for seventeen years and served two terms as a United States Congressman. He was always secretly one of my heroes; I just never got around to telling him.

◆ ◆ ◆ ◆

The formal announcement of the proposed cattle drive came on October 14, 1994, with a luncheon on the lawn of the historic Stockyards Exchange Building in Fort Worth's North Side. Texas Agriculture Commissioner Rick Perry flew in to make the formal announcement to reporters and about one hundred other people who had been invited. The mayor of Miles City, Montana, George Kurkowski, was there. The mayor of Fort Worth was not. McCasland had, at one time, made the remark: "When this drive is announced to the media, you won't be able to get within a mile of this office."

I did not hear any bands playing or people cheering, nor did I see any flags waving. *Where's the grand entry, the horns and fans? Isn't anybody coming to witness the beginning of this spectacle? I'll bet old Charles Goodnight and Oliver Loving are out there somewhere watching all this. Come on in, fellows, and join us for steaks and amenities.*

I was disappointed by the media turnout. I had pictured television cameras and clamoring reporters there, but I saw only two – one lonely reporter for the *Fort Worth Star-Telegram,* Art Chapman, who would write many articles about the cattle drive, and a Channel 5 television newsman. That was it. *Hell, I could always draw a bigger crowd in my little beer tavern.*

The excitement was not there except among the few of us who were like children on Christmas Eve. I wanted the whole world to feel like I did about the drive. I wanted to write about it and let all those at home know what was happening each day. My proposal got no response from the *Fort Worth Star-Telegram,* Fort Worth's only newspaper. I assumed that it was not interested in hiring a novice or that it probably would send its own reporter on the drive. Commissioner Perry made a short speech and was rushed back to the airport for another stop. Bud made a short speech about the work involved in organizing the drive and the donors of the steers, and he introduced the cowboys who were there. The long- awaited announcement to the world about the Great American Cattle Drive was over.

I drove away from the North Side with mixed emotions. I felt somewhat elated after the great luncheon, but a tiny voice inside seemed to be trying to tell me something. I just did not want to hear right then. Being the optimist that I am, I was already thinking about what had to be done before leaving on that cattle drive

Oh, I had misgivings about such an undertaking. My mind raced with thoughts of what to do first. I had a mobile home, a truck, and a few singing jobs - nothing that couldn't be handled with a bit of ingenuity and help. I would sell my home because I did not relish the idea of someone else using my furniture and living in my house for six months. I needed money, and I wasn't real gung ho on staying where I was living anyway. In December, I talked to Carolyn Hunter, editor of *Trails* magazine, a periodical written for the Texas Longhorn Breeders. We made a deal for me to write an article each month for the magazine.

◆ ◆ ◆ ◆

Four years earlier, a flood had destroyed my home in Palo Pinto County. My fans, friends, and family rallied around and raised enough money to rebuild my house. A warm feeling welled up in my chest, remembering. . . .

Paul and Jo Burns, Big Moe and Nancy Dowler organized a benefit party for me. Other friends organized a golf tournament. Arnold Palmer, my friend and hero, sent one of his putters for an auction held at the dinner party the night after the tournament. Jim Trinkle, my beloved friend and writer for the *Star-Telegram*, gave his golf clubs to be auctioned. Fellow entertainers, B.J. Thomas, Mickey Newberry, Red Steagall, and Roger Vee not only played in the tournament, but entertained at the dinner and auction.

The aftermath of the flood brought drastic changes in my finances and priorities. I feared another flood. I was bankrupt and saddled with debt and knew I had to get back to Fort Worth, where offers were open for my performances. I needed a new challenge. I had dreamed, for years, of going to college. What better time than now. *You are backed in a corner financially; you have lost many of your material things, you are over sixty years old, and time may be running out. What have you got to lose?*

I sold the house and acreage and moved back to Fort Worth. I put the rest of my belongings in rented storage and moved to an apartment close to school – my first time to live in an apartment. Soon after, several of the storage buildings burned, including the one containing my belongings. I lost everything. The storage building owner's insurance paid $1900 for $50,000 in personal things, including all my family pictures and antiques. I was back to square one, with nothing left but a bed, dresser, table, and what clothes I had in the efficiency apartment. But I had my dream of earning a degree. *What the hell, you can't take it with you.* I shook off the despair, looked at my options and the future, and pushed my losses somewhere in the attic of my mind.

I lived in apartments for two years and finally bought the little mobile home when I could no longer tolerate apartment dwelling. So now, the thought of selling that mobile home was not a blip on a screen. The cattle drive took priority over everything. It had to work, no matter what.

The lack of interest in the drive from the businesses on the North Side around the Stockyards, the heart of the West in Fort Worth, bothered me. I knew almost everyone over there. I had performed in the Maverick Saloon and General Store for most of 1989 and '90; also, the Longhorn Bar and the Stockyards Hotel. I had played for Chuck Connors and Leslie Nielson and a host of stars at Billy Bob's when we had participated in a celebrity golf tournament together. I knew that all those businesses should have been right in the heart of what was going on. Nobody seemed remotely interested. Alan Luskey, owner of Luskey's Wear on North Main Street, said that he would have had fliers all over his store had he known about the Ranch Rodeo and Celebration that was held at the Stockyards Coliseum for our sendoff.

The salesman who had sold me my saddle and tack was blunt, less diplomatic, and very emphatic. "They came around here wanting everything free and told us what we could give them. They were just too damned arrogant for me. I'll bet they never make it. Hell, they been talking about this drive for four years," he said.

As I walked away from an empty coliseum after the rodeo, those conversations hung like an ominous black cloud. I quickly shook it off and thought about the glory of riding down Exchange Avenue on a white horse behind those longhorns, on the way to Montana. Hell, that wasn't the first time I had heard someone say that something couldn't be done or that something that I was a part of was crazy. I seemed to live in those kinds of situations, and I thrived on every one of them.

Life is full of snags, set-backs, and skeptics - you just have to go around them.

Which reminds me, Ma was a bit skeptical about some of my antics.

◆ ◆ ◆ ◆

I was in gym class in high school. We were learning to do handstands and headstands. I went home and got down on our big living room floor with a pillow and practiced standing on my head, or at least attempting to. Ma came in from the garden and stood with hands on hips.

"You cain't stand on your head! There ain't never been a Milford born yet thet could stand on their head. They're all too damned clumsy and big-footed!"

"This one will!" I knew that I would do it then if it killed me, and it damned near did when I fell through the glass-toped coffee table and cut my leg to the bone. I bled all over Lettie's throw rug and had to stand and listen to Ma's "I told you you couldn't do them monkey shines." But I did learn to stand on my head, and I still can because I try every once in a while just to make damned sure.

◆ ◆ ◆ ◆

After the first night on the drive, I knew that I needed a place to keep my gear apart from the rest. I knew that something had to be done to protect my sound equipment, guitar, clothes, and gear. Right then, other things came first.

Night closed in on the pageant of a modern cattle drive, and barbecue was served. Red Steagall sang songs and told stories in poetry about cowboys and horses and the first Old Blue, Charles Goodnight's legendary lead steer that made many trips across the West leading herds of longhorns in the 19th century. Red's deep, melodic voice came from the heart of a man who loved what he was doing, and he did it so well. Outriders, visitors, and cowboys danced on the grassy pasture we camped in; the campfire painted silhouettes of dusters, Stetsons, and coffeepots moving in rhythm to the notes and beats of the guitars. As the curtain fell for the first time upon the children of the twenty-first century as they relived the history of the last cattle drive of 1886, I wouldn't have traded places with the next lottery winner. Exhausted, I lay in my bedroll, too excited to sleep. *Here I am, running away again, following a dream. Ma was right. I am a harebrained drifter, a non- conformist, and a Gypsy.* As I stared up at the murky sky, my mind went rowing down the river of my yesterdays.

◆ ◆ ◆ ◆

The first time I saw him, I was jumping the school-yard fence on a paint stallion that belonged to the constable in Commerce. He was standing in the street talking to another man. They had eyes only for me on that stallion, bareback, jumping that four-foot chain link fence. I was eating up the attention. He called to me, and I rode over to them.

"Will he ride double?" he asked with a twinkle in his gray-green eyes. He was rugged, with a mouth full of crooked snow white teeth. I learned later that he was sixteen years my senior. His jet-black hair was thick and curly, and his hands were broad and strong.

"You might fall off," I said, with foolish aloofness. He grabbed a hand full of mane and swung up behind me with little effort.

"You are about the cutest thing I have seen in a long time," he said, and pulled me tight against his hard chest. I knew how to breed cattle, hogs, horses; how to deliver calves, turn breech colts, drive a tractor, a team of mules, or fight. I knew absolutely nothing about the rush of adrenaline or some strange feeling that was coursing through my child's body at that moment.

Months later, I was going with him to rodeos all over East Texas, with or without Lettie's permission. Mack did not approve, I am sure, but he never said anything that he thought would make me unhappy, no matter what he felt.

I lost track of time, my head, and my innocence that year, amid the excitement of riding and winning cowgirl barrel races on Lady, that cowboy's roping horse. I discovered that my body was something besides a rack for jeans and shirts. His name was Gene, and he was a brakeman for the Cottonbelt Railroad, a rake, and a lover of horseflesh, calf-roping, corn whiskey, and women. He was my Gene Autry, Roy Rogers, and the Lone Ranger all wrapped up in Levis, white starched shirt, boots, and Stetson. He pitted me against accomplished barrel racers on trained barrel horses, and I won him money on side bets from one cow pasture rodeo to another. I lived to please him and to ride. My blood ran hot, my good sense flew, and my naivete entered college.

I graduated from high school in 1948 and had our child in '49, six months after our wedding. When Virginia Lea was six months old, I packed in the middle of the night and left after Gene had gone to work. I had discovered there was someone else in the world to love and care for. A tiny, completely dependent someone, whose chocolate eyes and constant smile looked up at me and wiped out all my fears and self-doubt, someone who did not abuse me or deceive me, or lie to me, or cheat me. I had grown tired of hiding my bruises and scars from Mack. I had grown tired of days when Gene was in a drunken, fighting stupor, bragging about his conquests. I cried for a year, but I never went back. I looked up the road and kept going. Gene and the years from out of the past faded from my thoughts, and I drifted into exhausted sleep.

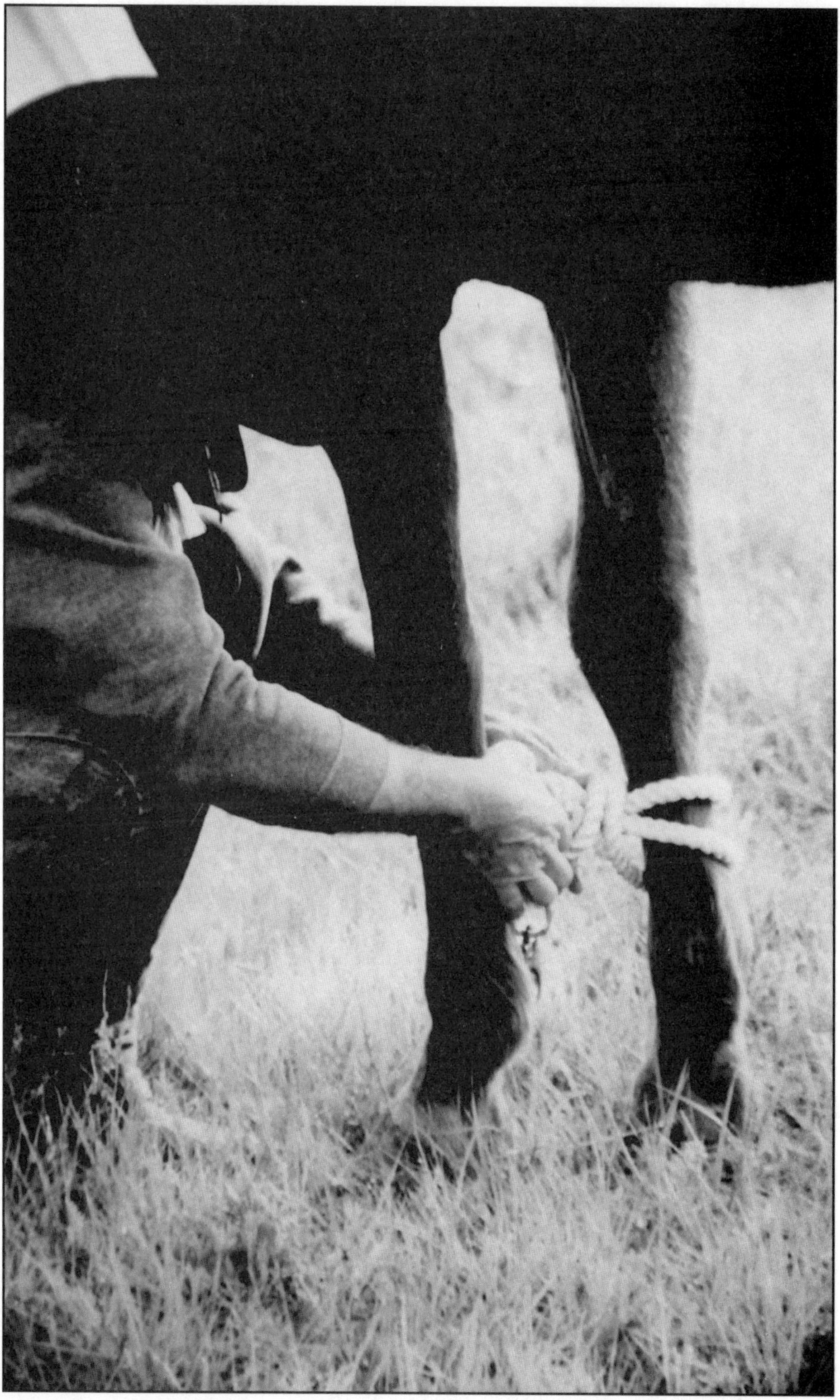

4

MOTHER NATURE'S POWER, NEWARK, TEXAS

The howling wind and the sound of my chattering teeth woke me around midnight. I fumbled in the darkness for more clothes. *Damn! It's colder than a well digger's butt in the Klondike.* When I reached outside my goose-down bedroll, the air was like ice. I pulled extra clothes inside and struggled to pull them on. I had difficulty making my fingers work in the dark and cold. I had pitched my bedroll in the top of one of the goose-necked trailers where the canned goods, boxes of plates, and kitchen pots and pans were stored. I had found a place to store my sound equipment and squeezed the bedroll in beside my speakers. That, for the time being, was the "private quarters" that I had been promised. Hey, it beat the hell out of being outside that night.

The freezing rain came down in bitter, icy sheets, rocking the big trailer like a buoy in the ocean. I could hear the outriders and people who had camped for the night yelling above the scream of the wind and trying to gather up and get out to dry ground before the mud trapped trailers and trucks and cars. Tents blew down like white dominoes, smothering exhausted cowboys curled in fetal positions in sleeping bags. The longhorns prowled through camp, bawling for early breakfast to ward off the cold wind and sleet.

At dawn, cowboys began crawling out from under the giant

green army surplus tent where some of them slept. It had blown down in the night. We were up at six, cutting out mounts for the day, saddles and halters were stiff and unrelenting. The horses were spooky and hungry. They stood stiff-legged and cranky and hard to saddle. Outriders huddled in knots. Some said, "To hell with this," loaded up, and went home. Others had left in the night. The wood was wet, so we couldn't build a fire. Coffee was finally brewed in pots that were plugged in to a generator at the souvenir trailer.

Breakfast was cold rolls with the hot coffee and we searched for any windbreak to stand or squat and eat and suck down coffee to warm our bodies.

"I got up, and the damned ice fell on me when I lifted the tent to crawl out," Will Miltimore, Oklahoma cowboy, told me later.

When we broke camp and drove those 262 descendants of the wild *cimmarones* out on Farm Road 718, and the icy wind hit us head on, the cattle scattered like popcorn skittering across a tile floor. Gathering them in was done in short time by the cowboys. I was proud of them. *Let Oliver Loving and Goodnight look down on us now.*

I was riding on the right side of Walt Secrest and the chuck wagon, just behind Walker Lawrence, and we traveled ahead of the herd. I didn't know just where to ride because no one had told me. I was just trying to stay out of the way and yet be a close part of all that was going on. I wanted to be more than a blip on a giant screen, but I decided to give it a few days until I learned who was boss, and some sort of routine was established. Things were really chaotic. That day the animals were cold and moved at twice the speed of the day before. I was just glad that I could move at all.

As I rode into that wind, I thought of the men who had ridden along that trail over one hundred years before me. Men who broke trails never before traveled, riding on half-broken mustangs, and existing on sowbelly, sourdough bread and beans, driving cattle that were about as tame as the coyotes and buffalo.

Like Ma, who had raised her children through the depression of the '20s and '30s, alone after losing Pa to tuberculosis, those men had tamed a frontier with guts, grit, and determination. The cold soon wiped out my thoughts of the past and its pioneers, and brought back the present with stern reality.

My body believed I would never be warm again. My face felt like it had been encased in concrete. My feet weren't numb – they screamed in sheer agony somewhere down there within two pairs of wool socks and wet boots. I wrapped my kerchief around my face, but my nose was dripping, and I believed it must be freezing and sticking to my face. I thought of hot coffee, a warm fire, and dry boots more than anything else. *Lord, I'm not asking for a big cowboy with a gray beard snuggling close, keeping me warm. Hell, I'm so cold I couldn't get ready for Gregory Peck – no bottle of Hennesey Four Star brandy to warm my innards – just good old hot coffee and a roaring fire in the fireplace. Damn! I must be getting' old!*

Just when I believed I couldn't go any farther without getting down and walking, and just when I began to wonder if I might have been just a bit insane to go on the drive, I heard a voice from the crowd standing along the sidewalks, thirty-five miles north of Fort Worth, in Boyd, Texas:

"Annie Golightly, you and those cowboys will never make it to Montana with that bunch of longhorns!"

"Don't you put any money on it, mister!" I retorted, instantly feeling warm and alive and ready to go another hour in that blasted cold and rain. Suddenly I wanted to prove to all the doubters that we could indeed make it against all odds. I wanted to get on my soapbox and tell that guy that history was made by the eccentric, the daring, the so-called nuts, and loners of the world. We were making dreams come true. We were "cuttin' trail," and he could follow or sit on his laurels and say "It can't be done" for the rest of his life for all I cared. I love a challenge. Gus felt the adrenalin began to course through my body, and his ears flicked backward, and he stepped higher as if to say, "Yeah, we are out of here, man!"

We made camp in Boyd with hundreds welcoming us along the streets. Ray and Marylon Jordon, who owned Boyd Building there, put us on a beautiful green pasture of wheat with giant rolls of hay for the hungry cattle and horses. The Jordons were old friends. I had met them through Ray's brother, Kenneth, who had been a fan years before and a regular in the little spot where I performed nightly in Fort Worth. I was glad to see them and was delighted when they took me home for a life-saving bath in their giant Jacuzzi tub, in water that was so hot it would have turned a grizzly bear beet red.

The blood began running through my veins again. *Hey, where in hell is Gregory Peck now – and pass that brandy bottle.* One outrider's horse slipped and flipped over backward. He caught his foot in one stirrup as the horse dragged him a way before the others could help. Paramedics discovered he had suffered a pulled groin and ample bruises and scratches, but no broken bones. Outriders were those who paid to ride with us a short time along the way. They were charged one hundred dollars a day if they had their own horses, or two hundred if we rented them a horse. Jamie Nail, off the famous Nail Ranch in Albany, had brought a string of horses for just that purpose. The money from outriders was the only income for the drive and later became vitally important to our staying the course.

Back in camp, the hot bath was history. We couldn't get warm. We were wet, the wind blew without letup, and we weren't allowed to build a fire in that pasture for fear of fire. Without a fire Dennis Dodson, the cook, could not make coffee for the cowboys who would be there later with the herd. I knew they would be as cold as I was and looking for hot coffee. Dennis, a rugged, handsome thirty-nine-year-old, was friendly and fun to talk to. He worked for Global International as a computer systems analyst but looked like he had stepped out of a Zane Grey book. He also worked part time on a ranch at Poolville, Texas. He and his dad had rebuilt an old chuck wagon a "few years back," and he had used it on the ranch for parties.

"My friends called me to do their parties, and it just sort of snowballed," Dennis told the cattle drive reporter.

I was sure that many people would find it hard to understand why a man with a job such as his and a family would go on the drive. However, many of the other cowboys had left jobs and responsibility to indulge in the experience of a lifetime. They left their wives, mothers, and fathers in charge of making a living and raising children.

Those young cowboys had more responsibility and people waiting back home than did this old gal. I had left behind only a casual social relationship, my kids, who were busy with their own lives, and all the stress and the humdrum life of the city.

Things had been different when my husband, Kenneth, was alive. I would not have thought of leaving him for six months, and he never would have considered making a trek such as this one without me and the kids. Kenneth was a plodder. That is, he loved going to work each day from nine to five, coming home to me and the kids, supper, and his favorite chair. He loved me and the kids and home and "sameness." He used to plead with me: "Mama, - he called me Mama, like the kids - don't get up so early and run the vacuum. Stay in bed with me." I was ambitious, antsy, tireless, and constantly looking for adventure. I remember reading where land was still available for homesteading in Alaska. I wanted us to buy an old truck, pack up the kids, and go to Alaska and homestead. Kenneth thought I had lost my mind.

"Mama, we can't take these kids and go to Alaska without a job. We would starve." I could not make him understand my way of thinking. I didn't even understand it myself. I only knew that we would not starve in Alaska, and I knew that Kenneth and I could do anything we set our minds to do. I had more confidence in him than he did. I knew that there was something out there that called and intrigued me. Just thinking about going was like a "fix" for me. We never went to Alaska. We lived each day like the last - until one day, it was the last day for him.

While I mused about Dennis and Kenneth and the absence of hot coffee, I shivered in the cold along with the rest. Besides having no campfire, we had no hay for the horses. This prompted the first of many meetings in the big green tent. Bud McCasland and two of the private investors were there. Mike Garrison, a Wyoming cowboy, was raising hell about the lack of hay.

"These animals can't perform in this cold weather all day without feed and hay. The steers will not make it to Montana if they aren't fed well, and I cannot ask my horse to work his ass off without grain and hay. The horses and steers are what this drive is all about, and I want feed for my horse every day." Garrison was a Vietnam vet with years' experience as a working cowboy. Abrupt and short-tempered, a man whose emotions were close to the surface much of the time, he was honest, to the point in all things, and his complaint was legitimate. Garrison had come to Fort Worth weeks before the drive started and had taught many of the younger cowboys the art of driving cattle. He was deft with a rope, hardworking, and careful to stay close to camp at all times. Besides being a driver, he helped Walt Secrest harness the Shires each morning and also worked as a farrier.

Secrest brought up the fact that the cattle drive owed him money. One investor stood and told Walt that if he didn't like the way things were going, he could simply go back to Montana.

"Your complaints about hay for a herd of steers are not what this is all about, men," the investor said. "We are talking here about money! Lots of money! Now if some of you are unhappy with the way things are going, I suggest you pull out now. I can tell you – we are going to Montana. We are going to take these cattle there, with or without you. There are plenty of cowboys who would give their left nut to get to go with us."

Walt did not flinch at the man's "who needs you" attitude toward the cowboys, but came back at the investor with confident force and a threat.

"If I leave this drive, you will not cross Montana with these cattle," he spat. "I know each and every one of the ranchers there, and they will not permit you to cross their land with the herd." Gone was the humility in his voice. We weren't sitting in an air-conditioned office in comfortable chairs discussing a cattle drive. The wind howled outside, and the angry words spewing forth from their mouths came out in steamy clouds in that cold tent.

"You don't seem to understand," Garrison stood close to the investor. "If any one of these cowboys should leave this drive, we all go. We are a unit and we are together." I loved those words. I wanted to say "yea, yea!" but kept quiet and listened. I watched men who came from different lifestyles and cultures, engaged in confrontation that bordered on physical combat. *Damn! I would like to get into this shit-throwing contest, but these guys wouldn't listen to anything a woman had to say. I'll bet I could yell louder than any on them anyway, and maybe make some sense too.*

"That's fine," the investor said. If that happens, then it will just happen, but I can tell you, it won't stop this drive."

It was a standoff between the leaders and the men. No other cowboy spoke. Bud and his investors appeared to hold a distinct advantage over the cowboys because of the cowboys' desire to make the drive to Montana. They were earning $1,500 a month and found (food). More important, they were making a statement to the world that they were capable of doing what most thought impossible.

I felt proud of those cowboys. Men who had done day work on ranches most of their adult lives were now moved to the limelight and were writing a new chapter in Western history. I believed that they understood the feelings of the investors and Bud and their desire to make a huge profit on the drive, but Bud and the investors did not understand those men, who loved and worked with animals and who were leading with their hearts, their pride, and their egos – men to whom this drive meant much more than making a lot of money. To them it meant tradition, being a cowboy, presenting an image of cowboys as they originally were. Suddenly, I felt the presence of those cowboys of yesteryear in that cold tent. I could almost feel them smiling down on that group of men as they defied the investors and their desire to establish the drive as being about "money." I also believed that every man had his limits. I wondered how long the standoff would remain a standoff. *And just who is leading this drive? Are these guys a couple of pompous asses from behind mahogany desks who may or may not know the difference between a cow chip and a paper clip? Is Bud a guy who is so wrapped up in self-importance he does not have the courage to stand up to investors for the men making his dream a reality? The animals have to have feed to survive. The cowboys are right about the feed. And I wonder why they owe Walt money, and we ain't even out of Texas yet?*

In his journal, one cowboy expressed concern over organization, management, and power struggles even before the drive began. On March 1, in Fort Worth, he wrote:

"Jamie met me coming back and he was pissed big time. The cattle had not been caked so we put out 25 bags of cubes and penned a steer that had jumped the fence. We then decided to go to Cattleman's Restaurant and eat a steak. Bud came to camp while we were feeding and him and Jamie talked about something but I went to water and don't know all the details of their talk. Stony Burke, that temporary cook, got drunk going over to Dallas to eat the free dinner for us and cussed and pissed in the corner of the cafe, I heard. He was terminated the following Friday. There is trouble in the pecking order of the command, but not the cowboys or wranglers. This will work its way out, but it is hard for us hands to know what to do. Too much work for such a small staff."

Here we were only days into the drive, and big egos in cahoots with lousy weather and frustration had brought on the big confrontation in the green tent. It was the first time I had really gotten a look at the bare emotions of those men, and when Bud spoke, his words left me slack-jawed. He told us that he had called John Justin, the western clothier and boot king in Fort Worth and told his contact man that we needed a sponsor for the drive to Montana. Justin's man said that he was indeed interested, that he wanted the exclusive boots rights, and he would give each cowboy two pairs of boots.

"I told him that I wanted three million dollars, and he could take his boots and stick 'em up his ass."

I thought I was so cold that I was having hearing problems. I looked around to see the impact of his words on the cowboys, but I couldn't read thoughts behind those cold faces in the dimly lit tent. *I would have asked Justin's man which cheek of my butt he wanted Justin Boot Company tattooed on. John Justin could buy Montana if it went on sale, and he would probably have furnished us a place to keep our clothes and gear too. Maybe even some Scotch or brandy, too. Well, I knew this wasn't a family picnic when I joined up. These guys are really funny with their pride and egos. I can see right now I am going to have to buy feed for Gus and Red to be sure they have it all the time, especially in this damned infernal cold. Maybe Bud doesn't have any money. Maybe he is bluffing, then again, maybe he is like the rest of us – scared but scrappy and determined to go to Montana at all costs.*

This was the first of many such meetings that never seemed to provide anything except the opportunity for a group of men to blow off steam and flex muscles and voice discontent. I was always present at those meetings, like some piece of furniture or a horse that someone was holding in the background. Only much later did I ever speak up and become involved in the discussions, and arguments. At one of the meetings, an investor seemed to notice my presence for the first time. "Annie, this is a meeting with the cowboys." His tone and obvious meaning stirred an instant resentment within. I had rather he had looked me in the eye and simply asked, "What the hell are you doing here?"

"I am aware of that, sir, and I am always present at the meetings," I answered, rather tersely. He made no further comment to me.

At each of the meetings, Bud made promises and agreed with many of the complaints. Sometimes he was complacent, and sometimes he was aggressive. When the investors were there, he let them run the meeting.

I wanted to believe that Bud was sincere and really was

concerned about the cowboys' needs, but nothing was ever done about most of the complaints. He made cameo appearances in camp, never saddled up and rode with us, seldom ate with us, and when he was there he was constantly on the portable phone in the Ford van he drove or "holed up" in the souvenir trailer.

The meeting at Boyd came to a "dangling" end. Bud promised hay for the horses, an unspoken truce was established, simmering anger was put on the back burner, and we went back to our tents. A campfire had been built by then, and after supper we crawled into warm goose down and slept.

WHEN YOU ARE FILLING YOUR
BUCKET WITH REALITY

LEAVE A COUPLE OF INCHES AT THE
TOP FOR DREAMS. . . .

Annie Golightly

5

ON THE TRAIL AND MEMORIES OF SIDNEY

Our modern-day cattle drive was not unlike a carnival traveling cross-country. We averaged fourteen miles a day. Longhorns travel at their own pace and will not hurry for man or horse. Each night we had to set up camp, and each morning we had to tear it down. We had approximately fifteen pieces of equipment that had to be moved each day to the new camp. All equipment was gooseneck with the exception of the portable toilet trailer.

Ford Motor Company, as one of our sponsors, had lent three Ford pickups that we used to pull the equipment. Those lightweight trucks pulled those big thirty-foot van/trailers, with numerous drivers (several of whom sometimes failed to shift the trucks out of overdrive when pulling a trailer). It blew my mind that we went through all the mud and bad roads and that they lasted all the way to Montana. It also made me proud because I have always loved my Ford trucks. There has been a friendly debate between Sidney and me for years. He drives Chevrolets now. I couldn't wait to tell him that an old Chevy truck couldn't have taken such treatment and lasted past the Texas border. And if Sidney were here right now, I would probably have to eat those words, because he would remind me about Mack's old '49 Chevy truck. . . .

◆ ◆ ◆ ◆

Our neighbors and close friends used to say that "Mack gets about 10,000 miles to the fender." Between Mack driving through a Bourbon Deluxe haze and plowing down fences and running off bridges, and Sidney climbing telephone poles and jumping bar ditches at 70 mph in that old blue truck, Mack put seven fenders and three transmissions in it over a period of twenty or so years. My rebuttal to that would be to remind Sidney about the time he and Lefty Branum out-ran Sam Matthews, the city constable in Commerce, in Sidney's Ford. I'll tell you about it. It all began one Saturday night in Commerce. . . .

"Hey Lefty, I bet I can set Ol' Greeny between those columns in front of old man Peek's bank! Whadda you think?"

"Shit Sid, I just saw Sam coming up Park; he'll get your ass if you do that."

Lefty's words were drowned in the squeal of whitewall tires as Sidney hit the brakes and spun the steering wheel knob, (with a picture of a nude holding a fuzzy puppy on it). The Ford careened crazily, jumped the eight-inch curb and came to an abrupt stop, snug between giant Ionic columns with a scant four-inch clearance on either side. Lefty let loose a gush of breath and slouched lower in his seat.

"Sid, you've ripped your drawers this time. Sam'll put us in that stinking jail now!"

"Take a deep seat old buddy, here we go! Sam's old Chevy couldn't catch this baby if someone was pushing him!" Sidney had no hang ups, no inhibitions, no fears, and no frustrations. He took the world by the horns and ran gleefully through life like a stone skipping across a clear pool of tranquil water midday.

Saturday night in Commerce on Main Street was bustling with country folk who had gathered to buy groceries, visit with neighbors, get hair cuts, buy horse and cow feed, eat good old greasy hamburgers at "Miz Tranthams," see Gene Autry or Roy Rogers subdue the bad guys at the Lyric theater, and walk around the square enjoying a double-dip banana-nut ice cream cone purchased at Oliver's drug store for a dime.

Sam Matthews, city constable, cruised in the Chevy, spotlight on the driver's side and ominous red lights and siren behind the grille. Like all Saturday nights, the usual group of older men sat on the curb in front of the City Café or leaned on the fenders of parked cars and spat brown splotches in the gutter while discussing corn and cotton prices and the new calf crop. Mamas with children in tow browsed in JC Penney's and the five and dime store, or exchanged recipes and dress patterns at the soda fountain at Oliver's.

Tranquility came to an abrupt end with the piercing screech of tires and the roar of twin Smitty mufflers blazing down Main Street, attached to Sidney's 1950 Ford convertible with the top down. His blond curls and defiant smile that charmed even the most straight-laced, bible-toting do-gooders were brilliant as he made his grand entrance and exit from Bruce Peek's Security State Bank.

Mamas grabbed tiny hands, old men stopped telling yarns and spitting, and all eyes were riveted on the Ford. Many recognized it immediately as belonging to "that wild Burrell kid."

Heads twisted in the other direction as Sam came barreling down Main Street with muddy smoke – balloons of oily breath from the Chevy. Sidney pushed the gear shift into reverse, bounced backward off the curb and laid a black trail of rubber. He and the slow-thinking, impressionable Lefty led the way up Main Street, turned right at the end of the square. The Ford bounced over the railroad tracks, dropped off the steep hill, and headed cross country with two cars in hot pursuit, lights flashing and sirens screaming in the still country night. Jim Latham, deputy sheriff, had joined Sam in the chase.

The center of the windshield seemed to explode on the chartreuse Ford.

"Oh double shit, Sid! They're shooting at us! You really screwed up this time!"

Sidney twisted the knob and laughed and rocked back against the seat, high on the excitement of the moment. Pow! The right front tire on the Ford went flat, and the car bucked and floundered and listed slightly to the right.

"Hang on Lefty, we gotta do some driving to put those assholes out of sight."

The road twisted through rows of cotton and maize, pastures, and across wooden bridges that had been built at the turn of the century. They were mostly used now for tractors moving from field to field. Fence posts going in the opposite direction looked like bits of string in the air as the Ford, running on three legs, widened the gap between the guns and flashing lights and the Chevys staggering in the mountain of dust behind.

Lefty huddled in the seat, head down, his heart beating like a trip hammer. He could hear each bullet as it hit the Ford with a dull thud. The minutes seemed like hours as they bounced and twisted and careened, around sharp corners, over deep ruts and across the ancient bridges. He had visions of twisted metal, and their bloody bodies riddled with bullets. And worse, "That stinkin' county jail in Greenville with its stinkin' toilets and that stinkin' runny oatmeal with a big stewed prune that they served for breakfast."

Suddenly they came to an abrupt halt, the engine died, and silence reigned. They were behind an old abandoned house, in sunflowers that towered over the Ford. Somewhere far in the distance, the sound of sirens, like the low moan of an approaching train, could be heard. When Sam and Jim finally gave up the search, Sidney drove down the road, across Willow Oak Creek and home. Sidney's car had nineteen bullet holes in it. The boys were arrested the following Monday when Mack took Sidney into town to the sheriff's office. I never knew what it cost Mack, in addition to the time Sidney spent in jail. Lettie raised hell about "the law shooting at little kids!"

I'll bet that old Ford convertible was tougher than even the trucks we had on that drive. Yeah, about the drive. . . .

◆ ◆ ◆ ◆

The day after that confrontation between the cowboys and Bud, the weather was nice. The sky was the bluest this side of Montana, and the breeze was soft and cool. We left Boyd, Texas waving goodbye to hundreds of new friends. We traveled at a leisurely pace down country roads where smiling faces waved from porches, at fences, and in cars and trucks everywhere, all expressing a desire to go with us.

We arrived at camp, a beautiful meadow where we basked in the warm sunshine, while hobbled horses grazed on patches of green. I gazed out on squatting cowboys as they ate sandwiches and repaired tack with onlookers strolling through camp. There were the young, dressed in cowboy regalia, holding the hands of grandpas and grandmas, taking pictures, getting autographs, and sighing over the longhorns. I wrote in my journal, penned letters home, and felt at ease with the world, There were no newspapers, radio, or television to invade my contentment. A tall man dressed in black, who answered to the name of Hoot, played his guitar and sang ditties around the campfire. I joined him and encouraged a sing-along with the crowd. We yodeled "Goodnight Irene," "Red River Valley," and many old Western songs while Dick Kennedy played the Jew's harp. Life was good.

As I sat in front of that campfire, spotlighting the faces of happy people, singing together, my mind went back three years to the Great Smoky Mountains and a backpacking trip I had taken with my geology class in college. One of the teachers had carried my small guitar sixty-one miles across those splendiferous mountains, and each night I would play around the campfire to the class. Music will bring people close as nothing else will – a meshing of souls that shuts out inhibitions, doubts, and anger. Music blurs race and social status, tending to put each of us on a more even keel.

All good things soon end. As that magical day on the cattle drive ended, the bitter cold came rushing back with constant wind, shivering nights, and short tempers. Dennis Dodson was canned. McCasland said Dennis would not cook for the crew.

Dennis said he would cook if he had groceries to cook with. I heard no conversations, only rumor. I was sure Dennis's firing would have a definite impact on the drive. However, I believed we would find a solution to the problem just as we had all the others that came before. We had not as yet had to worry much about food. Folks along the way had been great to cook and bring food to us. Things would change in the chuck wagon soon.

News of Dennis's firing came to the drovers last. I had begun riding with the herd, working as a drover. Gus and Red were both great cowponies, and I had no problem herding the cattle. I had raised longhorns for years as a hobby. I was familiar with their temperament and habits. Learning to drive them down a highway came easily and quickly. It was fun but very slow, and it made for a long day. The cattle moved about two miles an hour, and it was difficult to stay alert for seven to nine hours in the saddle.

Most of the cowboys respected and trusted my ability to "make a hand." A few seemed to just sort of tolerate my being there, and they were polite and distant. I was sure that that group was simply waiting for the day when I would grow tired and go home. I forgave them because they just didn't know me.

Because the herd came in at least two hours behind the chuck wagon, we were the last to know much that happened ahead of us. The news always came secondhand. It was amazing the things one heard in camp. Stories were plentiful and never the same as the last ones heard, although they might concern the same subject. Much of the gossip came via Dancer Davis, who rode with Walt and the chuck wagon. The chuck wagon arrived in camp hours ahead of the herd. Dancer told us he owned and edited the *Cowboy Gazette*, a small newspaper out of Dublin, Texas. He said the *Cowboy Gazette* was distributed in fifteen states and several foreign countries.

Dancer was small in stature, a picture of the old-time cowboy with his weather-beaten hat, high-top boots (that were so run over he walked on the sides of the high heels instead of the soles).

His greatest love seemed to be the sound of his own voice. He had a glib tongue and a friendly smile, and no subject could be broached he had not experienced firsthand, no profession that he had not worked at, at least temporarily, and no event that he had not had a hand in, be it war, famine, or making big money.

The crowds liked him and loved listening to his yarns although most, I'm sure, did not take Dancer seriously. He made sure that his picture was on the front of every newspaper and his stories were at least partially repeated in print. He was averse to bathing, as one's nose would quickly note, and he smoked almost continually. He ate little, and he kept the same congenial, upbeat attitude each day. I did not know what his job was and never learned if he was on the payroll, but he was adroit at being wherever a camera flashed, and his picture was to be in many papers along the way to Montana. Skip Nelson, who was our commemorative photographer on the drive, said of Dancer later, "Dancer was friendly and made me feel welcome when I joined the drive. He was good at public relations." I tended to agree with Skip, because Dancer greeted everyone with the same genuine smile and handshake. He was also a good writer.

I could touch and find every single muscle in my body from the waist down. My knees were screaming in agonized protest, my new saddle was a beautiful torture chamber, and I had not been really warm since leaving Fort Worth. My feet had been wet for days, my clothes were wrinkled and muddy, and I looked like I had been dropped out of an airplane at ten thousand feet. *How in hell Maureen O'Hara looked so damned pretty for John Wayne after crossing the desert in a covered wagon is beyond me. I'll bet I couldn't get a date on a troop train with fifty dollars in my pocket.*

Days later, we camped five miles south of Bridgeport, Texas. The steers were really tired and sore-footed. Eldon Winn, a Kansas cowboy and our farrier, was hard at work shoeing horses after a day in the saddle. This man said little and did much. Tall and slender as a reed, he had a warm, boyish face, soft voice, and gentle nature, which led one to believe that there was no fire underneath. He was a perfectionist in all things and cared much about the more than one hundred horses whose hooves he was responsible for shoeing and trimming and caring for. He never complained about any job that was asked of him. He had a ready smile each morning when we spoke, and I was always glad for him to ride Red – which he did quite often – because he had a gentle but firm hand with a horse.

The pace, the confusion, and the tempers were settling down to a soft hum. Beneath it all was a quiet determination to make it to Montana. I was having the time of my life. There was something wondrous about what we were doing. I could not help but feel the presence of the cowboy of the nineteenth century as we followed those bony bovines each day. Asphalt and man-made structures failed to obscure all the beauty of nature seen between a horse's ears. I felt good. I was responsible for keeping my strip of the herd in place and out of the way of motorists either zooming by or slowing to photograph the steers and cowboys or just to talk with us.

My bones were beginning to stop screaming, and my muscles were loose and not rebelling so much. I felt comfortable with the job I was doing in spite of the nagging feeling inside that some of the cowboys would prefer that I be somewhere else. I was gaining confidence in my physical abilities, which tend to wane with age, and this boosted my self-esteem. I liked myself better. I sucked up the sights of nature like a thirsty sponge and thrilled that I was a part of it all. My own real or imagined shortcomings seemed insignificant there under the open sky, without spotlight or flair.

Like a kid again, I would pretend I was there with those pioneers, and I would get lost in fantasies and facts. What a splendiferous place the Old West was. Those who saw the West as a place where nothing existed but lizards and prickly pear failed to see the rich nutritious buffalo and grama grasses that could withstand long drought and the hot sun – the same grasses that supported seventy-five million buffalo until they were almost completely destroyed by man. The 350,000 longhorns that moved north on cattle trails between April and October of 1876 had given birth to the American cowboy. One hundred and nineteen years later there I was, topside a White Horse, riding flank on a twentieth-century cattle drive – one old gal among thirty or so cowboys on the way to Montana with a herd of those legendary brutes.

Like those who had cut trail before us, we weren't concerned with material things beyond our horses, rigging, and equipment. Our horses were our most important tools and a major element of our self-image, and I owned two of the prettiest and best on the trail. I refrained from using a rope, although one nineteenth century cowpuncher named Joe Mora once said that the rope is a vital tool that allows a 140-pound man to snare and control a thousand-pound animal. I had no intention of proving or disproving my expertise with a rope, and besides, I did not want to be tied to something that I might not be able to turn loose of quickly. I made sure that the steers traveling in the area I worked were moving in unison with the others. Gus and Red were equally eager to nip any steer on his rear that got out of line, to warn him about the straight and narrow. If one bolted, which they often did, I made sure I retrieved it myself, without the help of one of the boys.

Without his horse, the cowboy was "just a plain bowlegged human who smelled horsey, slept in his underwear, and was subject to boils and dyspepsia," Joe Mora said.

I knew that both of my horses performed well, and I was smug and proud of them. I was determined to carry my load on that drive and to leave no room for any man to complain about my performance. I knew I could throw a rope. I had roped in competition forty-five years before, when Gene would get drunk after paying his entry fee, and I would have to take his place or lose the fee.

In later years, when I was married to Kenneth, I had pulled used railroad crossties from the Trinity River bottom with a horse. Sometimes they could not be reached with a truck. I had been big and pregnant in those days, but crossties don't fight back or bolt and drag lightweight horses and careless riders through river bottoms.

To my knowledge, only one cowboy ever complained about my work on that drive. I heard little or no praise, but I expected none. I felt comfortable and content with being there – sucking up the smell of leather, horse sweat, and cattle, mixed with sagebrush, wild flowers, and manure – on an even keel with those cowboys. Besides all that, I loved them all!

There is more to cowboys than folktale and legend. There must be a sense of depth of their hearts in all those who admire them. Those riding on the GACD were not unlike the nineteenth-century cowboy. The only things we loved better than the creatures we were riding and driving was the glorious sense of freedom we felt with the sky for a roof and the earth for a floor, though that floor sometimes was carpeted with asphalt or concrete. Cowboys have the spirit of the deer, the agility of the panther, and the heart and stamina of the Texas longhorn. They are funny, tender, daring, and tough as nails. They love women, horses, music, leather, and each other. With all those thoughts skipping through my mind, I scribbled a poem in my journal:

What is a cowboy?
the whole world wants to know,
He's legend and lyric
tornadoes and snow.
He's a two-legged varmint
brought here from another time,
God made him out of cactus,
mesquite thorns, and brandywine.
He comes in all ages
grizzled, young, or in his prime
covered in Stetson, leather, and denim
and high-top boots needing a shine.

Poets gather fancy words
and place them all in books,
telling stories of his antics,
his courage, and his looks.
He'll likely break your heart
then humbly pick up the pieces,
sing you songs about his horse,
broken promises, his legacy.
He loves beans and sourdough,
stray puppies, and good women,
bar fights, dun horses, his freedom
and day dreaming.
He hates deadlines and time clocks,
neckties and shoes,
possessive women, responsibility,
and most of all, the blues.
He's here today and gone tomorrow,
and like the wind he'll move on,
he'll be indelible in your heart
and you'll never forget him,
when he finally rides
away in the dawn.

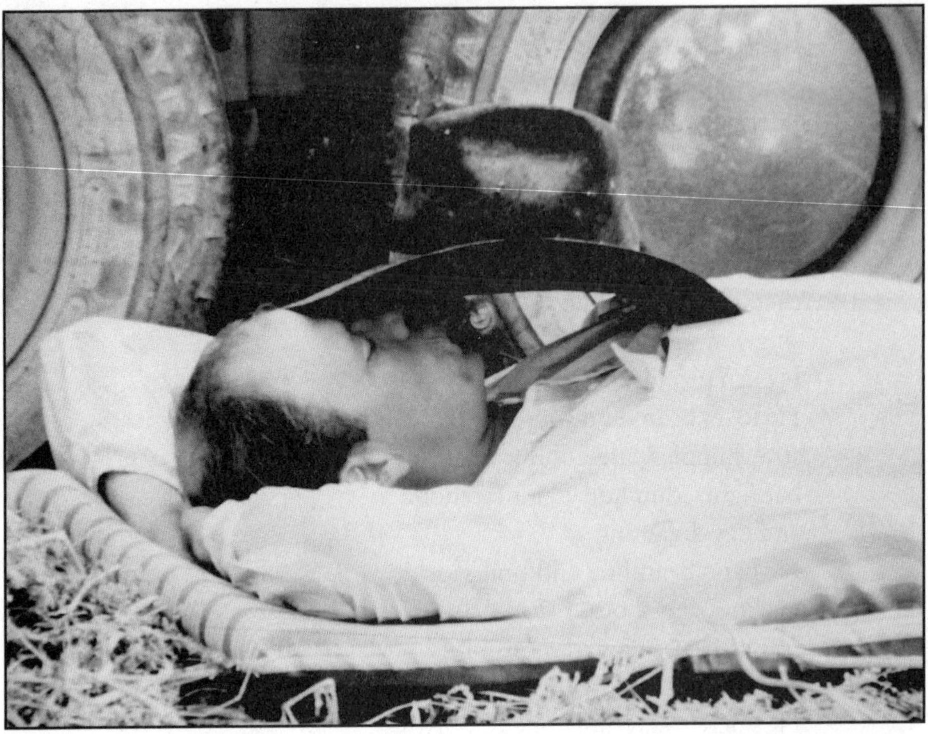

6

OKLAHOMA AND WILL MILTIMORE

On the eleventh day of March, I rode swing. The steers moved slowly, and I had time to gaze across the country and see the slow changes in the land. It looked much like the day before but "gettin' to look more like Oklahoma everyday," Will Miltimore said.

This old Oklahoma cowboy became my best buddy every mile of the way to Montana. He looked like Hollywood had groomed him for a John Wayne movie. With gray whiskers, eyes the color of Montana sky in the winter, he had hands as big as saddle blankets, gnarled with years of wear and tear in the saddle. His voice came from deep in the earth and belied his body, which was like twisted wire. He was as natural on a horse as the hair on its back. He was the oldest of the cowboys and the toughest. He spoke the least, and he could drink more whiskey than most could drink water on a hot day. The only thing he liked as much as whiskey was coffee, which he drank hot, cold, luke, or iced even when it was the color and consistency of tar. When we lesser mortals huddled in goose down, long johns, wool socks, and extra blankets in the cold, Will rolled up in a bargain-basement-special cotton-stuffed sleeping bag, wrapped a serape around his abundant gray hair, curled up on a tarp on the ground, and slept like Baby Jesus.

His gelding's bridle might have bailing wire patches or binder twine splices, and he once trimmed off a piece of tire he found on the side of the road and made spur straps from it. His gelding had a laid-back attitude and acted like a kid's horse, but he would buck like hell without provocation - a disposition very much like his own. The horse was totally honest, stayed mostly to himself, ate anything offered, got by on little, and performed well without fanfare or frills. These two – this animal and this man – came from out of the past, when man and beast lived with nature and not against it.

Will and I had great times sitting by our bedrolls, sharing whiskey, books, bitching, and tales. We looked out for each other, and Will rode my red horse much more than I did. He loved Red, and Red performed like a champ under him. He was one of only about three cowboys who ever recognized me as a "fit" hand with the herd. Others possibly felt comfortable with me working, but they never voiced an opinion to my face. Will was quick to mention me to the media, and I loved that courtesy and strove to be all he said that I was.

My other buddy hailed from the Kansas /Nebraska border. I dubbed Dick Kennedy, Will, and myself the Three Musketeers. Dick was a veteran of Vietnam, one hundred percent cowboy, hot-tempered, and deeply in love with his wife, Diane. The three of us had great times sharing stories. Dick played the Jew's harp while I sang and played the guitar. He was quick to express anger, but I really liked his overall attitude, and the rest of the cowboys liked him also. Dick was somewhat a loner and shy, and he seemed to feel more comfortable with just the three of us together. His greatest possession on the drive was his blue roan horse, Joe, one of two blue horses he brought. Joe was easy on the eyes and obviously well trained. He told us about finding him in the slaughterhouse just before he was to be shot because "he was too much horse for those sonsabitches."

"I took him home, and when we established just who was boss, he made me a great horse. He will still kick the shit out of you if you don't watch him, "Dick said.

Dick had had heart surgery before coming on the drive and had been having some respiratory problems for a few days. I was worried about him. When he felt bad, he wanted to go home. He was unhappy with the way things in camp were being handled, and the lack of leadership and direction. He missed Diane, and I was afraid that when we reached Kansas, he would not stay past there. I knew we would all miss him if he should quit the drive. I was happy with my "chosen brothers." We communicated easily, disagreed civilly, and I felt comfortable with the camaraderie between us - unlike my biological brother or father.

◆ ◆ ◆ ◆

I have so often wondered at the chasm between myself and my brother and father and how we could all have the same blood flowing in our veins but could never really communicate with each other comfortably or without disagreement. All my life, I had had boys or men for best buddies. I was more comfortable with the male species. I could talk to a man with more ease than with a woman. Maybe it all started with Mack, who was not only father to me, but also best friend. We had fun together, just the two of us, out in some old hot cotton patch with a team of horses or mules and the good earth. The cattle drive and my relationship with Will was a daily reminder of the happy days with Mack, because Will sometimes made me think of Mack, with his sky-blue eyes and his long periods of silence. Like Mack, he was a good listener, and I love to talk. That made a great combination. He and Dick and I ate together much of the time. We would cuss and discuss camp gossip over food, sitting on the ground someplace out of the cold wind when we could find one.

March 12, 1995, from my journal:

I am sure that at some point in my life I have been more tired, but I simply can't recall when that was. My knees feel as if they are detached from my body, hanging in mid-air screaming. I started to climb in one of the gooseneck trailers with my plate of barbecued chicken and fell backward on my ass bone and took a bath in BBQ sauce. I hit my back on a generator sitting in the doorway. My bruises were making themselves known, and my face looked like a lobster. I hope to hell that Sam Elliott or James Arness don't show up in camp tonight and see me looking like this.

For most of our meals since leaving Fort Worth, the country folk had brought all sorts of great food for us, but when food was cooked in camp, it was chicken. Chicken that was cooked seven ways from Sunday and several ways I had never heard of. That day, we had chicken again. The cowboys were complaining vociferously.

"I ain't eating another piece of that goddamed chicken," Garrison said. "Oh shit! Not chicken again," another cowboy said. I was beginning to cackle myself, but we were having fun anyway. The crowds seemed to double at each camp we made. One day there was a young man in a wheelchair, all decked out in cowboy regalia, who planned to ride on the chuck wagon with Walt the next day.

For the second time, my friend Marie Putt brought clean laundry back for the cowboys and me, at no charge, from one of the twenty-one Town & Country Cleaners stores in Hurst, Bedford, North Richland Hills, and Grapevine, Texas, that she and husband Frank owned. Everyone was thrilled, and one young cowboy said he had never gotten his shirts back from any laundry in a box with tissue paper around it. *Hey! That's my friends! They go first class!*

The next day was Sunday. After Bible readings, prayer, and talks, we rode fifteen miles, heading the steers toward Bowie, under protest because of their sore hooves. A fine rain was falling, and the air was heavy. Yellow slickers dotted the highway like a G. Harvey painting, and for seven hours we pushed those brutes down Highway 287, farm-to-market roads, service roads, under the freeway, over a viaduct, across several railroad tracks, and finally down a gravel road that was sheer torture for them. The narrow ditch on each side of the fenced lane gave small relief, and it was boggy.

One steer turned and jumped a five-strand barbed wire fence. He was so sore and weary, he got only his front half over. There he stood, half in and half out of the pasture, woven in between strands of barbed wire. J. Frank Dobie said the longhorn is the smartest cow animal of all breeds.

Mr. Dobie, that old steer looked around at me and the cowboys and his buddies passing on by and very carefully, one leg at a time, gingerly stepped out of the fence. In order to accomplish this feat, he had to weave in and out of each strand of the wire. He never panicked, and he did not hurry. We waited and watched in wonder as he deftly and deliberately got himself out of his predicament.

That was the beginning of an even deeper love and respect for the longhorns for me. I was not alone. The thousands who came to see us loved them. They gaped and sighed and gasped and pointed.

"Oh that one there is mine!"

"No, he's mine; I saw him first." A boy and girl, bright young faces peering out a van window as we passed down the streets of Tuttle, Oklahoma, made their choice of the horned wonders nonchalantly lumbering by. The streets of Matt Dillon's Dodge City, Kansas, were lined with curious onlookers seeking a glimpse of the descendants of those hearty, horned creations of God who helped to place their city in the archives of Western history. They were waiting everywhere – the young and the old, the affluent, the working men and women – with cameras loaded. They walked through green pastures, weeds, and grass burrs to get close enough for that special picture of Old Carrottop, the big red-headed steer from Ed and Nan Creel's Triple N Ranch near Cedar Creek, Texas, or of Old Blue, Walt Secrest's blue roan, who competed for lead steer with Carrottop. Walt had brought him to Texas to walk back to Montana. They loved the giant, docile old black, whose horns would have made even the most worldly turn around in awe.

How did we, human creatures following them across six states, feel about the ridgebacks? I can speak for only one. I chose the most intelligent, the most stubborn, stoic, the most fearful, and the most harebrained ones that intrigued me each day. One scrawny black-and-white spotted one, with black face and horns too big for the rest of his body, seemed to work at trying the patiencc of those of us who rode flank on the left side of the herd. He insisted on walking on the pavement when all the rest were on the grass. He put space between himself and the more aggressive steers to walk alone in the clear. We could not trust him to stay put, because if we let him be, he would wander across the highway. Most of the cowboys had expressed their personal descriptions, some unmentionable, about old Spotted Ass, the name I had tacked on him.

The big black-faced, white-bodied steer with trophy horns walked in the center near drag (the rear of the herd). He did not veer to the right or the left. His face exuded boredom and monotony as he walked at the same speed all day. Any steer that got too close was promptly gored and pushed aside like a pesky gnat in hot summer sun. That stoic bovine had the look and muscle of a bull, a coat that would be the envy of any who did not have it on display, and I imagined beneath his beautiful hide were delectable steaks and roasts. They were hidden because he never wasted one ounce of energy on such things as other hairy beasts or two-legged creatures. He simply had turned northwest at Fort Worth and headed for Montana, and he never bothered with much else after that.

Some of the steers with lethal weapons and weight were really wimps who were pushed around by smaller ones. Some would risk almost anything for a quickly purloined patch of clover or greenery. The smaller and weaker ones spent their time finding a space away from the tougher bullies. They all learned to trudge in a long line through heavy traffic, over viaducts, down streets of small towns without missing a chew on the cud. They were not intimidated by truck air brakes, helicopters that hovered, or a train's whistle. A running horse or sudden movement, on the other hand, would spark a stampede quickly.

Longhorns have personalities, just as people do. I had a bull on my small ranch in Palo Pinto County, Texas, who was a fifteen hundred-pound lap dog. "Chief" would have gotten into the cab of my pickup had he been able to get his forty-eight-inch horn span through the door. He was as gentle as a puppy, but he could hurt you bad just trying to get close to you. The cows were as gentle, except when they had a new calf. Longhorn mothers are as fierce as tigers about their young. Those animals were a joy to my stressful life. On weekends, I could not wait to go out to the ranch. I would fill my ice chest with bologna, a jug of red wine, a hunk of cheese, and a box of crackers. When I closed my nightclub on Saturday nights, I headed for the ranch. I slept in the bed of my truck and cleared brush in the daytime. I was happy and content to be out there with those critters.

Before Chief, I had purchased my first bull when he was only fifteen months old. "Bevo" was not the pet that Chief became, but he was a "stay-at-home" until my neighbor put some Hereford heifers across the fence from Bevo without a herd bull with them. I told Charles, my neighbor, that he should put a bull with his heifers or Bevo would help him with his breeding program. Charles procrastinated a bit too long and Bevo jumped the fence, and Charles had the best calf crop that year that those Herefords had ever thrown. When he finally put a bull over there, Bevo jumped over and whipped his butt. I could not keep Bevo in the pasture anymore and pulled him out and had him castrated, thinking he would make a great trophy steer one day. His horn span was already forty-six inches, and he still had much growing to do.

After Bevo healed from the castration, I turned him back in the pasture. He promptly jumped the fence and damned near killed Charles' bull, which I might add, outweighed him by about four hundred pounds. Longhorns establish supremacy, and castrating one does not lessen their aggressiveness. Bevo reminded that Hereford bull that those heifers still belonged to him.

There have been many stories about the longhorns and their

intelligence and individuality. J. Frank Dobie wrote about how the longhorn is systematic and habitual. He told how they get up in the night about the same time for a drink, how they lie down in practically the same spot, and graze in the same vicinity.

He told the story of Old Sancho, an orphan calf raised by a Mexican woman named Maria, who worked and lived on the Esperanza ranch. She fed him tamales and chiltipiquin peppers, which he learned to love. He became addicted to hot peppers and human companionship and his little world close to Maria's house. When he was three years old, he was sold and driven to Wyoming from that ranch, which was south of San Antonio, Texas. He tried to turn back south so many times that the drovers began tying Sancho each night.

In Wyoming, Sancho was branded with the CR brand by the side of his 7Z Texas brand. The drovers went back to Texas and left Sancho, who was still looking south. Three months later, Sancho showed up on the Esperanza ranch, where he found his "mama," Maria. He had worn his hooves to the quick, but he made the trip back from Wyoming.

Dobie wrote, "As far as I can find out, Old Sancho lived right there on the Esperanza, now and then getting a tamale, tickling his palate with chili peppers in season, and generally staying fat on mesquite grass, until he died a natural death. He was one of the walking Texas longhorns" (*The Longhorns*).

I cried when I read that story. I couldn't help it. I don't believe anyone could have lived with those critters for six months as we did and not have developed feelings for them. There is a monument on a hill in Addington, Oklahoma, overlooking the Price Ranch, dedicated to the memory of the Chisholm Trail. Written on one side of the monument are these words:

Millions of Longhorns were driven northward
across the plains to railheads in Kansas during
the period 1867- 1889. The great cattle drives
not only helped to feed a nation just after the

Civil War, they produced one of the nation's
most enduring heroes – the cowboy .
The brief era of the open range and free grass
generated the greatest cattle boom in world history.

The longhorns are like the earth, the sky, and the mountains. They will live on with us or without us. Long live the Texas longhorns.

I cannot think or write about longhorns without thinking of my late, great friend, Ace Reid, cartoonist, creator of *Cowpokes,* the legendary, bony cowboy misfits, their cattle, and their antics and mishaps. Ace was world renowned and a household name for four decades. He still is, with legend now tacked on to that.

We met in Kerrville, Texas, in 1968 at the Inn of the Hills. My children knew his face immediately and pointed him out to me in the restaurant, begging me to let them go and ask for his autograph. That was the beginning of a friendship which prevailed over twenty-five years of doing shows together, sharing fun, friends, laughter, booze, and tears. Ace spilled more whiskey than most people could drink, loved pulling practical jokes on those he loved, was always optimistic about life, and although he walked with kings and paupers, he treated all with honor and respect. He told me that he held the distinction of being the only living survivor of leukemia in its last stages. I am sure that he simply "pickled" the disease. Whatever miracle happened, Ace and his magic pen brought laughter to millions from continent to continent. If you mention Ace to my children, my son will tell you about the time Ace came to the house after he and his sisters had gone to bed and drew cartoons on their navels while they slept. Kenny was then about four, and he refused to bathe for two days. "Mama, it'll wash off my longhorn," he moaned.

The first time I performed in Kerrville, Ace introduced me at the *LaBazaar,* a small shopping center with art shops, a crystal and glass shop, a leather shop, a music store. Ace owned La Cantina, where beer, popcorn, and peanuts could be bought. I was to perform for the grand opening of the center. With local television cameras rolling, the mayor of Kerrville presented me with the key to the city. About four hundred gathered around the fountain in the middle of the center to hear me sing.

Ace, standing six feet four in his ostrich boots, western cut suit, silver belly Stetson, and a belt buckle the size of a football field, told the crowd: "Folks, this here's a real live Indian! She don't eat nothin' but German Shepherd Dogs!" When Hondo Crouch, owner of Luchenbach Texas died (before the world heard of Luchenbach), Ace cried a bucket of tears. He loved Hondo like a brother. He stood up at Hondo's funeral and said: "The reason they cremated old Hondo was to git all the ticks off him." The three of us did many shows and shared much laughter together over the years.

Ace Reid's wit and awesome art will live forever for me and the millions who have relished his calendars, cookbooks, and daily cartoon in one hundred thirty-five syndicated newspapers for over forty years. He depicted the longhorn as the ornery, bony, persevering creature that he really was. He took the hardships and poverty of the cowboy, and the dry, barren land in West Texas and made them poignant and funny to the world.

7

BOWIE, TEXAS AND THE QUIET BEFORE THE STORM

The Bowie, Texas, Sheriff's Posse Arena Grounds was the nicest camp we had had yet. We had stalls for our horses, water, good grass, and shelter over the tents. Hordes of people came in the rain to greet us. They were impatient for autographs and could not wait for us to feed and water our tired ponies, for the answers to hundreds of questions.

The wind was blowing a gale. Between questions, we signed the big maps of our route which were being sold in the souvenir trailer to those standing in the cold in lines and groups. There was no place to lay the papers, shirts, maps or whatever we were asked to sign, so we just used the backs of those wanting autographs while others held the maps, borrowed pencils and hugged, thanked, and congratulated us.

All that was like a warm fire and sweet words from home, in spite of my aching bones. I had to learn to walk all over again. My knees refused to respond to my brain. I couldn't find Dick to see if he was OK, and someone told me that he had gone to the hospital for a checkup and a treatment for severe cough and possible bronchitis. He then went to a motel in Bowie for rest and medicine while we had downtime. I decided I would also get a room for the time we would be down.

Wow! A motel, and with heat and maybe a drier for all my wet clothes. So what if it doesn't come equipped with Gregory Peck or James Arness? Who cares, so long as it has a hot shower. I couldn't wait to get into a shower that was hot enough to scald my dirty body and to get into some dry clothes.

The Travel Inn in downtown Bowie reminded me of the old tourist courts, of the forties. It was managed by a couple who lived in the back of the office. They were nice, friendly, and accommodating. Their trusting nature was apparent and pleasing. After breakfast, I walked five blocks in a steady rain to a health food store for herbal tea. Less than half a block from the motel, I walked past a service station (where they still give service). A man, perhaps thirty-five years of age, came out and yelled: "Hey, them old cows wuz really cranky yesterday, wudden they!" He had a bright face with a small mustache and dark hair. The patch on his Exxon shirt said "Richard."

"You know, I took my little girl down at that railroad crossing where yall went under 287, you know, when that ol' steer took off a-running up the tracks and that cowboy took off after em', well, my little girl ain't but two and a half years old and she's a cowboy, see, not a cowgirl, she's a cowboy, see, well, she don't never say it, and she never said it before, but when she saw them steers and cowboys she said, "My God, look at them cowboys." He laughed a full-throated laugh with pride and satisfaction and admiration.

"You know, my cousin – he's dead now, died with cancer – he's a redhead and the sun was bad for him. He had 3,600 acre ranch and worked out all day and got skin cancer and it killed him." He took a deep breath, which gave me time to interrupt and ask where the health food store was, although I had directions already. I felt another long, detailed story coming forth, and the rain was soaking my goose down and seeping into my shirt. I bid Richard a good morning and soon found the store and tea. Richard is one of life's little hidden treasures.

Later, I went to camp to tend to Gus and Red. It was a bog hole. All the horses in the remuda were turned out after we arrived, and they were tearing around the pasture like children after being cooped up in the house. They were glad to be out of the hock-deep mud in the stalls and corrals. Dick Allen and Garland Hartley brought hay for the steers from across the road. I believe they are partners there in Bowie, and they were responsible for us camping at the posse arena and grounds.

Everyone was friendly and generous with food, feed, and accommodations. Jack's Café in Montague fed us three meals. Locals brought smokers and meat to camp. Longhorn breeders were quick to offer any assistance needed. The big chuck wagon horses were turned out because the arena was a mire of mud. Those aggressive half-broken creatures fought with one of Jamie Nail's horses and broke its back. It had to be destroyed. Those big horses averaged a ton or more.

On March 16, the outriders began pouring in to cross the Red River. We would cross on the bridge. Not because the river was deep, but because the banks were so steep the animals would not be able to climb out of the river after we were in. I was relieved. I would have attempted it if the rest had, although it would have scared the ass off me, but I had doubts that all the horses, including Gus and Red, could or would swim the river. I was sure that if Goodnight and Loving and all the rest of the old cowboys had had a bridge to cross on, they would have used it without hesitation. To hell with egos which seem to propel men to do crazy and senseless things.

The life of a cowboy gets tedious, but it is never boring, and we weren't far removed from those whose cold trails we were following. For every cowboy ever born, there are ten stories about his antics and adventures. That may be another reason that I am so content to be with men – for no other reason than to listen to their tales and adventures. I haven't reached the age when I am bored by those tales, even the ones I have already heard. I have been known to tell a few myself, and I basked in the stories of the Old West in my research paper written in college. A nineteenth-century cowboy, Fred E. Sutton of Oklahoma City, told George

W. Sanders, president of the Old Time Trail Drivers Association, about a personal experience he had:

"It took place in the fall of 1881, when fifty other punchers and me were rounding up some thirty thousand head of cattle for Jesse Evans in New Mexico. We had considerable trouble with a bunch of outlaws and cattle rustlers headed and controlled by Billy the Kid. In the latter part of '80, a then-noted frontier officer by the name of Pat Garrett was detailed to bring the Kid in, dead or alive, and he knew our boys had been bothered a great deal and had lost several cattle. He came to our camp for help. I was detailed as one of the posse to go with Garrett, and we finally located the outlaw in a ranch house about forty miles from White Oaks. After surrounding them, a halt was called for a parley. Billy the Kid sent word by a Mexican outlaw by the name of Jose Martinez, one of his leaders, that if Garrett would send the writer, who was known as "The Crooked S Kid," and Jimmy Carlyle, a young cowboy, to the house he would try and come to some kind of an agreement. Garrett readily consented to this as he knew his men and those of the Kid, and he knew a battle meant death to many.

Leaving our guns behind, Jimmy and I went to the house, where we found as tough a bunch of outlaws, gun fighters, and cattle thieves as ever infested a country, or were ever congregated in a space of that size. After an hour spent in propositions and counter-propositions, we agreed to disagree, and started back to our own crowd with the promise of not being fired on until we reached them. But we had only traversed about three-fourths of the distance when there was an avalanche of lead sent in our direction and poor Jimmy, Sheriff William Bradley, and a ranchman by the name of George Hindman were instantly killed. Our posse then withdrew. (Trail Drivers of Texas).

There were no gunfighters in the vicinity of our cattle drive, but we had our own twentieth-century so-called "hills to climb" and our first big one wasn't far away.

The most dreaded of all the trail hazards in the nineteenth century was the stampede. It could be caused by thunder, lightning, a wolf's howl on a still night, a stick broken, a pot rattled, or any unusual noise in the night. Instantly, the whole herd would be up and off in a panic, usually scattering in all directions. This brought all hands into action.

In his book, ***The Chisholm Trail***, Don Worcester relates tales of storms along the trails, including one account of a disastrous stampede that occurred when two thousand steers belonging to the Wilson brothers plunged into "Stampede Gully" and every animal was lost. Rainstorms might wash away a trail for days and turn the prairie into a mire, making horses weak and causing cattle to lose weight. The cooks could not prepare food because everything that would burn was wet. The cowboys were soaked and wet and exhausted.

One such crew was driving a herd of yearlings north when a blue norther struck in the night near a dry lake bed that was covered with large tumbleweeds. Soon the tumbleweeds were flying among the bawling yearlings that scattered in all directions. In the dark, it was impossible to tell yearling from tumbleweed, and one cowboy was said to have chased a bunch of weeds for half a mile trying to force the leaders to turn. We knew it could happen to us. When one is dealing with animals, anything can happen at anytime, and it did.

In Ringgold, Texas, the cattle balked at an overpass and scattered on the grassy bank instead of going under it. We quickly gathered them and started the leaders to milling until they quieted down, then drove them back on the highway and under the overpass. I was riding swing about twenty-five or thirty feet behind Dick Kennedy. When the front half of the herd broke into a run, Dick yelled and turned his horse at the same time.

"Cut 'em! turn 'em!" he yelled. I followed suit and swung Gus to meet the steers head-on before they had time to realize that the front part of the herd had bolted. We cut the herd in about half and kept talking and soothing the restless ones in front and kept them milling. I looked and saw the front of the herd going out of sight over a small hill, the cowboys in pursuit at breakneck speed.

There were cars lining the shoulders of the highway, and people standing in the middle of the highway gawking and pointing at the thundering herd quickly widening the distance between them and the half we held back. On Red River Bridge about four miles away, a crowd was waiting, including the senator from Oklahoma, to greet us as we crossed the river.

There had been no crack of thunder in the still of night, no gunshots, no scream of a panther or puma to set those leggy bovines into a wild race. There were no prairie dog holes to worry about your pony falling into, no mesquite trees to dodge, no cliffs to fall over, no tumbleweeds to chase – only hard, deadly slick asphalt, broken bottles, litter, automobiles, and people.

My heart was pounding with excitement and dread. I had a vision of cowboys or even steers strewn along the highway injured or worse. Asphalt is no place to run a horse.

One lady made a hasty decision to pull her Lincoln across the highway and stop the herd. Those steers went over, into, and around her, without slowing or hesitation. Bud McCasland and one of the investors in two vehicles tried pulling their cars into a vee to slow the leaders, but to no avail.

On the Texas side of the river, James "Jim" Donaldson, an Oklahoma cowboy, finally turned the ridgebacks into the valley on the east side of the bridge. With bleeding hooves, sides pumping, and tongues spitting froth, they stopped at last, about thirty feet short of the bridge. We, the children of the twentieth-century telecommunications world, had for the first time heard the thundering beats of yesteryear when cowboys of the longhorn range ate the dust of stampedes – while we chased the steers down an asphalt path, leaving a trail of small patches of blood.

Do not believe that the modern longhorn isn't tough. Do not believe that one hundred years have bred the fiery *cimmarone* blood out of him. Those horned racehorses with hearts of eagles and the ancestral blood of legends wrote another chapter in their long history, equally as exciting as the past.

We gathered all of the steers, except two who managed to hide in the brush and drove them out of the river bottom and across Red River Bridge to a crowd of over five hundred Texans and Oklahomans who must have seen the end of the stampede. We set up camp right on schedule, at Terrell, Oklahoma, where the warm and hospitable citizens of Terrell were waiting for us with barbecue and all the trimmings at the small community center. The next morning we cut out the sore-footed steers to be treated and hauled a few days until they became fit again and headed the rest to Ryan for the next camp.

Tales about stampedes aren't the only kind of stories told around campfires or in books, because rap sessions along our trail around the campfire and tailgates on the trailers were like balm for frustrations, lousy weather, and cold, wet feet.

Tall tales, jokes, and discussions were great therapy, and some were funnier than cross-eyed pigs. In camp at Ryan, the next afternoon after the stampede, we were sitting around Eldon Winn while he replaced worn shoes on one of the horses, when one such rap session was in full swing. One cowboy told a great joke, (I assumed it was a joke).

"We had hauled loads into California and couldn't get a load out, so we headed for a bar. We were drinking and having a good time, and this gal began to get real friendly with us. We sort of figured after awhile she might just be commercially interested in us. She assured us that she was not gonna charge us a dime, no matter how many there was. She told us that her husband was sitting at the bar and he liked to watch. Man, I didn't want no part of that kinky stuff, and I headed for the motel room. I had just got my boots off when Charlie came charging into the room and said, 'Man,' he says, 'can you believe what them people wanted us to do?' I said yeah, that goes on here quite a bit. 'Man,' he says, 'they don't even do *that* in Amarillo!'"

This story earned a roar of laughter from the whiskey sippers and bystanders, Dick, Will, and me. We all bent our elbows as a lady walked up and asked if I was Annie Golightly. She was a friend of a fan, and later that day she took Gloria Shaefer and me to her house for life-saving showers with real hot water and soap and dry towels. It was very close to heaven. When we got back to camp about an hour before sundown, I went to feed Gus and Red. The damned gap was wired so tight that I had to pry it open. (A gap, for the uninformed, is an opening into a corral or pasture made out of fence posts and barbed wire with a loop over the corner post that fits over the stationary fence post to lock it into place). A friendly couple came down and said they were from Mineral Wells, Texas, and had heard about me for years but never seemed to be able to find me.

"We finally named you the Phantom Lady because everywhere we went we were told that you had just left. We heard you were on this drive, and we were determined to find you, and here we are with you at last." I was astounded and thrilled. Recognition always warms the heart and makes one feel a bit taller.

In 1974, I was in Panama to sing for President Demetrio B. Lakas. I had a body guard who drove me everywhere I wanted to go, and one day I asked "Lopez" to stop at a store so I might buy some film. I was walking down the street when someone yelled, "Hey, Annie Golightly, what are you doing here in Panama!"

So there I was in Oklahoma, miles away from home in a grassy pasture, and there were two people who had come a long way to see me. Life was good. We had a great visit, and I knew some good fairy was sitting on my shoulder.

The long, cold day led me to turn in early to get warm. I fell asleep almost instantly and awakened later to shouts and cursing and finally giggling – male giggling. I sat up and peeked through the tent flap in time to see five or six figures running through the night clad in hats and boots and nothing else. The glare of headlights on a car turning into camp outlined the nude cowboys and the squeals of delight or fright (I never learned which) were heard throughout camp. Two cowboys and their visiting wives were in the car and had just returned from town in time to catch the scanty display of western humanity. It seems, as was told the next morning at breakfast, that some of the nude pranksters had poured sweet feed on bedrolls of their sleeping comrades and had driven the steers in close for treats, then "streaked" through camp for curtain calls. I called it the Weenie Festival. I could only guess who the culprits had been; because of darkness, I could not recognize faces – only gender.

8

OKLAHOMA AND KANSAS

I never latched onto many women in my life, but once or twice in my travels, I have met some unforgettable women, and Mary McCauley is one of those women. At Waurika, Oklahoma, Jim and Mary McCauley and their friends, the Brisindines, all from Fort Worth, were waiting for me when we got into camp.

"Annie, I brought you a fresh supply of peanut butter and jelly. I think you are crazy as hell, but I am really proud of you," Mary exclaimed in her deep, throaty voice. Is that diametrical or what? I'll explain about the peanut butter and jelly before I introduce you to Mary and Jim.

◆ ◆ ◆ ◆

Until I was thirty-five years old, my experience with alcohol consisted of holding my nose, downing a straight shot of bourbon, and chasing it with a cigarette and a Grapette soft drink. In high school, once in a blue moon about six of us "rebels" would buy a quart of White Rose wine from the bootlegger and get puke-sick on it and feel really grown up and worldly until we gagged up our cereal and milk off a soured stomach next morning.

Later in life, I tended bar for seventeen years and never drank any of the merchandise. But at the ripe old age of thirty-five, I acquired a taste for Scotch, and since that time, I have done my part to keep corn prices near the top.

In the ensuing years, I often said that I had, in my adolescent years, believed peanut butter and jelly to be the greatest stuff in the world and that the first time I tasted J&B Scotch with water, I believed that it undoubtedly must be peanut butter and jelly. Thereafter, my fans and customers would always see to it that I had a plentiful supply of "peanut butter and jelly" in my glass on the bandstand.

◆ ◆ ◆ ◆

The McCauleys were there, in that muddy camp, laden with warm greetings and a half gallon of J&B Scotch. Shades of prosperity! Life was good. Mary and Jim McCauley have been my friends for a long spell. We have had some good times together in my club and great restaurants and other clubs. Mary is one elegant lady who knows how to laugh and live, and Jim is laid-back, witty, soft-spoken, and a bundle of fun. They were fascinated with the drive and made several visits along the trail, and Mary wasn't hard to spot strolling among the denim, boots, longhorns, and manure with her multiple gold bracelets, diamond rings, high-heeled "bitchy" boots, fur, and suede. She tramped through the mud with all the class and majesty of Queen Elizabeth, her rich laughter making music throughout camp. She meets the world head-on and accepts people for what they are, culling those she dislikes and giving her all to those fortunate enough to meet with her approval. She picked me a long time ago and that makes me pretty damned rich.

There's nothing like friends, small talk, and Scotch to warm the insides after a cold day in the saddle. I often wonder why I didn't start earlier. But the farther I go, the better the trip becomes. Let's get back on the trail. . . .

Tuesday, March 21, and we moved on past green pastures with angus cattle like tiny black polka dots. We narrowly missed another stampede when five curious horses came in a dead heat across the green at the city limits of Addington, Oklahoma. Cattle respond to excited horses by running headlong.

I had been uptight for several miles because two of the young drovers put their ponies into lopes which instantly excited the cattle. The young men became bored with the turtle pace the longhorns set each day. Their yen for excitement or change made me nervous. I am an expert on knowing what devastation one tiny impulse can cause.

The Price, or Monument Ranch as it was called, was sixty thousand acres of rich grass and rolling hills just east of Addington, and twenty miles south of Duncan. The Chisholm Monument stood on a hill just above where we camped. We were there three days and went out of our way to get there because Bud and the investors thought the ranch would be a great place to sell souvenirs and promote the cattle drive. They were wrong.

The business at the souvenir trailer was a nil. We had a sprinkling of people as I set up my computer on a small table in the rear of the souvenir trailer to write a story for *Trails* magazine and bring my journal up to date. One of the investors was attending the trailer and sales of the souvenirs. A tiny lady, quite possibly an octogenarian, came to the window and asked the price of Steve Schick's tape. Steve had written a song about the drive which was adopted as our theme song, and it was for sale out of the souvenir trailer.

"My, but $13 seems real high to me for this tape," she told the investor.

"Take it or leave it, lady, it'll be higher farther down the road." I felt a bit uncomfortable, and I was glad that tiny lady couldn't see me. We were treated with utmost kindness and sometimes near worship along the way. Everyone seemed to be thrilled with us and wanted so much to be or to have a small part of the drive. We should have learned a lesson from the cowboys of yesteryear, who were polite to ladies – especially older ladies. My country upbringing, though sometimes crude, was always sprinkled generously with kindness and courtesy to all. My grandmother would have swatted the snot out of that big arrogant man had she been the one commenting on the price of that tape. I scurried off to better things and put off the writing until later.

All of a sudden I wanted a bath. I found a towel and soap and headed down the road to the creek we had crossed with the cattle. The water was colder than a witch's tit, but running clear. I shed my clothes and took only scant minutes to bathe the grime off my goose bumps. I vowed then and there that for the rest of my life, I would never complain about the hot water, or lack of it. There is something humbling about bathing in cold creek water.

I caught a ride with a couple of cowboys in one of the equipment trucks and took laundry to Duncan and bought batteries for my camera. We ran errands and wandered through the stores and drew attention everywhere we went with our jingling spurs, Stetsons, and high-topped boots. We encountered people in sneakers, skirts, slacks, and business suits. Duncan was not a western town.

The ideal weather in the early afternoon reminded us of the scorching days of summer ahead of us. Flocks of wild geese chanted to us across the sky on their way north. There is a very special corner in my heart for wild geese. I love the fact that they mate for life. I love their beauty and wildness. *I am flying Northwest, just like those critters up there. Ma always did call me wild, but I have always felt a kinship with the wild creatures, and the Canadian honkers never cease to thrill me.*

Dick and I played and sang in camp, and the Duncan newspaper reporter came out and wrote a story about us, complete with our picture on the front page. Some little man came to camp as a representative from the Arbuckle Coffee Company and declared that the company would furnish all our coffee for the rest of the trip. Well, it wasn't the best coffee I ever drank, but it brought back some memories of the days when I worked in the City Cafe in Commerce, Texas. . . .

I was a teenager in high school, and the Cottonbelt Railroad crew would come in, and one of the men would always say, "Gimme a cup of Arbuckle." He never said, "coffee," just "Arbuckle." He was short and ugly and sort of grouchy, but he always left me a quarter tip. After I left Commerce, I never heard of that coffee brand again until we camped on the Price Ranch.

That little Arbuckle man wore a Canadian Mountie hat and sang and played the guitar and hung Arbuckle Coffee banners on the chuck wagon and brought that awful coffee to our camp, to my chagrin. In all fairness, I must add that some of the terrible coffee we drank in camp might have been due to the fact that Dancer simply never cleaned the coffee pot. Never. I remember while still living at home that Lettie wasn't the greatest housekeeper around, but she cleaned the coffee pot once in awhile. That old adage about "it will ruin the camp coffee if you wash the pot" is so much horse manure as far as I am concerned. When you look down at your morning coffee and see grease floating on top, the damned coffee pot needs cleaning.

One of the nights when we were down, Will, Dick, and I confiscated one of the trucks (no small feat because only three or four of the cowboys seemed to have access to the trucks) and went to town for steaks and drinks. Will and I drank whiskey, and Dick ordered coffee. We had a great time, and Dick made several calls, one to a friend who came to camp the next day with a trailer. Suddenly, without warning, Dick Kennedy was gone. Will told me later that Dick had told him of his plans to leave. I was sad to see him go, but not surprised. Will and I missed him and wrote to him several times. One of the Musketeers had "lit a shuck for home."

One of the days we were on the Price Ranch, Will and Ace Wright combined their talents with hammer and saw and built partitions in the equipment trailer. I would finally have a small space for just *my* stuff. It was like someone bringing me a new set of Samsonite luggage; like the first time I had my very own dresser in my room. The compartments were about thirty-six inches long and about two feet high and deep. There wasn't enough room for all my belongings, but it was better than searching for my bedroll and clothes under a mountain of bags and buckets and boots that belonged to someone else.

I put my footlocker with the stuff that I didn't need each day and stuffed all the rest around it. I copied Will and drove a nail into the front board to hang clean laundry on. I learned to have the laundry fold my shirts, but I liked to hang my coats and a couple of shirts that might survive the crowd in the trailer for "special" occasions. There was something wonderful about putting on a stiffly starched shirt and jeans with a crease in them. Like when you were a kid and put your Sunday-go-to-meetin' dress on for that special day when you got to sing "Jesus Loves Me" in church. You just knew that everybody out there in the congregation was admiring your outfit. All the ruffles and pleats were starched and ironed and stood out crisp and pretty. And out there in the wide open spaces, there was something about that "George Strait" starched perfect look that made me feel great.

When I went to pick up my clothes at the cleaners in Duncan, the bill was twenty-seven dollars. That almost loosened my teeth. Hell, I didn't want to buy them again, just get them cleaned. Gloria told me later that her bill was $32. Well, we were clean for a day or two anyway, and donning those clothes was right up there with white table cloths, candles, soft lights, and good red wine. I cleaned and oiled my tack, and Gus and Red got new shoes while they were basking in green grass and three days of freedom and rest.

March 23, we left Price Ranch at the Monument, and back tracked three miles south. We rode fourteen miles and ended up in Hastings, Oklahoma, three miles farther south. *God, what a drag when you know you aren't getting any closer to Montana but still spend nine hours in the saddle*. It took an hour just to round up the cattle in that beautiful ranch before hitting the road.

The weather continued to batter us. In Hulen, Oklahoma, a storm blew down the big tent before we arrived with the cattle. The camp was moved to higher ground and set up near two huge grain elevators. We had a "wreck" near Sterling when ostriches at a ranch raced out to the fence, curious about the chuck wagon, and the Shires bolted and ran for several miles before Walt got them under control. One horse was being ponied on the back of the wagon, and it was dragged until all the hide was gone from its side. The horse made it but was later sent home to Texas, I believe.

I thanked my stars that I was working as a drover that day and did not have to witness that horse being dragged behind the chuck wagon. I am pretty squeamish when it comes to seeing a horse hurt. They are such fragile and tender animals. Their hides are as tender as human skin and as easily torn. A cow will survive running through a fence whereas a horse will be torn to shreds.

Outside Sterling, Oklahoma, we camped on Curtis and Peggy Scruggs' ranch. Peggy took me across the highway into her beautiful brick home for a wonderful shower. I looked in the mirror at skin that was rough and red and hair that needed a bit of "shoe polish." She called a beauty shop in town for an appointment to get color back into my then-white hair. I met her sister, Jolanda, and her grandson, Robert, a big strapping boy of seventeen, clad in bib overalls and wearing a brilliant smile. After that heavenly shower, I sat at the kitchen table and drank coffee and talked with those delightful and friendly people.

That night in camp I met Beuna and Earl Heston. A tiny couple, both octogenarians, towering almost to my rib cage, came to camp and stood in the blasted cold and wind and rain to listen to my guitar and voice, which wasn't too good because of a nagging cold and chest congestion that had been plaguing me for days. They begged me to go home with them. At first, I politely declined, thinking of my horses and my cold and sore throat. They refused to accept my weak "no," and I crawled into their pickup. I slept in a warm bed surrounded by hundreds of teddy bears. Beuna's walls were lined with tiny whatnots and pictures of children and grandchildren.

"He gets to be boss between October and January when he is one year older than me," Beuna beamed as she held Earl's hand. They looked and acted like high school sweethearts. In sixty-one years of marriage, they had survived the Depression, had two children who came down with polio two weeks before the Salk vaccine was approved by the FDA, suffered heartbreak from the loss of another child, bankruptcy, and the general hardships of life. Their delightful, positive attitude was as refreshing as spring water on a hot day. Beuna cooked a wonderful breakfast in an airy kitchen, and we ate on bright red plaid oilcloth with hot coffee and laughter. I forgot my cold and the constant cough that had set up housekeeping in my chest. I was reminded of how simple life could be and how little it takes to be happy if one is kind and good and caring and content with what one possesses. How sweet the feeling of meeting the warm, caring people along the trail.

I was learning brand new lessons about life, or perhaps I was simply being reminded of lessons I had been taught and had forgotten. I began to count all the adjustments I had made since leaving home, and I remembered one day many years ago being brought to a standstill by something that Fat Albert, a funny little animated cartoon character, said on television: "It's de little things in life dat count de most. Like de plug in de bathtub!"

I had come a long way from the days when I carried a couple of grand in my wallet for "spending" money; when I had a financial statement with six figures, two automobiles, a ranch, cows, money in the bank, and a business that was the envy of many. Back when I counted "roughing it" as slow room service and unironed sheets. But then again, it hadn't always been that way.

◆ ◆ ◆ ◆

When I met Kenneth, we were both floundering around in our broken marriages and found something wonderful in our love for each other. Ten years later, on the eve of our anniversary, Kenneth was killed in an auto accident, and I was left with five children, a mortgage, and furniture and cars which were worn out and still not paid for. Kenneth and I, like many young people, most always spent more than we made for things that we could have probably done without.

There was little time for self-pity; I had too much responsibility. I also had my fierce pride to contend with. I was sure of one thing – filling out a credit application is like baring one's soul to the world. I knew for sure that I was not going to be poor the rest of my life. I vowed to myself that the day would come when I would never fill out another application telling my financial secrets to some pompous ass I had never seen before, sitting behind a seven-foot mahogany desk. I'd as soon have dropped my BVD's on city square.

Without formal education, I had a limited choice of jobs available to me. I went to work at five in the morning in a café in Plano, Texas, where we lived. When the kids were home from school, fed supper, and busy over lessons or TV, I drove to Dallas, twenty-five miles away and worked in a club tending bar. My two eldest girls helped take care of the three babies. There were babysitters also. We made it through the next few tumultuous years, not without many heartaches and emotional scars, but we stayed together and made it on our own, never asking help from anyone.

In 1978, I bought a nightclub in Fort Worth. That club prospered; I accumulated land, a house, cattle, Western art, and friends. My children spread their wings and flew from the nest, all with high school diplomas and a couple of college degrees that they earned on their own (with some help from me, mostly in the form of my love and admiration and cheers). Fate had other plans for me. Because of the flood, the fire, and a business failure within the span of four years, I lost everything except tenacity, chutzpah and the love of my children and friends.

◆ ◆ ◆ ◆

Now, I was in the middle of Oklahoma, sick with a blasted cold, but deliriously happy and without problems of any significance. One's priorities change with circumstances. My big concern now was keeping warm, dry, and uninjured and doing my job as well or better than the cowboys I was riding with. The world in which

I had once lived was far away, out of reach, and unimportant.

Hell, I was getting to be good at being a cowboy. I could brush my teeth with less than a half cup of water. I could change clothes in a thirty-six- inch sleeping bag that was zipped up. A piece of cake, you say? Try it. I am five-feet-ten, my legs being almost three-quarters of that. Let me explain. When dressing in a sleeping bag inside a one-man tent, you must lay everything that you intend to wear tomorrow on the right side of your body, outside the bag. This applies to right-handers; the opposite applies to southpaws. Lay your shirt, pants, long johns, socks, and boots in the order needed. Did I mention that all this is performed in total darkness? It is tricky business shrugging out of jeans that are tight enough to resemble a body tattoo. Now work them up the side of the sleeping bag across your face and out. Be sure to put them on the left side of your bag. Now snuggle a moment to re-warm your hands. Reach for your clean jeans and bring them inside. They are stiff and cold next to you, so take time out to shiver and gasp and get circulation going again. Getting your knees drawn up around your ears in a sleeping bag to pull on your jeans is a feat that would have meant stardom on *The Ed Sullivan Show,* with a little promotion. By the time you are dressed, your blood is moving at a pace to warm the body, and you are ready for the day.

And speaking of the day, mine began at 4 a.m. on the drive. All the years of growing up on that cotton farm in East Texas came roaring back, and I was a kid again and loving every minute of it. In those days, we would hit those cold linoleum floors at four in the morning, when it was as cold as an Eskimo's butt, grab a bucket of water to wash the cow's teats and head for the cow lot to milk those Jerseys. I would be rudely awakened when that cow whopped me in the face with a tail full of cocklebururs while I was busy robbing her of that warm, frothy white.

On the trail, after dressing, I rolled up my bedroll, took down the tent, and went looking for Gus and Red to feed and care for them. Sometimes the horses were in pastures which covered thousands of acres. That didn't mean they were far away. The horses were so people-oriented that they had to be driven out of camp when we were in the same pasture with them. They were like children who wanted to be close, and they were always looking for tidbits of food that might be lying around.

Most of the cowboys had to chase their horses or even rope them to catch them. Not so with Gus and Red. They had only to hear the sound of my voice to find me, even in the early-morning darkness. They were always together and away from the rest of the horses. What a joy when I called and they came running and poked their heads into their halters. They had to have time to eat; therefore I fed them even before I had my coffee. Gus was so like a little boy. He was always happy and thrilled just to be loved and touched. Red was all business and ate with gusto. He cared not one way or the other if I petted him.

I trained my kidneys to function only early morning and late afternoon. We were in the saddle an average of seven hours a day, nonstop. How great it must be as a man to be able to simply stand behind a tree, bush, or your horse to get rid of the morning coffee. By the way, have you ever tried to find a tree or a bush in Kansas when you need one?

In Rush Springs, Oklahoma, the Comanche Indians came with fried bread to go with the saddle-blanket-sized steaks the townspeople had brought us. Remember the big Indian who scalped the mule skinner in the classic movie, *Dances with Wolves*? That was Lalo, chief of the Comanches. There he was, in his leather breeches, moccasins, vest and arm band, with no coat, no shirt, and there we were, in our long johns, wool socks, thick shirts, pants, goose down jackets, scarves and caps, shivering in the cold. Indians are as tough as longhorns.

The Comanches played their drums and chanted their songs, dressed in beautiful native dress. We stood in a circle around them huddling for warmth, fascinated by those brown bodies gyrating and flowing in the cold wind like the supple deer and antelope and panther. It was March 29 and so cold it seeped into the marrow of my bones. I had endured weather that was warmer in February. The wind blew in gusts of thirty-five to forty miles per hour, and the people came in droves.

Dancer cooked the steaks on the campfire, and there were three eight-foot tables covered with dishes, cooked at home, and every kind of dessert one could think of. We each could have had our very own pie. I was amazed at the love and admiration those people, young and old alike, brought to us. In spite of my congested chest, headache, and numb feet, I felt the warmth and kinship of those country folk strengthen my resolve to finish the trip, and my faith in humanity was enriched and rejuvenated.

◆ ◆ ◆ ◆

I stood just outside the glow of the campfire, gazing into the flames, I saw visions of my childhood and all the good country folk who cooked and brought dishes for school activities and the end of each school year in the small community where I grew up and attended elementary school. It was called "dinner on the ground." All the mamas would bring a covered dish - fried chicken, potato salad, and delightful deviled eggs. A deviled egg ranked right up there with chocolate pie, and ice cream and fresh strawberries. Everybody cared for their neighbors, and knew each other's kids and where they were at all times. They looked out for each other.

Yeah, and what about the time Sidney got burned? I will tell you. . . .

Country kids played in the road as much as in the yard. We found cattails on the small lake in the pasture and soaked them in kerosene. They made great torches. Lettie said that it was all right to play with them as long as we stayed close to the house. Sidney and I were about ten and thirteen, respectively. Mack and Hippy Herron farmed together on some leased land they had, and we were playing with the children of Hippy and his wife, Lelabelle.

"I'll go get summore coal oil," Betty Jane said, and dashed for the tractor shed where the oil was stored in a fifty-gallon tank beside the tractor gas tank. A south wind was blowing a pint-sized gale, and dry puffs of dust swirled in the twilight across the deep-cut ruts in the black gumbo road. Waffled tractor tracks decorated the road like giant doodles in the dirt. The shadows danced eerily in the dark from my bright torch. We heard Betty coming up the road before we saw her. The sun had made its exit, and its last remnants of light had disappeared beyond the horizon. She came running up the road with liquid sloshing over the rim of the bucket and down her arms.

"Okay Sidney, hold out your cattail, and I will start it back up," Betty said breathlessly. Sidney held out his still smoking cattail, and Betty threw on the gallon of liquid.

Sidney erupted into a human torch. Lettie had always been emphatic about what to do if we should ever catch on fire.

"Don't never run! Lay down and roll!" She reiterated many times.

The can Betty Jane brought back from the shed was full of gasoline, not coal oil. The kerosene tank was low and the gasoline was handy, so she simply filled the bucket with gas instead. Sidney was burning from his waist down. The south wind was behind him and kept the gas from blowing in his face. He sprinted like a sheet of fire across the ditch and into the cotton patch and lay down and rolled in the soft dirt and stalks of cotton. Fifteen-year-old Phil, Hippy's eldest, reached him first and tried putting his socks out with his hands. Together, we finally got his britches off. Lettie and Lelabelle were there by that time. I can't remember ever hearing Sidney utter a cry or sound. Maybe he did, I don't remember. I don't remember going to the hospital. We were just there.

I walked down the corridor of the Commerce hospital alongside the rolling gurney, my skinny, long fingers clutched by Sidney's small ones. His face was tiny and gaunt and white. His lips were a thin line, his teeth clinched, and he held my hand tightly, needing our closeness for strength. He was not crying.

The doctor told Lettie that he was in shock. Sidney was not crying because he was tough, even then. He was tougher than any junkyard dog's old man.

I don't remember what anyone said after that. I don't remember how the doctor dressed Sidney's legs or Lettie crying or Mack holding her and Hippy pacing the floor outside and the other kids sitting like cornered rabbits in their dirty little bib overalls and the smell of gas still strong in the antiseptic waiting room.

I just remember the smell - the smell of burned flesh. I can close my eyes today and still smell it. I remember the tall waste basket sitting by the hospital bed in the operating room, with the charred remnants of the skin off Sidney's legs and thighs, and I remember how his legs reminded me of over-roasted marshmallows.

Commerce was a small farming town where everybody knew everybody. Saturday night, in town, you got to buy a double-dipped banana-nut ice cream cone and walk around the square and flirt with the guys and girls who walked around the square. You could go the Ralph's Newsstand and hide behind the counter and read Captain Marvel and Flash Gordon comic books free, if you didn't get caught. The old man who owned the grocery store at the end of Main Street kept his old Model T truck backed into the curb where he loaded it for home deliveries. He was so stingy and particular about that old truck, he hot-wired it to keep the old men from leaning on it while they talked and spat. Past Ralph's was a barber shop, and the domino hall, then the City Café with the high curb where neighbors sat and squatted, or leaned and talked and watched the sidewalk traffic. Everybody was talking about Sidney. Everybody was out hustling blood for him.

"Say John, did you know Mack's kid almost burned to death Wednesday night? He's at Lebermann's hospital and he needs blood."

"I'll be there, Chester. You be sure and tell everybody at the barber shop, and they'll give blood. They need anything else?"

Lettie stayed at the hospital during the daytime and Mack stayed at night. The crops grew, the weeds grew, and the days grew long and hard. Sidney's legs looked like giant rolls of dirty gauze with pinkish-gray splotches leaking through, permeating the rotten odor of dying flesh. After eight weeks, the doctor told Mack he could do nothing more. Sidney was admitted to Scottish Rite Hospital for Crippled Children in Dallas. There, the doctors told Mack that Sidney had gangrene in his legs and they would likely have to amputate them.

They didn't.

He was there for nineteen weeks, had twenty-two operations when the doctors removed skin from his chest and upper thighs to be grafted onto his legs. One little brown nipple ended up just above his ankle, neat and intact, just as if it had grown there. The giant leaders that run behind his knees were burned completely in two. He had to learn to walk all over again.

The kinship and brotherhood of country folk is born of hard times and short rations. There were no televisions, telephones, videos, faxes, or computers. Instead, there were dinners on the ground, barn raisings, hand shaking, hugging, word of honor, hog killing, canning, quilting, Amos 'n Andy on the radio, and fried chicken after church on Sunday.

I remember lying in my bed next to the window facing the east that September morning. All was quiet just at the breaking of dawn. Lettie had left to relieve Mack at the hospital, and Ma was still in bed. At first, the sound was like a giant airplane far in the distance. The bed began to vibrate slightly, and I heard Puppy Dog stirring on the front porch. I rose up and leaned on one elbow sleepily from my pillow, looked down the road toward the creek. A convoy of tractors roared toward the house like a row of prehistoric monsters heading for the watering hole.

These were our neighbors, our friends, coming to gather our crops. They picked the cotton, gathered the corn, baled the hay, and went back down the road home with waves and smiles and support. My, how time does fly. . . . Sidney has grandchildren now, who sit on his knee and listen to his stories. He carries the scars from that night on his legs and chest. He carries all the memories in his heart, of meeting Helen Keller when she visited the hospital; of all the letters and cards and money in his piggy bank at the hospital, and of the twisted and hopeless children who lay side by side with him in Scottish Rite. He is a grizzled old grandpa whose favorite joke in the local tavern is the bet he always wins.

"I bet I can do something ain't no woman in here can do!"

"What Sidney?"

"Stand in water up to my tit without getting my ass wet!"

RBUCKLE
ARIOSA COFFEE

9

THE GOOD DOCTOR IN TUTTLE, OKLAHOMA

Things change, but somehow stay the same. As I watched all those people at the campfire, I knew that that old "country selflessness" still lived. I knew that were it not for the people there, and all those we had met on the way to Montana, we would surely have failed and faded into the land somewhere back along the trail.

I didn't feel good. For days things were fuzzy, I was disoriented, coughed much of the time, and walked around in a fog. I rode with Jim McElroy in the equipment trucks during the day because I couldn't get warm or dry any other way. I fed and cared for Gus and Red and slept little because of the constant cold and wet, and I had difficulty breathing. When I finally admitted to myself that I was very sick, I was running a temperature. With Gloria's help, I found a doctor in Tuttle, Oklahoma, and she loaded me into her van. We met the good doctor at his office on Sunday afternoon.

"You have acute bronchitis, and I suggest you go check into a hospital today." He was a slight man, balding and soft-spoken, and I am sure he was curious about this old gypsy, dressed in muddy boots, dirty jeans, jacket, and felt hat, sitting in his office on Sunday after church with a high temperature and infected lungs.

"I can't go to the hospital, Doctor; I am with the cattle drive."

"Well, tomorrow, when it is over, you should go then," he said, matter-of-factly. When I told him that the drive wouldn't be over until September, he was aghast. He said that he had heard of "some trail drive," vaguely, or "saw something on TV about it," but he was not aware of it being in Tuttle.

He gave me a shot in my lower extremities and a prescription for pills. He then rummaged around his office and found samples of the pills because Tuttle had no pharmacy, and he felt I should get some of them down as soon as possible. I thanked him with words and a check, and Gloria and I left. He stood in the door and watched us drive away, thinking, I'm sure, that the old woman was totally nuts to leave a warm fire and bed and opt for the cold and rain and to sleep on the ground. I wasn't sure that he wasn't correct.

The pills made me even more goofy and drowsy, but I took every one of them, and those pills, combined with the determination not to be a candy-ass and give the cowboys a chance to call me a weak old woman, made me soon begin to feel like a human again.

Something very nice happened on April Fool's Day. About six of the cowboys went back to Sterling, Oklahoma, with a plaque and flowers for the Lions Club and the city of Sterling in appreciation for the nice things they had done for us while we were in the vicinity. The cowboys asked Will if he would make the presentation because he was the oldest Oklahoma cowboy.

"They asked me if I would be able to make the presentation, and I assured them I could handle it," Will told me. "And they thought old Will was pretty laid-back!" He laughed. I think many of the cowboys underestimated old Will and me a lot of the time. Walt, Will and I were the oldest members of the drive. I am convinced that the younger drovers looked upon Will and me as excess baggage that had to be tolerated, politely. We were able to contend with the elements, inconveniences, and hardships, because we both had been around the world more times than most of those on the drive had been around the pot looking for the handle. We had many laughs along the way because of that "tolerance" from the younger drovers. Thinking back now, we could have been reading the young ones completely wrong, but it seemed that way at the time. I wasn't present when Will presented the plaque to the Sterling townspeople, but I'll bet he was just the right one for the job.

Goodnight and Loving and all those pioneers of the Old West would have thought that the stove in the cook's trailer that Bud had had rigged up along the trail, was a wonder. In truth, it was a 1950 vintage, with an oven door that had to be propped shut. I'll bet they would have been amazed at the bologna and pressed ham hugged by two pieces of sliced bread and a dab of mustard for color that we had everyday for lunch. I'll bet even lobster and steak can get tiresome if it is served every day. A large percentage of the food on the drive was either lunch meat or something fried. We sometimes had a candy bar, packaged sweets, and occasionally a piece of fruit. Beans were served often, but were not a staple, as I had assumed they would be. I am not a lover of beans, so I did not miss them. When the public fed us, there were always beans. Dancer prepared several tasty dishes during the short time he did the cooking, but they were heavy with grease.

The pots were iron and washed in cold water the bulk of the time because no one bothered to heat water to wash them in. It would have been a bother and would have taken a lot of time. Walker Lawrence was the cook's helper and did most of the hard work around the kitchen. He rode with the chuck wagon each day, which meant he had to saddle early, and much of the time, the pots and pans weren't washed until we arrived at the next camp. I had a difficult time enjoying the "green" scrambled eggs each morning. The men bitched to each other and to me, but I never heard complaints to Bud when he made his rare appearances in camp. Cowboys aren't famous for bitching much. They take life the way it is handed to them.

Things that had seemed so important at home just weren't high on the priority list out there in the great outdoors. I nagged about the food to Will and Gloria, but never to Bud or the leaders because I did not believe that anyone there had the faintest idea what to do about it. Complaints seemed to fall on deaf ears, especially if the ears belonged to Bud. He was attentive to Gloria, but she did not complain to him either. *I will eat the things I like, and do without the rest until we get to a town or someone cooks for us. Who cares about breakfast anyway. Just so my horses have good food, and don't get any of that lousy hay that is sometimes fed to the remuda. Bad hay can and does kill horses, by causing them to colic with twisted guts.*

When I got sick and rode with Jim McElroy in the truck, we gathered garbage after camp had been dismantled and moved. This was a daily job. While loading the dozen or so sacks and boxes and cans, I asked what happened to the vast amount of garbage we created each day.

"We just find a Dumpster somewhere and dump it there," he said, to my amazement.

"You mean we are going to dump all this shit in someone else's Dumpster?"

"That's what I am told to do, and I do whatever Bud tells me."

Damn! Like what happened when I owned my club, and all those ne'er-do-wells dumped their old tires and carpet and crap in my Dumpster that I paid plenty for each month. Now we are doing the same thing. Poor Jim, he is always dressed neat and clean, and we are like transients in back alleys. Wonder what Charles Goodnight would have done? The best he could, just like we are doing I suppose. God, this reminds me of when I was in business. . . .

One night I drove up behind my club and caught a man methodically unloading sacks of garbage from his truck into my Dumpster. I scalded him with expletives and wrath until he tried to self-destruct right there. He called me by my first name and apologized sheepishly, loaded all the sacks back on his pickup, and drove off. I thought to myself I had just lost a customer or a fan, but I was still mad as hell.

It was easy to see mistakes that had been made in the planning of the drive. It is difficult to think of everything. I was quick to judge Bud and his planning, but had I been the planner, the situations could have been worse. I thought about a lot of things that night as I lay in my sleeping bag. I did not envy Bud and the heavy responsibility on his shoulders.

I was naïve enough to believe that all the people along the way welcomed us. I thought they all felt like those people who brought food, feed, firewood, prayers, and hugs. Wrong!

Six and one-half miles south of Tuttle, we camped in a pasture next to a beautiful, gabled house with a manicured lawn surrounded by silos, barns, tractors, and equipment lined up in a near-perfect row. We heard about the man who lived there. Jack Boles, our campsite scout, met him when he stopped to ask where he might find the man we were to deal with for our camp.

"He called us leechin' sons-o-bitches and ordered me off his place. He warned me that we were to leave no tracks on 'his' right-of-way on the east side of the highway," Jack told us.

We had already heard about the man in the meeting the night before. Someone said he was notoriously hostile, and Jamie assured us that he had talked to the sheriff, highway patrolmen, and deputies. The man, not us, would be in trouble should he make any complaints. I felt uncomfortable. I wanted to go over there and tell that man that we were not "leechin sons-o-bitches." I remembered the garbage dumped in someone else's Dumpster and the lack of management and the arguments and the undertow of discontent in camp, and I felt naked and exposed. It was as if that man had seen an ugly side of us that I did not want to admit even existed. I had become a master at evading reality. I was learning to face my frailties and those of others. We were human, subject to mistakes and wrong decisions. We were stumbling along a cold trail for the first time in over one hundred years, and we were making mistakes. Maybe that man just did not like to see someone veer from the conventional. Perhaps he resented those who dared to be imperfect.

Human frailties are numerous and sometimes difficult to swallow. One of the hardest things I remember facing as a child was the first time I discovered weaknesses in my parents, the first time I realized that Lettie wasn't always honest with me. She used to tell me that the cows were out and that she and Mack had to go get them, when they left me at home with Ma to go out. I must have been four or five before I began to put two and two together and got less than four. I was crushed and blamed myself and wondered what I had done to warrant her lying to me. I believe that somehow I would have better understood things if she had simply been honest and told me that I was too young to go out on the town with them or wherever they went without me. In my adult years, I have been called an idealist, and when that happens, I always say, "Thank you."

◆ ◆ ◆ ◆

Oklahoma always made me think of that great philosopher, Will Rogers, who once penned: *Always drink upstream from the herd.*

Oklahoma was red sand, wheat fields, and alfalfa growing green across spacious fields dotted with neat houses, huge combines, tractors, and Angus cattle. The highways and roads were lined with well-wishers waving and saying hello to us. We had to fight the steers out of the rich green stuff tempting them on each side of the road. I was riding swing between Claude Voiles and Eldon Winn. Claude hailed from Wyoming, where he worked an eleven thousand-acre ranch there for a great lady I was to meet later. Claude was divorced, father of a grown son and daughter. At first glance, he was not a handsome man, with his crooked teeth, thick glasses, and small stature, but he was supple, tough as nails and fearless. The more I was around Claude, the more I felt the depth and warmth of the man. He was unmatched in his abilities and knowledge as a working cowboy. He was quick to help anyone, and I noticed early in the drive, that he did much to help Walt each morning and evening with the harnessing and hitching of the Shires. He talked little, complained seldom, and minded his own affairs.

The day started all wrong when Red ran backward as I was saddling him and knocked me down. He was probably pissed off because his stomach was empty. There was no horse feed. It is hard to explain to a horse that he has to work but can't eat. We had to wait for someone to go buy horse feed. Jerry Owens said Jamie wouldn't let him buy but one ton of feed at a time. I was sure that Jamie had an excuse explaining that it was someone else's fault. *We have expert buck-passers here. But hey, I wonder if there is no money, and these guys are just covering for Bud? What we need is a woman running this outfit. Wouldn't that start some shit if I said that out loud to this bunch of macho cowboys! Man, wouldn't those old feminists have a field day with this bunch. Hey, I'll take the cowboys any day over broads, but damned if I like not having feed for my ponies.*

I was angered again when I discovered that my spurs were missing from beside my tent. A special friend had given me those spurs twenty years before, and I was furious that someone would walk off with them. I was sure that was what had happened. When I found out later that Jackie Foe Donaldson, a young Oklahoma cowboy, had inadvertently picked them up with his numerous pairs of spurs, I felt ashamed of my first assumption.

Nonetheless, that morning was a bitch, and I had a fit of cussing because there wasn't enough room for my gear. I reverted to a silent prayer for Sam Pack to hurry and send me the new truck I had ordered after realizing two weeks out on the trail that if I didn't get my truck I would have nothing left by the time we reached Montana.

When I called Sam, he told me that they had sold my old truck four days after I left. I ordered that new truck and wondered if I would have any money left from the sale of my house when I got back to Texas. My old truck had brought top price, but I still had to put several thousand with that money to buy a new one. At that moment, I didn't care how much one cost if it was just there for me. *Well, I guess I will be broke when I get to Montana, but I always wanted to be a bum anyway. Besides that, someone once said that you can't take your money with you when you die. I wonder if I can take my truck? And maybe I can drive around up or down there and find some of the men I have lost along the way.*

Thinking back, the men of importance in my life, with the exception of a few, would not have stirred many hearts beating inside female chests. I learned just inside my teen years that I was very much a girl and was geared like a girl, but somehow put together different between the ears. In spite of some forgettable events in my life in relationships with the opposite sex, my love for men has not waned. I have met some unforgettable ones who probably had much to do with the person I am today. Some of the men on the drive are unforgettable - some aren't, but I will take the warts along with the rest.

In Minco, Oklahoma, the media were in camp in force. They came from Tulsa, Oklahoma City, and even Houston, Texas. They all talked to me that day. I had stayed in the background since leaving Texas. In each camp, there were reporters from local papers and radio stations. The press and television were always there. Jamie, Dancer, Walt, and a few others were always in front of the cameras or microphones.

JW Beeson was an Oklahoma cowboy, saddle maker, fine poet, and a singer. He liked himself very much, which is helpful if one is in the entertainment business. With his handlebar mustache, he looked like an old-time cowboy. He wore a "Montana" hat, leather wrist bands, and carried a bull whip. The pretty girls who came to camp liked him too.

JD Blanton hailed from Texas and looked like he had been "pulled green." That is, he was short in stature. Ma used to say that about her four-foot-eleven stature. JD loved to sing more than anyone I have ever known. He would sing for hours, as long as he had an audience of at least one. He gave his all to his audience. JW and JD played the guitars and sang and read cowboy poetry. JD was sure as hell no Sam Elliott, but he must have had hidden treasures because his bedroll seldom slept just one. Could be he just had warm feet.

I was happy to let those two cowboys take the spotlight. Mack would have said, "My, but you have changed." But then, I had been in the spotlight for twenty-eight years, and I was amused and pleased when others were getting more attention than ever before. No one ever mentioned my name in interviews. Neither Jamie nor Bud ever told the media only one working woman was on the drive. Dancer and Walt talked primarily about themselves. Beeson and Blanton stated numerous times that they were the entertainment on the drive, with no mention of me. They were backed up by Bud and Jamie. I said nothing, although deep inside it hurt my feelings. I was accustomed to being recognized everywhere I went at home. *Well, let them roar, Gus and Red think I am the cat's meow!*

It became somewhat a joke to the cowboys who were less inclined toward constant attention and recognition that whenever a microphone or camera appeared, Dancer, Walt, the two singing cowboys, and Jamie ran over each other to get in front. So I was surprised when the cameraman from CBS cornered me in camp for an interview.

Jim Moore looked like he had just stepped off a golf course somewhere. He was tall, slim, in his mid-forties and dressed in slacks and knit shirt and neatly shined shoes. Adjusting his camera, he wanted to know, "Just what in hell makes people love those cowboys so much?" I couldn't answer that question, but I attempted to explain my theory.

"I feel that we are all more or less searching for our roots. The cowboy is a link to our past. Today, he is portrayed as daring, colorful, romantic, and living the life we all secretly wish we could live. In the beginning he was a man in a particular time and place who lived by a code that combined hard-fisted frontier desperation and Victorian-era social values. He still had to deal with harsh nature. He did physically impossible jobs against wild mustangs and fierce cattle, cougars, bears, and rattlesnakes. He dealt with a scarcity of abundant water in a land raw and untamed."

In our modern world, there is something about living in the out-of-doors, with God's creatures, that is just exciting and wonderful and somewhat intriguing to the millions who live in a world of stress, asphalt, calendars, and watches. That is what we are doing."

That theory seemed not to be enough for Jim. He went another route with the sixty-four-thousand-dollar question:

"Annie, why is this drive such a two-bit, rag-tag organization? I believe that it should be televised and publicized daily to the world." Bingo!

I could not bring myself to say one word against the situation. I "rode for the brand." I felt loyalty to Bud and the cowboys.

"Jim, I think perhaps our public relations people are more cowboys than politicians. Perhaps the media have been misunderstood or discouraged along the way by some who are in charge here," I answered.

"Annie, do you know when CBS got word that you people were leaving Fort Worth on this drive? Two days before you left. It is absurd to believe a huge network can or will cover a story with two days' notice. With something of this magnitude, it should have been a year."

Jim asked me to introduce him to someone in charge and suggested that he might piece together the beginning of the drive and began to film the day-to-day events from then on. Bud was not in camp. One of the investors was the only one there with any authority. Later, when I asked Jim Moore what had transpired, he told me:

"He said they would be interested if I wanted to do some filming of the drive. I told him that I was just a lowly cameraman, and the drive would have to get a sponsor for CBS to do a documentary, but I assured him that many sponsors would jump at the chance to finance coverage. He told me they were not sharing the profits of the drive with anyone." Jim shrugged and told me he thought the man was arrogant and not very smart. I made no comment, shook hands, thanked him, and headed for my tent.

We rode into El Reno, Oklahoma, on April 7, and I was sick as hell. Frank and Marie came and put me up in the Best Western motel. I slept or stayed in bed for the two days we were there for the Oklahoma state celebration. Margaret Bean and more of my friends came from Fort Worth, and I ate with them but did not want to do even that. I was glad to see everybody but just too sick to want company.

I did not attend the rodeo, and my name was not on the program to entertain, even though I was asked to do so in the beginning. JD and JW's names were there, but not mine. My chest was congested, my nose was dripping, and my feelings were lower than a whale's belly.

JD came to me in camp and said that Bud had told him to tell me that I would be singing. I told him I would not, as I had not been included on the program. Assuming I would not sing, I had made other plans. I was pissed that Bud would send a "messenger" to tell me what he should have told me himself. I was secretly glad that I was not on the program because I could not have sung anyway, but I was hurt and angry. It was as if I had been an afterthought to Bud. I felt as if I were in a vacuum, and I believed the cowboys felt intimidated by me, especially the boys who entertained. There was no intention on my part to do that. When one is sick, one tends to nit-pick. When we got back on the trail, I helped drive equipment trucks for a few days to keep dry and warm until I felt better.

Will Miltimore added his own brand of spice to our cattle drive world. To anybody who looked at that grizzled Oklahoma gypsy, who must have been born in a saddle on a horse throwing a rope, he was a kaleidoscope mirroring the faces of cowboys from another time. He got drunk on some of the whiskey that friends had brought the two of us. Jack Daniels for him and J&B for me.

At a sale in El Reno, he bought a gelding. The horse threw him because he mounted him without saddle or bridle. Everyone got a great laugh - Will got a sore hip and broken ribs. If he had been sober, he probably would have fared worse. He was a pain in the ass when he was drunk, but he was the best friend I had on the drive, and I felt blessed by his friendship. His dry wit and great sense of humor were a constant joy. He did not gossip, and we used each other as sounding boards for our bitching.

The morning we left El Reno, I awoke early and lay listening to the silence inside the big green tent. I had pitched my little Omar inside the big one with the cowboys for a bit of privacy, because there I had just a bit more shelter from storms and cold. In the night, the cold wind had calmed, and the air was warm, silent, and heavy.

I could hear the men snoring, and I was dressing when the first big drops of rain hit the tent. By daylight, rain was pouring inside through big holes, soaking bedrolls and cowboys still curled asleep. Lightning and thunder danced around like eerie gypsies around a campfire, and wet cowboys began rolling out, grumbling. Just as sudden as sunrise, the temperature began dropping, and the north wind came back in full force. In only moments we were standing in water in the big tent. We rode that day with wet butts, and camp morale was at low tide because the Oklahoma state celebration and ranch rodeo had been a complete flop.

Damn! Here we are, freezing our asses off, suffering with blue mokus, bronchitis, sore throat, and stiff joints, but we are making history. I wish I knew what was really going on with our leader, and why he doesn't square with us on many things – why he doesn't shoot from the hip with us. We had a poor turnout for the state celebration, on top of having no feed for our horses that have to buck cold rain and wind, but we are making history. We are doing what nobody thought we could do. I can live with all this for that. But my soggy mind reeled with unanswered questions.

While we were in El Reno, I lost a white satin jacket and my favorite goose-down jacket. Both were hanging in the equipment trailer by my compartment. I was angry and asked if anyone had seen the jackets. The white satin one had been made in Fort Worth. I had the back embossed with "Cowboys, Longhorns, and Fords! That's Texas Baby!" On the front was my name. I had not worn the jacket yet. Most of all, I wanted that old goose-down back. Nobody knew anything about them, so I kissed the jackets goodbye, kicked the dirt, cussed, and thanked my stars that I had another goose down.

One evening about three weeks later, after we moved to a new camp, I went to set up my tent, and there on the floor in front of my compartment was the old goose-down jacket. Someone had had a change of heart. But I never saw the white satin jacket again.

Indelible in my memory is the Chain family, their warm hospitality, their history, and the wonderful impact they had on the drive. Oscar Chain was twenty years old, driving a team of mules with worldly possessions consisting of an auger and $35 when he came to the Cheyenne/Arapaho territory in 1894. He lived in a dugout until he met and married Laura Hickok from Missouri in 1898. He built a two-room house out of native lumber from a local sawmill for his new bride, and they lived there for ten years, until he built the house that still stands today. He was too young to homestead a claim, so he traded his shotgun and $50 for 160 acres, and the Chain Ranch was born.

I had the pleasure of meeting the present *el jefe* of the vast Chain Ranches, which now are in eight units located in Dewey and Woodward counties in Oklahoma and in Barger and Harper counties in Kansas. Ralph, grandson of Oscar, and his family run the ranches and employ twenty full time men who live on the ranches where they work.

"The men who work for us are like family, and they simply do not leave. We have some who have been here for thirty years," Ralph said. The ranches run 6,500 to 7,000 head of cattle, including 2,000 mother cows, with the balance as yearling steers, and replacement heifers. They have one of the oldest Texas Longhorn herds in Oklahoma, and they farm approximately 7,000 acres of wheat, alfalfa, and hay for the yearling and commercial cows.

We stayed on the Woodward County Chain Ranch through two camps. I went to the main ranch house, which was not far from our camp, and was invited in to shower. Ralph's wife, Darla, and Andrea, their daughter, took Gloria and me on a grand tour of the ranch and the historical landmarks there.

At my invitation, the Chain family and their friends came to our camp on Easter Sunday for sunrise prayer meeting. I sang for them. Our services were conducted by Reverend Curtis Reynolds, pastor of the First Christian Church, and a friend of Jim Peck, Oklahoma cowboy, and his wife, Lisa. We had communion, and I thought of the little town of Ladonia, Texas, and of the First Christian Church, where I had been baptized so many years before. I sang "The Old Rugged Cross" and "In the Garden," standing in a pasture just outside of Seiling, Oklahoma, to that group of cowboys, our guests, and the longhorns, and I was once again singing to Ebb and Gertrude Bartley, Lettie and Mack, and the rest of the congregation at the old church, and most of all, to Miss Lucy Parsons, who played the piano and accompanied me from the time I was eight years old. Life was good.

10

TRAGEDY STRIKES THE OKLAHOMA, CITY FEDERAL BUILDING

We live in a nation where my generation for over a century had been free from tyranny, oppression, and fear. My generation grew up without locks on doors or on the spare-tire racks on our pickups. Everybody knew everybody's kids for miles around in the country, and in the small town where I attended school the neighbors looked out for each other and all the children. We knew the banker, doctor, lawyer, insurance man, tractor dealer, grocer, and the local drunk by his or her first name, and wars were fought in other countries across the ocean. We saluted the flag, said the pledge of allegiance each morning, and bowed our heads in prayer before each and every ball game at school. We had the courage of our convictions, and honesty and courtesy ruled then, where political correctness rules now. The worst that could happen to you in a bar fight was getting your ribs kicked in with a number twelve brogan or boot. If someone hurt you or your kid or your dog, you either cussed him out or whipped his butt soundly, or he came to you like a man and apologized and paid for his crime. Lawsuits were as scarce as "word of honor" is today.

Our big fears were the effect of weather on crops, the note at the bank, and Lettie's heavy hand on our butts. The stark realization that those days were gone forever smacked me in the face when an unheard-of-tragedy struck nearby, and waves of shock permeated my surroundings.

When the Oklahoma City Federal Building was bombed, Gloria and I were sitting in a small café in Woodward, having breakfast. Chills ran down my spine when the small radio sitting on the waitress' pickup window told of a twelve hundred-pound bomb that had been hidden in a car or truck and parked outside the front door of the building. Oklahoma City was only a couple of hours away from us. Suddenly breakfast did not taste quite so good. The contentment of being out in the open, away from the chaos of urban civilization, suddenly was snuffed out, and I was back where people did horrible things to other people for crazy reasons. I wanted to turn off that radio and run to camp and hug Gus and Red and pretend that the world I had lived in for a large part of my life was the only one there was. Maybe the huge and frightening problems we face in our winter years are God's way of making us content to grow old and to welcome the thought of getting' the hell out of this crazy world.

◆ ◆ ◆ ◆

The mind has a way of suppressing trauma as deftly as an umbrella turns rain. After thirty years, even after the morticians put him back together, I can still vividly picture my husband Kenneth's broken body, after he and two friends were killed in an auto accident. I close my eyes and see the tiny limp body of the black child that Sidney and I played with everyday, after his father had accidentally run over him with our tractor. When I lay under another tractor years later with my back broken, gasoline pouring on me, the engine still running, my first thought was how to get my foot loose where it was pinned and get the hell out. I jerked it loose, leaving ankle bone and hide, and began trying to get on my feet.

That same "something" pushed the Oklahoma bombing somewhere in the attic of my mind there in that small café - in Woodward, in the rain. We left there with a pall hanging over us, and headed back to camp to tend my horses. Between broadcasts about the bombing, Jamie and Bruce and JW Beeson were interviewed on the local radio station in Woodward. We were down for three days at the next camp. During that time, some of us mended tack, bogged in the mud, wrote in journals, drank whiskey, ate "real" food in restaurants in town, and the bosses talked to disc jockeys and posed for the cameras. I pondered the problems at camp while sloshing around in the mud and thought of one of the stories I had read about nineteenth cattle drives and their problems with Mother Nature.

The problems facing nineteenth-century cowboys differed considerably from ours, but they were equal in importance to morale and physical comforts. Human emotions have changed little for two thousand years. I am constantly amazed with the growth of problems, cures, diseases, doctors, specialists, diagnosticians, and answers to all things, yet emotions remain the same.

◆ ◆ ◆ ◆

There was hostility among all at camp, mostly stemming from simple frustration at not being able to do anything, and we felt that the management *wasn't* doing anything. All those frustrations were intensified by the cold and the ever-present mud, and things began to happen as the weather showed no promise of improving. Outside of Woodward, the big green tent was surrounded by a lake. Several of the cowboys' saddles were in it, including Will's. I had stashed mine in the top of one of the trailers, in the feed compartment. It was as dry as it could possibly be under the circumstances.

Unrest increased when Jamie McClain left for Texas in the latter part of April. Scuttlebutt was flying that Bud and Susan had accused Jamie's wife, Donna, of stealing from the drive. Many said that was preposterous, that Jamie was simply a patsy; that Bud and Susan were going to skip to Mexico with the drive money. *What money? I wonder if there is any money around.*

Man, if there is, why in hell don't they just take it and haul ass and let us go on with this drive the best way we can. With a little help or the wonderful people along the way, we can go to Canada if we choose to.

The next morning after Jamie left, I asked Bud where Jamie was. He shrugged and said he did not know and changed the subject. I sensed that he did not want to discuss the matter further, and I just let it drop. *Don't rock the boat, baby, just ride for the brand and get to Montana.*

The Sunday paper did not cheer me one bit. A story said the TV media had tormented parents of the children injured in the Oklahoma City bombing. Oprah Winfrey and Forty-Eight Hours were two programs that were mentioned. They had representatives who posed as relatives to get into the isolation ward at the hospital. The paper further stated that these media people became angry when they found out that some of the children in the ward weren't victims of the bombing. The paper said they insulted the parents of these children. *God, I am so glad that I am out here in the rain and mud with my horses, away from the bulk of insane humanity.* I knew that I wasn't really far from it all, but I felt apart just the same. Animals and adverse atmospheric conditions have a way of minimizing human frailties and the effects of tragedy.

There was still no word from Jamie. I decided to wait no longer for my truck. I knew that Gloria was getting tired of having my junk in her van and having to haul me around everywhere. It was so against my grain to be dependent on someone else. She was going back to Texas, and I asked to go with her. I could make it back and miss only one camp.

When I returned from Texas with my new truck, Jamie McClain was gone. I learned that he had been back, loaded his horses, and gone home for good. Our trail boss was no more, but that wasn't the worst of it. Mike Garrison had had a run-in with the guy who ran the souvenir trailer and handled the money. Garrison was so disgusted with things, he said that if he had his paycheck that he would load up and go home. And the money man handed him his money and told him to "hook em." Unfortunately, he did. I overheard one cowboy grumble about the souvenir man: "That son of a bitch is beginning to bother me. He has too damned much authority, and he is too damned arrogant with the cowboys, and he is a goddamed bully to boot."

I had heard that the man received ten percent off the top of everything that was sold in the trailer. That seemed like a hell of a deal for him and not so good for the drive. We had no money, according to Bud, but the cowboys said this guy sat in bars along the way, buying drinks for the house, giving away souvenirs, and "high-rolling in front of the women," one said. He was certainly not popular with the drovers and wranglers.

I heard him dress down the cook's helpers and some of the younger members of the drive. He called himself the "trail manager." I did not feel comfortable around him, even though he claimed to have known me in years past as a member of my audiences at home. If all that I heard was true, it was difficult to understand why Bud took such good care of this man while the drive was going downhill. One cannot take gossip as fact, and gossip flew fast around camp.

I felt empty inside about Mike Garrison and Jamie leaving. When I was a child, when some member of the family died or went away, things went to hell in a hand basket. Jamie might not have been the greatest trail boss we could have had, but he was nice, honest, and friendly, and the men liked him. If he had a weakness, said one cowboy, "it was the fact that he was not enough son-of-a-bitch for the men to take him seriously." He did not have enough experience, but then, most of us were novices when it came to driving cattle down highways across six states. Mike Garrison would be missed very much. He was a great cowboy and a hard and dedicated worker. His hot temper had made him act irrationally, and the man who sent him away had to share in the blame. I believed the man running the souvenir trailer certainly could have been replaced, but I doubted that

Garrison could have.

Whoever said that cowboys were unemotional sure as hell wasn't ever on a cattle drive. Pride ran deep with that group of cowboys. Traditional values were of great importance to them. Some of them had egos bigger than a Texas tale, but had it not been for big egos, the West would probably never have been won, the cowboy would never have gotten the girl, and some of us would never have been born. God Bless Cowboys.

In Ashland, Kansas, Gloria and I rented a room in a small motel so that we could dry out and I could work A young woman of generous proportions assigned us a double, and when we opened the door to the room, we found a double bed and one of those small folding cots that are sometimes taken on camping trips for the kids to sleep on. Gloria said, "You can have the cot," and that is when she saw the other side of my jovial personality.

"If this is a double, I am a cross-eyed buffalo! Don't unpack, we aren't staying in this dump!" I headed for the office with Gloria trailing behind. The large young woman assured me that the room was a double. After I described to her just what a double really was, we were given a room with two double beds. Then we discovered that the air conditioning was controlled from the office and that all rooms were the same temperature - about thirty-five degrees. I stuffed the vents with toilet paper, and we settled down for the three days' downtime we had coming. At the request of the souvenir man, I sang in a little club downtown, where I watched him buying drinks for the house. *Hey, I believe this guy is the one who is making all the money on this drive. Looks like running that souvenir trailer ain't a bad deal.*

In the midst of all the controversy, bad weather, and crummy motels, there were moments of hilarity that bring sunshine to my days even now. One such moment happened at that motel in Ashland, Kansas. As with every inch of Kansas, from border to border, rain fell almost constantly, and we dealt with mud for the entire width of the state. The morning we were to leave Ashland, I had showered last and was not yet dressed, so I asked Gloria to go to my new truck and get my old rain boots from the front floorboard. I had a remote opener for the doors of the truck, and she picked up my keys and went for the boots. After she was gone for what seemed a long time, I opened the door of the room, looked outside, and saw her hanging over the back of the seat of a black supercab Ford parked next to mine, digging around in it. I ran out and asked what the hell she was doing in someone else's truck. She jumped and squealed and ran back inside and slammed the door.

"Son of a bitch, they may come and get me. Oh shit! I thought that was your truck. The remote opened the door," she said. We laughed so hard we could not talk. At the beginning of the drive, Gloria would never have expressed herself with expletives. Coming from her, they were hysterically funny. The other truck belonged to a couple in the room next to ours, and they had a black German shepherd dog big enough to eat tigers. He had growled at me when I passed the truck the day before. Gloria just knew that they were in their room watching out the window as she rifled their truck. It was 4:30 a.m.

"Well, hell! The remote opened the door to that truck; I heard it when it beeped," she said again, between fits of giggling.

"The doors were probably unlocked on that truck, Gloria." We laughed about that for weeks, and I reminded her that we should be glad the dog slept inside the motel and not in the truck.

One night at that motel, one of the girls riding with us came to take a shower. She was a small woman who came from an urban world and looked out of place on that cattle drive. When she came out of the bathroom, she said: "That was a great shower, but I ran out of cold water." Well, OK. Hey, she was serious. Ashland, Kansas was a funny little town, or perhaps we were the funny ones.

One of the treasures on the drive was Skip Nelson. A native of St Paul, Minnesota, Skip was head photographer for a major television station in ST Paul for 40 years. This talented man whose photos covered Viet Nam to the White House, also worked for the NFL simultaneously for 30 years. He had been retired for ten years when he joined us on the cattle drive as our official photographer. His twinkling blue eyes and always-cheerful and positive demeanor warmed my heart each time we met. We became instant friends, and that friendship increased each day. His partner was Derk Hansen, a delightful and multi-talented, nationally known artist who was, rightfully so, our commemorative artist. Derk hailed from Germany but now lived in St. Paul, just down the road from Skip. These two were filming the cattle drive for a series of three videotapes they planned to produce.

Outside of Dodge City, Kansas, Derk and I played and sang together in camp for a large crowd. Ford Motor Company representatives were there and had a grand party for us, complete with barbecue and all the trimmings. Fifty families named Ford were invited, and we were in Ford County, Kansas.

At the party, I met Jerry Thomas and did a double take when I saw him. It was like looking at the ghost of John Wayne. He is the spitting image of the Duke, and a more delightful man I haven't met. He was personable, fun, and interesting. I sent a picture of Jerry and me back home to the folks and wished I could be present when they opened the envelope. Jerry rode with us into Dodge City and joined us again on down the trail. He travels nationwide making appearances in over two hundred shows annually. His career began when he won a John Wayne-look-alike contest.

We couldn't wait for J R Lane, a Wyoming cowboy and devout fan of John Wayne, to see Jerry for the first time. J R soon came sauntering across the campground toward the chuck wagon, where we all waited with bated breath. Jerry greeted J R with "Hi, young fella" in the Duke's tone of voice. J R looked up, grinned, and said, "Welcome back, Duke!" and kept right on going. That master of dry wit, the funny man on the drive, had left us slack-jawed and bent double in laughter once more. J R was truly a gift to the drive with his quick wit and keen perception and upbeat attitude. He was also a master horseman, a great help with anything that went wrong with any horse, and a congenial companion.

May 6, 1995, I rode swing into Dodge, right behind Jim Donaldson. We probably had twenty-five outriders. The streets were lined with people, and by the time we got to the edge of town, the outriders were in and among us, intermingled with the cattle. There was a tendency to be overconfident about the longhorns and their docile countenance as they sauntered through busy streets. The outriders' enthusiasm made them eager to be "up close." They were politely asked to move back to the rear of the herd, and we pushed the ridgebacks down 14th Street in a sudden rain. I had foolishly left my slicker in camp because of brilliant sunshine when we left. I should have known by then that Kansas weather can change in a heartbeat. Red Steagall was riding with us before his scheduled performance that night, and he, too, had no slicker. Our cook rescued Red from the rain, and one of the cowboys took his horse to lead on into camp. Jim Donaldson turned around, pulled off his slicker, and insisted I wear it. The age of chivalry was alive and well in the GACD.

We lumbered through the town that has been called the Buffalo Capital of the World, Cowboy Capital, Queen of the Cowtowns, Wickedest Little City in America, and the Beautiful Bibulous Babylon of the Frontier. The city swells with history of the Old West. Dodge had a reputation as the wildest town on the western frontier. Bat Masterson and Wyatt Earp became legends in their own time as they fought to bring law and order to Dodge.

With Jim's slicker buttoned over my body, I watched the longhorns trudging on asphalt among hundreds of people. I chuckled, thinking about what some of the nineteenth-century cowboys would think had they seen our wet and cold crew. They would have wondered why the outriders were in the rear and why anyone would have paid to ride in that cold rain. I felt snug in Jim's slicker and patted Red and waved at folks as we left the city limits and headed out to camp just outside of town.

I heard someone yell and heard or rather felt the cattle lunge behind me. I was on the outside, which put me on the wet asphalt. I turned to see a horse tearing through the cattle, riderless, with pieces of saddle flying in all directions as the cattle broke. We managed to hold only a fraction of them, but the cowboys turned them quickly with the help of muddy fields on both sides. I had barely gotten out of the way of the thundering herd and off the pavement, because Red's first thought was to tear after them. When it came to stampedes, this old cowgal was a realist. I got the hell out of the way. One doesn't lose nerve with age; one just becomes more protective of gray hair and wrinkles and brittle bones.

One cowboy's horse stepped into a badger hole, did a complete flip, and went down on top of him. The mud and Someone Higher up saved the man from being hurt or possibly killed. The stampede started when an outrider's stirrup had broken and caused her horse to bolt. She was not hurt, merely shaken up and wet and muddy, but her saddle was in shreds. We rode into a wet camp intact, bringing to a close another day in the GACD.

We took great showers in the Best Western, did laundry, had pictures developed, repaired tack, shined our boots, and met and had fun with Renny, Walt Secrest's petite wife, who had driven down from Montana to see Walt. We saw the old boarding houses, walked through notorious Boot Hill, heard the echoes of gunfire, and thought we saw the shadows of Wyatt Earp and Bat Masterson walking the board sidewalks of Old Town.

I looked everywhere for Matt, Doc, Festus, and Miss Kitty. I called my son, Kenny, and told him where I was. Like me, he loved *Gunsmoke* and Matt and the wonderful cast of that great television show. It was fun, in spite of the rain. My old buddy, Red Wilkins, came from Wichita to see me, and we hugged and talked about Fort Worth and Dallas good times, and the old beer parlors I had sung in while Red tapped his foot to my music.

Camp was a proverbial mud hole. The horses and steers were

in a big pasture, but Red and Gus stayed close to camp and easy to find in the late afternoon, when they expected feed and hugs. I saw Derk and Skip there, and they filmed and recorded an essay I had written for *Trails* magazine, which was to go in their first video. On a clear, sunlit morning we said goodbye to Dodge and pointed the herd toward Nebraska and new adventures.

11

MORE OF KANSAS

The Butler Ranch is memorable. I rode with Walt and the chuck wagon that day, and we arrived in camp before the herd. An ambulance arrived about the time we rode into the Butlers' driveway and headed for the big tepee, which was already up. Vision Quest, the organization for dysfunctional boys, traveled with us. They came along with the hope that the trip would help to rehabilitate those boys. They slept in that tepee. The ambulance was there for Mr. Butler, who had suffered a stroke – his third one. I learned all about what had happened that night when I went over and sang to him at the main ranch house. He had suffered the stroke about the time we arrived at camp, but he refused to leave for the hospital until he "could see those longhorns walk through my gate." After the cattle arrived, he told the paramedic he was ready to go, but he refused to stay at the hospital overnight.

I talked with him for awhile after I sang. He was seventy-four years young, and other than slurred speech, he seemed to be alert and having a grand time. His daughter told me out of earshot that the doctor said it was just a matter of time, because that was his third stroke. Mr. Butler knew this, but he was a game guy who took it one day at a time. I really liked him and admired his acceptance of a losing situation. I sang for him on the front porch of his pretty house, wearing tee shirt, jeans, and sneakers in the clear, balmy evening. Next morning, the temperature was thirty-five degrees. I put my long johns back on, and we made twelve miles in the cold that day.

I sometimes forgot about home and family on the trail, so I was brought up short when I called my sister in California. The past and family came cascading over the wire to me halfway across the United States as she told me the shocking news about my close buddy, my baby brother, and the most delightful and colorful member of the family – Sidney. He could have been any one of those wild, rowdy Old West cowboys whose trails we were following.

I had often told Sidney that he was like a cat with nine lives. The only problem was, he had used up almost all of them. Sidney had had a heart attack while visiting her in California, was in ICU, but was feeling better.

I should have been much more anxious than I was, but I had been called so many times to be told that Sidney had barely missed death, it had become almost commonplace. In a scuffle with the law once, he had been shot with a sawed-off shotgun by the sheriff. A drunken friend had aimed a .357 Magnum at the sheriff, and the bullet had passed through Sidney's leg and shot the sheriff in the foot. Sidney had survived both bullets.

"Sidney, how in hell do you explain surviving being shot with a shotgun and a .357 and surviving both," I asked him when I arrived at the hospital.

"Neither one of them sons-a-bitches could shoot worth a shit," he said with blue eyes twinkling above a grin. Once, in a truck stop in California, another trucker had gouged out one of Sidney's eyeballs in a fight over a remark Sidney had made. It lay on his cheek, hanging by a blood vessel. He went to the restroom, looked in the mirror and put the thing back in its socket.

"I needed that eye to see how to kick the shit out of that big asshole," he said to me later.

My sister's news about Sidney was just the beginning of a series of foreboding events.

◆ ◆ ◆ ◆

May 16, we drove the cattle and horses up Highway 83, past shimmering wheat fields and huge towering grain elevators storing the world's wheat, then feed lots with sleek fat cattle, by neat farm houses with green lawns, pickup trucks, and giant tractors, and down the streets of Scott City, Kansas, where hundreds of smiling faces greeted us with excited cheers, salutes, and flashing cameras. A warm, comfortable feeling seeped into my tired bones, and I felt almost like I was coming home. That was only the beginning of a fun-filled day of festivities and great hospitality.

We set up camp in a beautiful park at the fair grounds where tanks of cool water awaited the thirsty animals. Don and Mona Herbers, young Jim Herber's parents, were there along with numerous people to see that our needs were supplied without fail and to tell us about the fantastic dinner planned for us at Marsha's Restaurant.

That evening, we sat down at elegant tables with impeccable white tablecloths and candlelight, listened to soft music, and were served delectable steaks that would make kings green-eyed with jealousy. Ron and Marsha Gordon were superb hosts and shared the responsibility for the wonderful evening with Terry Ryan with the Kansas Livestock Association, Loren Smith, councilman, the Herbers, and last but not least, Chad, who served delicious drinks along with congenial conversation. It was a moment in heaven just before all hell broke loose.

Gloria rented a motel room in town and then decided to go home to Texas for a few days' rest. She insisted that I take her room, although I had already picked out a tree to pitch my tent under. It would be close to my horses at the fair grounds.

"You take my room, it's already paid for, and you can work on the computer in the dry and get a decent night's sleep in a bed," she said.

I went to bed around eleven, and the sirens awakened me at midnight. I got out of bed and was standing in the door watching the storm when the phone rang. Bert, the lady who ran the motel, said, “Get to the shelter immediately and waste no time changing to street clothes; the tornado is on the ground.”

I had on shorts and a teeshirt. The air was heavy, humid, thick, and still as death. The tornado was seen on the ground somewhere, and in minutes the town was hit with winds seventy-five to eighty miles per hour. We stayed in the shelter until the storm passed. I found out next morning that Will had awakened the cowboys out at the fair grounds, and they all went to a shelter somewhere else in town. The tree where I had planned to pitch my tent had been uprooted by the storm. It just wasn't my time to get blown away. Two days later, when we rode along part of the path of that tornado, we saw twelve-story grain elevators wadded and twisted like pieces of paper and huge T-shaped steel light poles destroyed. Acres of wheat and corn had been sucked out of the ground. Mother Nature had sneezed.

Next day, after the tornado, I was invited to supper in Leoti, Kansas, and asked if I would sing at the Mexican restaurant there. Leoti is twenty-four miles due west of Scott City. We had a great dinner, I sang, and then shortly before nine, one of the cowboys went to the door and came back waving his arms and yelling: “Come look outside! You won't believe it, but it is snowing!” It was. It snowed four inches in an hour, which was less than twenty-four hours after the tornado. It snowed horizontally, blizzard fashion, in thirty-five mph gusts. Driving back to Scott City, I got behind a big semi and followed him back to the motel coffee shop. I went in and walked up to him.

“Driver, I apologize for tailgating you out of Leoti. I just couldn't see a thing,” I said.

“Hell lady, I couldn't see anything either!”

One night while we were in Scott City, Marsha's Restaurant cooked steaks for all of us. Complete with white tablecloths, candlelight, and great wine. I sat on the bar and played the guitar and sang after wrapping myself around several Scotches. Life was good.

But all was not wine and candlelight. My heart still ached in the aftermath of the tornado. Lightning killed Jeff Herber's beautiful paint mare the night before we left Scott City. I was heartsick. When I got to camp, it was raining and cold. I went to look for Red and Gus. When I saw the mare in the middle of the arena, she was in convulsions, and the geldings were standing at a distance, curiously watching as she writhed in her agony. I crawled through the fence and went out to her. No one was there. Everyone was getting ready to break camp and ride. I started out the gate, and Eldon met me and said that he had found her a few minutes before.

"We called a vet, and he is on his way I guess," Eldon said.

◆ ◆ ◆ ◆

As I stood there in the rain, feeling helpless and wondering where in hell the vet was, I remembered a scene fifty-five years before, in a muddy corral on a blackland farm in East Texas. A small frail girl of nine sat in the mud, an old gray mare's head cradled in her skinny arms. With hands that were blue from the cold, she scooped warm oatmeal from a tin pan and gently pried open the old mare's mouth and laid the oatmeal on her tongue.

"Little Mack, Old Nellie won't eat that; she is real sick and old. Why don't you come in for breakfast and get warm." Mack picked me up out of the mud and carried me to the house, my tears soaking into his rough black overcoat. I couldn't believe that he could not make Nellie well. I refused to believe I would lose my best friend out there in that cold and miserable mud. Nellie died from blood poisoning and old age, and a part of me died with her. I had my first real experience with losing an animal that I loved. That moment was as vivid to me as the moment I stood there in Kansas, watching that paint mare die.

◆ ◆ ◆ ◆

I did not want to ride that day. I had to write. Writing is great therapy. I had to write that beautiful dead mare out of my mind.

"This damned infernal mud symbolized much that has happened to us here in Kansas. God, how depressing it is. Daniel Webster defines mud as wet, soft, sticky earth. There was a continent of mud in Kansas, and it was simply a continuation of the rain and mud we had had since leaving Fort Worth. We were in mud from one border of Kansas to the Nebraska line. We were wet when we reached Ashland, Kansas with Oklahoma rain and cold. We had not dried out when we crossed the Red River into Oklahoma.

Mud humbles the most astute and beautiful. Mud cuts you down to bite-size. Psychiatrists and psychologists agree that mud is depressing to even the strong and stalwart. Gus abhorred mud. He would almost panic when he had to walk or run in a muddy field to herd the steers. I couldn't stay out of the way of their hooves as I led Gus and Red out of the pasture to camp just outside of Seldon, Kansas. The mud almost sucked the boots off my feet. Mud dampens the spirits of optimists to soggy sulking. Despair was written on some faces in camp at Rexford, Kansas, where we camped between a cemetery and a feedlot."

Kansas farmers were more than anxious because they should have had corn almost up in the field, but it wasn't planted yet. The wheat stood tall and green across the plains, but I knew that if the mud did not dry soon with warm sunshine, the wheat would fall over and be lost. I walked into a store in Rexford for coffee. A group of men sat drinking, and one asked: "Are you people gonna take this rain with you when you leave?" I felt as he did, that we had brought it with us. We were knocking on June's door, and since leaving Texas on March 5, we had enjoyed a mere six days of sunshine.

My childhood in East Texas, where the land was black and sticky when wet, came to mind. It would ball up on your feet and on the tires of a car. We lived on a dirt road one mile from the pavement. Ma swept the yard. We fought weeds and grass out of the fields so much that no one in the country had grass on the lawn. Ma had mud shoes to go to the clothesline and barn. To a child, the mud was fun to make pies and to play in barefooted in summer, but when it rained for days and we were literally cut off from the rest of the world, it was no longer fun. I vowed never to live there after I was old enough to find pavement and green lawns. There is something sinister and creepy about mud and mire and bogs. Horror stories are written about monsters arising from mud and muck, and Sherlock Holmes' most terrifying cases usually involved bodies found in swamps or devoured by bottomless quicksand. Mother Nature must smile at our frustration with Her work. Who knows, maybe she was responsible for putting the snake in the Garden of Eden.

◆ ◆ ◆ ◆

As I rode down Highway 83 later, on a morning that could have come out of a Disney movie, I gazed in wonder at the vastness and splendor of Kansas with her miles of green wheat and alfalfa, dotted with wildflowers, meadows, and gently rolling hills. Peeking out between wispy clouds, morning's sun made me forget for a moment that underneath it all was mud. I stopped and took pictures of that day, including Decatur Feed Lot and the lazy, lolling, fat cattle – twenty-four thousand of them sucking up the stingy sunshine on the few dry spots in the pens. I was still basking in the genuine friendship, generosity, and warm hospitality that had greeted us through the entire state of Kansas. I could still taste the delectable food the women and men had cooked and served to us in Scott City, Leoti, the Pyramid Ranch, Garden City, Buffalo, Ashland, and points in between. Dodge City was unforgettable.

So what is the big deal with a little mud? It harbors flowers, nourishes the little earth creatures, replenishes minerals in the soil, makes for great sinister movies and stories, and keeps pigs deliriously happy. It makes me appreciate smooth sand, dry weather, and asphalt. To have glorious rain, we must tolerate mud. Mud comes just before May flowers and rich Kansas wheat that feeds the world. I smiled, hugged old Gus, and rode on toward Montana.

When we left Scott City, we rode toward the Pyramid Ranch down a narrow, muddy road, which put us in a plowed field in mud up to the horses' knees. Just before we reached camp, we had to swim the Smoky Hill River. A crowd of people waited to watch the steers and horses cross, and they had prepared a royal feast for us. It reminded me of the last day of school when I was a kid and everybody brought covered dishes, and we ended that delectable meal with homemade ice cream. Shades of home!

The ranch could have been a scene from a great painting with its tall old trees, green lawns, and the river, corrals, and green pastures for the horses and steers. Steve Schick, J W, J D, and I played for all the folks. I interviewed Asher Crowley, a ninety-three-year-old cowboy who worked fulltime, riding pens at one of the livestock companies. Asher rode with us that day. He was lean, crisp, and a delight to talk to. He told me that he and his wife of sixty-plus years had moved to Kansas from Colorado to care for his father years before and had stayed. His sister had a ranch in Colorado City, Colorado, and ran two hundred head of cows. She saddled up each morning to check the herd. She was eighty-seven years young. I silently vowed never to mention my aches and pains again on the drive, except to Gus and Red.

Jess and Joy Cole were there. I had met them at Marsha's Restaurant in Scott City when I sang there, and they brought me a gift and my coat that I had left in the restaurant. Jess told the crowd that I could outride half of the cowboys. I loved it, but I was afraid his claim wouldn't enhance my popularity with the cowboys.

Next morning, I arose early and took pictures of the three hundred million-year-old monuments rising up like silent sentinels out there in the Kansas flatlands. I drove into Scott City, had lunch at Marsha's, and visited with her and her husband. They liked the letter to the editor I had written to the newspaper, which expressed thanks from me and the cowboys for the warm reception we had received in Scott City.

Back in camp, tempers were short, and because there was little or no leadership, the "troops" were at each other's throats about trifles. There were accusations, finger-pointing, and heavy resentments among men who had been friends in the beginning.

"When we get to Montana, I am going to whip his ass" or "One more word, and I'm gonna bust him in the mouth – he don't know enough about driving cows to get one to water." Angry words were everyday occurrences. Resentment toward the outriders, who took the liberty of riding in and through the herd, endangering themselves as well as the rest of us, was constant among us all. We so very much needed an able leader. The young men on the drive – and really everybody in general – wanted someone who had the last word; someone who said what he meant and did what he said he was going to do; someone who could tell us when and where and how, and someone who was respected by all.

Walt was looked up to by the younger men. He was tough, masculine, terse, and determined. There was much resentment between him and the management. He was branded an agitator who, several of the older cowboys said, "keeps some kinda shit stirred up all the time." He complained much of the time about situations in camp. Some took his side, and others leaned in the other direction, and some were simply staying quiet and trying to get through the days with as little stress as possible. But camp was a simmering volcano.

I wonder just who is gonna whip whom. Nobody, probably. When we get to Montana, we will all be drinking together and hugging each other, and all this anger and misunderstanding will be forgotten when we have our pockets full of dollars and everyone is getting ready to go home. We will miss this life we are leading now. It hasn't hit these cowboys yet that it will be over someday and that we will have to go back to the everyday humdrum. They had better enjoy it now and knock off this crappy fighting all the time. Besides, nothing is gonna be done about anything, or else it already would have been done.

12

CHANGE AND CONFLICT

In a dramatic meeting in Oberlin, Kansas, on May 29, Bruce Seidel was appointed trail boss, Jim Hooks became cow boss, and Jim McElroy became front man, the guy who went ahead of the drive to deal for camps and to meet the people who opened their hearts and pastures to us. Then all subtlety disappeared, and repressed feelings surfaced like ugly alligators.

Jim Hooks was liked and respected among the cowboys. Bruce Seidel and Jim McElroy, both retired lawmen, presented a different image. They had been on the drive from the beginning, but they had stayed mostly to themselves. Neither was ever "one of the boys." They seldom ate with us and seemed to have little in common with the rest. They had driven equipment trucks from the beginning, with the exception of three or four days of riding with the herd. These men were disliked and/or distrusted by many of the cowboys. I had no particular feelings for them at the time. They had always been polite and courteous to me, and I had no quarrel with either of them. Perhaps Bud's decision to put law officers in charge of a group of free-spirited cowboys created a boiling pot at that time.

At the meeting in Oberlin, Bruce read a letter from Bud that appointed Bruce as trail boss with the power to fire and hire. He was emphatic about his intention of "getting this outfit to Montana," and he said that those who were unhappy with the way things were going should simply go home. This statement was followed by a dynamite line: "I am damned sure a company man."

"That went over like a turd in the punch bowl," Will Miltimore said, later.

Bruce was telling them he was for the company. I believe that the cowboys felt that he separated himself from them with that statement. For the first time since leaving Texas, they really began to voice their frustrations out loud. Jamie Nail brought up the fact that he was owed over $6,000 by Bud. Walt also named a large amount of money and said: "Bud McCasland is a bald-faced liar."

Bud's son, Dax, who had recently joined us, sat in stony silence listening to his father being reviled by a room full of angry men. Walt's outburst was followed by words from the usually quieter members of the drive expressing their disgruntled feelings about lies and broken promises. Soon the meeting erupted into a shouting match. Bruce had talked himself into a corner. He suggested that the men write their complaints in a letter and that he would take it to Bud.

"Annie is the journalist on this drive. Why don't you ask her to write the letter for you?" Bruce said. They asked, and I said that I would be glad to write it if they would give me a list of grievances. They did, and by morning I had written the letter that was to become a controversial subject for the duration of the drive:

Bud McCasland and concerned leaders and sponsors:

We expressed our concerns, grievances, anger, and frustrations at an extended meeting last night in Oberlin, Kansas, called by your appointed trail boss, Bruce Seidel. We regret that these problems were not heard by those of you who are sitting in the driver's seat in this cattle drive to Montana. Please take a moment of your time and hear what we have to say. The following are some of the primary reasons for our concern and frustration:

For the past several weeks, we have been feeding inferior feed to our horses. Our complaints have fallen on deaf ears. The animals will not eat the feed until they have no choice other than hunger. Several have had colic. Many are lethargic, losing weight, and off their feed. I am sure you understand that these animals cannot perform continuously under these conditions.

The outriders have become an increasing problem to those of us who want to do our job and present to the world the true image of the American cowboy. We were hired to drive a herd of cattle to Montana from Fort Worth. We were screened for men who were cowboys, who were experienced handlers of cows under all conditions and circumstances. We are now surrounded by people from all walks of life who come and pay a fee to ride among us, cut the herd, get in the way, expose themselves to danger, and make us look like imitations of actors in a cheap B movie. They disregard polite requests to remain behind the herd and out of the way. We are told we must entertain these people. Then permit us to do so by doing our job while they safely look on from a distance.

In the contracts we signed in Fort Worth, we agreed to work for $1,500 a month and found, with two days off each week. We have worked many of those weeks without days off and did so willingly, in the rain, sleet, snow, hail, infernal wind, and extreme cold. We eat the same thing each day for lunch: meat and cheese between two slices of bread with a minute bit of mustard, nothing else, and sometimes chips, and rarely, a piece of fruit. Now you tell us when we have several days' downtime in a row, that if we want off several of these days we will not receive pay. Why? We worked straight through many weeks without our promised days off.

Some of us have not received our money for rented horses and entertainment, even though you were paid promptly by outriders for these horses, and we had an agreement about entertainment. Now you tell us there is no money, or you write checks that do not clear, or you fill our ears with broken promises. Why? Where does our percentage of this money go, and what do we tell those people who follow us, when they are waiting to hear us sing and entertain?

Our new trail boss, Bruce Seidel, tells us that if we are not satisfied with how things are going, to haul ass. How can we haul ass when we have invested more money than we can stand to lose in an undertaking we believed would work because we were promised it would pay off in history, glory, profit, and satisfaction of a job well done? How can we haul ass when we have been continually told that "next time" it will be better and 'there's going to be a big change,' and this time the 'check will clear.' How can we haul ass when we have invested heart, money, time, guts, and soul in something we want so desperately to work because we love what we are doing when it is being done as it should be done?

Communications in camp are almost nil. We seldom know where we can take showers, whether we have horse feed or hay until it is too late to shower or it is time to saddle up for the day. We are asked constantly where we will be tomorrow, how long we will be there, and when we will be in someone's town, and on and on. We seldom have answers for these questions. We are told there will be downtime, and then it is changed. We are not told of downtime in time for others to make plans to visit us. We are handed different orders and answers from many and never know whom to believe.

Bud, you promised many things that have not been given. You asked us to follow you, but you do not lead. You say you will return and spend time in camp, where we feel that you will learn that the demands we make are well founded, deserved, and needed, but you make only cameo appearances.

We are willing and able to give what it takes to make this dream of yours a reality. We ask only that you give us your support, confidence, and the leadership we deserve. Treat us as men who are on your team, not as tools being used to make a profit without investment on your part. We do not want to quit. We are not quitters. But every man has his limits.

I read the letter to the men and told them they could alter it or simply throw it in the trash. It was their words paraphrased and theirs to do with what they wished.

"I'll sign it twice!" Ace said, and the others followed suit until all who heard it signed it, and then I went into town and faxed it to Bud and the small investors.

Soon, one of the investors called me on the souvenir trailer phone and raged for twenty-five minutes about the letter.

"Those pansy sons of bitches are always whining about something. I could take those cattle to Montana by myself. I'll bet there ain't a single one of them who will stand up to my face and complain about anything. Bud McCasland is just a hired hand. I run this show, and what I say goes. I have put over $100,000 in this son of a bitch, and I am going to make it work, with or without those goddamned cowboys." I listened and never heard him take a breath during his tirade.

"Annie, you don't have any business getting in the middle of this," he said authoritatively and added something about "killing the messenger."

"Hey, don't worry about me. I have been taking care of myself for several years now." A younger me would have roasted his ears with a verbal lashing, but age breeds patience, and something told me just to shut up and mush on. I did.

I was not "in the middle." I knew exactly where I stood in that situation, and I didn't need some guy with a large ego four hundred miles away telling me how to think. The investors saw the potential to make a lot of money, possibly at all costs to human feelings, and the cowboys wanted to reestablish the image of the old cowboy and enjoy the glory in doing so. Two sets of emotions, worlds apart in conflict.

If these investors believe I can be intimidated, they need to think again. I don't owe them a damned nickel nor an apology. What strange things happen in the midst of history being made. What a shame we can't all enjoy this great accomplishment.

My sentiments were with "my" cowboys until hell froze over. I believed we would get to Montana with or without the investors.

In a small community in Kansas called Gem, we camped close to the community center, and the residents of Gem cooked steaks for us. There we met Lon Sowell. A seventy-two-year-old widower, this big, soft-spoken man was one of the nicest people we had met along the way. He had a beautiful place with a small pasture and corrals where we kept the horses. He was proud of his collection of buggies, surreys, and a sleigh. He was a lonely man who doted on his family and talked of a beloved wife lost to cancer three years before.

Lon joined us a bit later, and the "Montana Express," as I christened it, was added to the drive. Walt called his son and had him bring one of his wagons from Montana, which became the Express. It had bench seats on each side, and two of the Shires were hitched to it, and Lon drove them. He was a great driver and had such a warm and friendly countenance that everybody loved him, especially older folks and young children. This group could go along and ride the Montana Express if they could not ride horses. The extra wagon was Gloria's idea, and it later became the "water and snack" wagon for the cowboys as well as the outriders. That wagon was destined to change many things before the drive ended.

The rain continued; the mud got deeper; our clothes, tack, and horses were constantly wet. Will was driving equipment trucks, and I missed not seeing him as often.

I had purchased an old stock trailer in Oberlin, and while we were in Gem, I went back to pick it up from the owner, who had promised to repair the tailgate on it. I parked it in Lon's yard and camped there the night we stayed in Gem. I found the trailer in an ad placed in the local newspaper by a big blustering German named Wayne Zwickle, who owned and operated "Wayne's World," where he sold everything from ham to harness. That trailer became home to me for the remainder of the drive, and it was a haven for part of Gloria and Will's belongings as well as my own. It was a pain in the butt to hitch and unhitch each day, but without it life would have been much more difficult. My little Omar tent was no match for the adverse weather we encountered most of the time. I tied a tarp over the trailer to cover the openings on each side of it and had complete privacy from eyes, wind, and rain. It's funny how priorities change with circumstances. . . .

In 1974, I traveled to Panama and sang in the palace for Panamanian President Demetrio B. Lakas and stayed in the presidential suite in the Panamanian Hotel. I had a king-sized bed, a spacious apartment, fresh flowers, fabulous food, Scotch, and champagne every day. Downstairs, a private bodyguard sat in an old Cadillac, with a Tommy gun at his side for protection. He hauled me wherever I wanted to go.

That presidential suite and amenities could not compare with the luxury of that old 1973 stock trailer on the GACD. The fourteen-foot trailer was the epitome of privacy, luxury, and space unmatched in my sixty-three years. I wrapped a piece of fence wire around one of the openings along the side and had an instant clothesline. The "head" compartment up front, where one could place hay for a horse being hauled, was great space for storage. The middle gate separated my sleeping space from Will and Gloria's belongings. Yeah, I had two rooms. Life was great.

Oberlin, Kansas, and some of the things that happened there linger in my mind, like an old scar reminds me of something I would like to forget. I helped with a benefit for a young boy who had been hurt on a horse. He was sixteen and lay in a coma with extensive brain damage because he had lain out in the corral face down in the sand for hours before being found by his mother. Lack of oxygen was the main culprit. The locals combined their welcome to us with the benefit, and we helped to raise $6,500 for the boy's family. The boy died three weeks later, I heard down the trail. I was glad to have been able to help in that small way. In the middle of my part of the concert, the souvenir man set up two tables and began selling souvenirs for the drive. Jim McElroy came on stage and took the microphone and announced we would be selling souvenirs for the drive after dinner. I wanted to simply disappear from the stage at that moment. I expressed my incredulity later and was told: "That's the way life is, Annie."

One other strange thing happened in Oberlin. The morning

we left camp to ride into Oberlin, Bud told Walt to take the chuck wagon to downtown Oberlin and pick up the queen of the big homecoming festivities being celebrated there. But when we got to the crossroads where we should have turned downtown, Walt never veered and kept right on going to the next camp. I was riding scout in front of the wagon with Dancer. I turned back and asked Walt why we weren't going downtown to pick up the girl.

"I found out Bud does not have any insurance on us, as he promised. I am not going to pick up anybody and take a chance on a runaway or something else and get sued." Walt slapped the lines on the Shires, and we kept going.

Walt's explanation made sense, but I wondered why he hadn't expressed his feelings to Bud when he was given those orders. I rode on in silence, soon shedding the uneasy feeling in my chest, with the help of Gus and the early morning mist, in the dawn of a new day.

Walt had been congenial and somewhat of a clown with me all the way. He flirted with all the girls along the streets and towns and highways. They loved that big cowboy sitting high like a king on the chuck wagon, driving those huge black horses. He would tease me about us running off together or keeping each other warm on cold nights. We joked back and forth in fun, and I enjoyed it as much as I was sure he did. He liked to hear me sing "Ridin' Ole Paint." I always told the crowd that that was Walt's favorite song, and he would grin at the recognition it brought him. I would share any goodies I had with him such as an apple or cookie or candy. Walt loved to eat, and he could eat as much as six logrollers. He was always first in line at the cook shack at chow time.

Behind all his bantering, I sensed Walt's angry, rebellious feelings toward Bud. Also, Walt and Bruce seemed to absolutely hate each other. Walt was silent to me about their relationship, and Bruce attempted to be diplomatic on the surface, but he was later blamed for many of the miscommunications between the leaders and the cowboys. These confrontations, power struggles, big egos, and fights for limelight and personal glory grew bigger, like weeds taking over a meadow. Refusing to pick up the queen in Oberlin would surface later when Bud finally fired Walt.

In McCook, Nebraska, Bud called a meeting for everybody. To get away from the visitors, we had to go down into a gully in the pasture where we were camped. Gloria and one of the outriders were left in camp to "meet, talk to, and entertain" the visitors. That meeting was to discuss the letter I had written for the cowboys. Bud held it in his hand and took the complaints, one at a time, and discussed them with all of us sitting surrounding him. He promised to have special feed mixed for the horses. One more time he discussed the fact that the outriders were our bread and butter, but he said he would "see that they stayed in behind the herd." Bud reminded the cowboys who complained about days off that many of them did not stay in camp to help with things when we were down. He told us that he was broke and that there was absolutely no money to operate on. That was the first time I had heard him admit that we had a money problem.

He became irate when he mentioned the fact that he had been called a liar in front of his son at the meeting in Oberlin. He assured us that he was not a liar and had not lied to us about anything. Walt brought up the fact that Bud owed him money for the horses he had sold Bud before the drive. Bud said: "You brought those horses down here, and they were wild and poor and crazy and unbroken. They looked like hell with matted manes and tails full of burrs. You said they were good horses, and they weren't nothing but scrubs; they weren't fit to ride or do anything else with."

"You ordered those horses on the phone and agreed to pay me fifteen hundred apiece. Now, I can't get my money," Walt said.

"I don't figure I owe you for those horses because you misrepresented them to me. What do you think about a horse deal like that, Larry – you saw them horses."

Bud looked at Larry Orrell. Larry was a wrangler, a Texan in his mid-forties, rather surly to most, and a loner. He stayed to himself, rode drag most of the time, where he worked his horse more than driving the cattle. He was respected as somewhat of an authority on horses, especially by the younger cowboys.

"If you ordered the horses and bought them sight unseen, you should pay for them. A deal's a deal," Larry said. Several of the cowboys agreed with Larry's answer. There was little or no sympathy for Bud. Jess Herbers was adamant that Bud promised things and did not do them. J W brought up the fact that he and J D and I had been hired to entertain the visitors and "now you up and say that we will no longer be paid for our entertainment."

Bud said that no more would we be paid to sing for the visitors in camps. I decided to put in my two cents worth. When Bud said he was paying each of us $100 a performance, I corrected him by reminding him that I was not paid as much as the two men were.

"Well, whatever," he said with a wave of his hand and a shrug, as if to dismiss that part of the conversation. But I wasn't through.

"Bud, we are tired of being treated like idiots by the investors. Our complaints are ignored or brushed off as if we were one of the steers, bawling for hay. They seem to make light of the many problems plaguing this drive, and most of the time they are rude to the media, and the visitors." I told him that one investor had called him a hired hand to me on the phone and had said that Bud did not have anything invested in the drive.

I continued, "I believe your biggest problem is the fact that you don't know who your friends are. If you would only let us know where you stand, we want to be your friends and make this drive a success, but we can't figure you out or just how you feel or where you stand."

He never responded to my complaints or oratory in the meeting, but later, he asked me to accompany him to his truck and said we would call that investor together. I told him I was ready when he was.

That ought to be interesting. The investor will simply call me a liar. It will be his word against mine. We will accomplish nothing by arguing on the phone except to run up the bill. Bud asked those who had called him a liar to remain and the rest could go. I left; however, the majority of the cowboys stayed. After the meeting, when all the cowboys came back into camp, Jess Herbers and Bruce got into a shouting match.

"I was so mad and fed up with Bud and his lying, and I figured that Bruce was the one who had called Bud about what we had said in the meeting in Oberlin," Jess told me later.

"When you left the meeting after it was over and we stayed, I told Bud that I had been one of the ones who called him a liar, and I thought he *was* a liar. He invited me to whip his ass, and I told him that I would but that I still wanted my job after I whipped his ass. He really got mad then, but we never did fight, and the meeting broke up, and when we got back in camp, I just walked up to Bruce and asked him if he had been the one who had told Bud that I called him a liar in the meeting in Oberlin. Bruce said he had because he thought Bud ought to know. I jerked his hat off and threw it on the ground, thinking he would hit me. His buddy, Jim, walked over and hid behind a trailer. Bruce just picked up his hat and stalked off. He did not want to fight. Some buddy he had in Jim, who stayed hid behind that trailer."

Jess was angry, hurt, disappointed, young, idealistic, and probably warranted in his outburst. Bruce and Jim left camp. I guessed that they would leave the drive for good. I couldn't believe they would stay in the midst of so much resentment and anger toward them. They had been blamed for everything that had happened or didn't happen on the drive from the moment they became bosses. Their every word and action brought instant resentment and hate. I felt a bit of pity for them and thought that if they were gone it was best for all, including them. But they were back later, and I believe that everybody was disappointed. *God, they must have hides like an alligator or politician. I can't believe they are going to try to live with these cowboys until we get to Montana under the present circumstances. I would have already tucked my tail and hauled ass for home.*

Bud later dropped a bomb by telling me that someone had sent the letter I had written for the cowboys to WBAP Radio in Fort Worth/Dallas and that the station had been reading it on the air. I couldn't believe that anyone would deliberately hurt the drive by baring our troubles to the public like that.

Bud wanted to know if I could help him find some investors for an idea he had to market the souvenirs on television. He said he needed enough money to buy out the present investors and about a half-million to promote the souvenirs. I thought of all the times I had offered to help before the drive. Now that things looked hopeless, I was being asked to help. I made some calls and got three appointments for him to pitch his idea to friends. I made no recommendations to anyone, just arranged for an audience to hear his pitch. We never did call that investor.

The downtime in McCook was welcome. We began drying out. There had been no dry weather in weeks. The entire state of Kansas had been nothing but mud. I went to Juan Pertle with Vision Quest and got a jar of neatsfoot oil and started working on my tack. My saddle had not been oiled since leaving Fort Worth. The sun came out hot and wonderful, and I put down a tarp outside the trailer and spread the oiled tack out to dry in the sun. I spread out my bedding along with clothes that had not been dry in days. It really felt good to sit out there in the sun and to clean and dry everything. I was happy to watch everyone working or playing, visiting, and talking to the visitors.

Eldon and J D and the Donaldson boys were hard at work shoeing horses, including Gus and Red. Jerry Owens and Jeff Christenson had a horse race. Jerry had bought a mare somewhere along the way. While they were shoeing the mare, Jeff wondered why Jerry made such a fuss over "that club-footed mare." Jeff was immediately challenged by Jerry to a race. Jerry's "club-footed mare" proved to be the faster horse. We all took pictures, cheered, and enjoyed the downtime, the sunshine, and the horse race.

Then, like an old enemy sneaking up on the blind side, the

rain came back in the middle of the night. I got up and hooked the trailer up in the dark and got out onto the road before I got stuck in the mud. One pleasant thing happened in McCook. Dick Kennedy came back. He looked rested, and his attitude had made a 180-degree turn. He was happy to be back, and his positive feelings were a great boost to the cowboys' morale.

The countryside changed dramatically, and I read the words engraved on the crude, concrete monument.

Oregon Trail Marked
by the state of Nebraska, 1912
Trail 30 Feet East

We drove the longhorns of the twentieth century along remnants of the historic Oregon Trail through Ash Hollow, surrounded by rolling sand hills dotted with cedar and waves of lush green grass enriched, some natives claimed, with more rainfall than ever in history. Wheat was the palest of yellow, just beginning to turn golden for harvest. Plowed, manicured fields were cream with a touch of ochre and lay in sharp contrast to the wildflowers growing in canyons. Centuries-old rocks and clutches of cottonwoods jutted out between giant firs where gullies fed abundant water. In the background, stretching for twenty-six miles, lay McCaughey Lake, shimmering in bright sunlight, rich blue-green from its depths of more than 150 feet. It was Tuesday, June 27, almost four months since we left Fort Worth.

I was riding scout in front of Walt's wagon. He had the brake partially on as we traveled downhill on the asphalt to that valley where one hundred-plus years before, windlasses were used to pull the pioneers' chuck wagons up to higher ground because of the steep inclines. Those pioneers struggled with rocks, mud, treacherous trails, bandits, and cattle thieves. Today, Will and the cowboys were enjoying the magnificent scenery and playing with the steers.

"The cattle ran today, and some of us tried to get the lead

men to let them go," Will said. "I was cuttin' out one steer at a time and gettin' it away from the herd, and then Dick would fall behind it and play with it until it cut back into the herd. But those damn steers got smart, and it was difficult to cut one out then. The boys on the swing and drag started roping steers; then a couple would get off and mug it and get the rope off. Dick started them to running, but the point checked them before we could run hell-bent. We are getting pretty undisciplined because we don't have no leadership."

Hell, Will, you were probably born undisciplined, you old coyote. I'll bet you guys had a ball today playing with those steers and never worrying about the consequences of a stampede or traffic. What a hoot you are.

I was glad I was not riding with the herd anymore although I loved that, too. It was still fun to watch those cowboys cavorting with the steers when they should have been more disciplined and concerned with things in general. Men just don't seem to worry about things like women do. They are simply little boys inside big bodies. In spite of the fun with the cowboys, it was more laid-back up front, and I got into camp earlier, leaving more time to write. I was by myself much of the time, out front of the chuck wagon, and I liked that.

In Ash Hollow camp, Eldon was attempting to put shoes on Will's mare, Penny, when she kicked and dragged a horse shoe nail into his hand. The wound took four stitches to close. Mishaps, mud, and the fact that our horses were a half-mile from camp, made for frayed nerves that were somewhat soothed when the locals came and cooked for us again. One cowboy expressed pure glee at the thought of having a respite from chuck wagon fare: "I am sure glad these people are gonna cook for us. Them Vision Quest kids work in that kitchen and never wash. They run around camp with their jeans down around the cracks of their asses in them baggy clothes, and it really looks bad as the film crews are here making documentaries most of the time. This will look bad in the magazines and other publications because this is supposed to duplicate the old trail days, where they didn't have to baby-sit a bunch of pissant criminals."

I understood how he felt. He expressed feelings that were shared by many of the others. I just stayed apart from the boys as much as possible and never really minded them much. I believe the cattle drive was good therapy for those kids who had never lived outside the urban life. Living with creatures can teach us much about living and tolerance and honesty. They are honest and predictable, and they love you unconditionally.

13
BEAUTIFUL NEBRASKA

Ash Hollow made me feel like I was nestled in a warm blanket, surrounded by Nebraska and her beauty. I loved it! The weather was changing, although we got several more days of floods, and the wind never seemed to stop. I was thrilled by the country nonetheless. The wildflowers were breathtakingly beautiful, and most were orchid in color - the richest orchid I had ever seen. The right-of-ways were solid carpets of wildflowers, and I hated walking on them and crushing even one. A car pulled up alongside the chuck wagon, and the lady yelled out her car window:

"May I ride on that wagon?"

"Yeah!" Walt said with a grin.

The lady was ecstatic. She climbed aboard with a boost from her husband and rode half a mile while listening in rapt attention to Walt. He was a great talker when he talked about himself. He was a one-man show and a good one at that. I am sure that lady is still talking about that short ride on the chuck wagon with a big cowboy. They were from Washington state, and she insisted that her husband take pictures before she got down to "prove I really did this." We rode nineteen miles that day. In Lewellen, I visited the Volunteer Center and had a great shower and then had dinner with Dick, Will, Claude, and JW.

Oshkosh, Nebraska was a small but busy farming town. There we had downtime, and the Eastern Star ladies brought homemade apple pies and cooked the greatest hamburgers we had had so far.

I met "Muggie," who owned the Print Shoppe and a car wash. She was a pint-sized dynamite lady who printed new business cards for me, and we had coffee and talked about Texas, where she had lived for a while with her husband. The S&S café, where we drank coffee, was a gathering place for farmers and ranchers and other locals to cuss and discuss crops and the weather. We enjoyed good food there, too. Next door was a motel by the same name, where I set up and wrote stories and called home and slept in a dry bed. I washed clothes, cleaned the truck and trailer out, and watched my horses run and play in plush grass.

Later, we saw foothills and centuries-old sand pyramids jutting up out of green pastures behind arrow-straight rows of corn and fields of alfalfa. The roadside was sprinkled with purple spiderworts, another Nebraska wildflower. While in Broadwater, some of the cowboys went to nearby Bridgeport to the first night of a two-day rodeo while we had downtime. They entered the wild horse race and put on a show for the crowd. They caught one pony and got JR mounted. When he got off, Jamie Nail jumped over the rail and mounted the pony on the run and rode him to a standstill. They had to remove the saddle from the horse to qualify. The pony got away, and Jess Herbers jumped over the rail and caught him. They were disqualified for having too many riders in the arena at one time, but everybody loved the show anyway. They came back to camp laughing and rehashing the night and fun.

Skip and Derk were filming again, and we had great times around camp, singing and sharing brandy and Scotch and whatever we had to drink at the time. We told tall tales and played guitars, and life was indeed good. As I saddled up on the Fourth of July, I thought of Texas where everyone would be cranking up smokers for barbecue and donning bathing suits and lying around the lakes, basking in the hot Texas sun. I put on my goose-down jacket to ward off the chilly north wind and thanked God for being where I was. I rode by fields of sugar beets, some of them right in the small towns we passed through. I could think of nothing I needed or wanted, and I rode tall in the saddle with my thoughts, my White Horse, and my dreams.

That night in camp, a young, Montana couple were joined in holy matrimony under cloudy skies, next to a campfire, surrounded by Texas longhorns, cowboys, and Nebraska's land.

We were camped at the eastern edge of Broadwater, Nebraska, when the animosity between Bruce and Walt began to fester. Word came to Walt that the people of Torrington, Wyoming, were furious because the GACD had canceled that camp (Jim McElroy was named as the culprit). The Wyoming people cancelled plans for a steak supper for us and other activities that had been previously planned. Walt had scouted all of Wyoming and Montana before the drive for our scheduled camps through those two states.

Walt could not reach Bud on the phone. While Walt was trying to call Bud on a pay phone in town, Bud was calling Walt on the phone in the souvenir trailer. Walt distrusted the man who ran it. He was livid. I believe that Walt despised Jim McElroy with a passion. He talked in camp about the "great folks in Torrington."

"I had all the camps set up, spent my own money and time traveling across two states, and that pale son of a bitch has changed the camp and made those people mad at us."

When the rest of us finally got the scuttlebutt about that episode, we learned (secondhand) that Bruce and Jim had changed the camp site because "the livestock would have been on gravel, and the camp was not big enough," Bruce told Bud. Walt said that he had told Bud in Fort Worth about the size of the camp, and Bud said he did not remember anything about it. *Hey, who said there was no communication in this organization?*

We were riding on the downhill side of our journey, and tempers were growing hotter. The weather, the culture, even the time had changed to Mountain Standard. There was a sense of urgency within us all. We were feeling an inner excitement, knowing we were getting nearer to our destination each day.

Many of the horses were crippled. Jamie Nail and others knew we would need every horse available for outriders as we got closer to Montana.

I was still worrying about the same thing that I had been worrying about since leaving Texas. Water. I had asked Bud several times if we were going to get a water truck. I knew that when we reached Wyoming, we could not depend on the towns to send a fire truck out to camp with water at our request. The small towns were sometimes sixty miles or farther apart. It was growing hot, and the steers and horses could not go without water.

Bud had finally gotten a water wagon that held five hundred gallons. Five hundred gallons was a drop in the bucket compared to what we needed just for the steers, much less for the camp and horses, but it beat hell out of nothing. Amid all the bickering between Walt and Bruce and Jim, the old man who drove the water wagon turned it over and caved it in just outside of Oshkosh. It had to go in for repairs. Walt blamed Bruce and/or Jim for any delays, problems, or changes, as did some of the other cowboys. When it came to stirring things up, Walt was better than the agitator pole on a Maytag washer.

I thought PMS only happened to women.

I had decided by that time that I was going to Montana, with or without cattle, cowboys, or chuck wagon. I concluded that the frustration, anger, and hard feelings were not going to wane, but perhaps become worse.

I remembered a story I had read in a book about the nineteenth-century cattle drives. A group of cowboys was going up the North Platte River and cut across to Sweetwater, following the old California immigrant trail, by the Enchanted Rock and Devil's Gate. The cook had broken one of the ox yokes, and they had to camp and cut a small cottonwood tree to make another yoke. The axe was dull, making it almost impossible to cut the king bolt of the wagon. It took all night to burn six holes in the yoke. They were short of grub and had forty miles across the Rocky Mountains or two hundred miles if they went around them. They chose to go over them. The first night in the mountains, it came a snowstorm, and they lost twenty-five horses, and the cattle scattered. They had no salt, flour, or coffee, and lived on nothing but beef for over a month. Remembering that story, I wanted to tell those cowboys that our problems were small potatoes compared to those whose footsteps we were following. But I said nothing. That was totally uncharacteristic of me.

Out there on the trail to Montana, I wasn't in charge. I was merely a speck on a great big wall, and what blew me away was that I didn't even care. I was so happy riding down that road, behind those longhorns, surrounded by cowboys and sleeping under the stars with my horses, it wasn't necessary to be in charge anymore. I took care of Gus and Red, looked out for my buddy Will (as much as he would permit me or anybody else to look out for him), and rode on in a northwesterly direction.

Chimney Rock in Nebraska was awesome. That natural monument had been a landmark for the early settlers and trail drives. I visited the Tourist Cabin, an information center that was surrounded by wildflowers, and bought two books by Rick Steagar, entitled *Cowboys* and *Oregon Trails*, and watched a movie about the history of the Rock. I closed my eyes and heard the rumble and rattle of the wagon, felt the earth tremble beneath me, and listened to the longhorns bellowing when the pioneers and trail herds of the nineteenth-century plodded beneath the monument. The pioneers must have stopped and gazed in awe at that million-year-old pyramid standing three hundred feet in the sky, like a dusty lighthouse – always there, always waiting to guide them toward their destination. Perhaps they felt they would never see anything like it again. I wasn't sure that I would, either.

In Scotts Bluff, we were served hot doughnuts and coffee by Grampy's Pancake House from tables set up in an open field across the highway. The steers and horses grazed contentedly nearby, waiting to push on to the next camp. Hundreds of people gathered to take pictures, ask questions, and visit. One of Walt's mares colicked while we sat enjoying the coffee. I was sitting on Gus when I noticed her trying to lie down. Walt got down off the wagon and made her stand, but only for a moment before she went down again. He unhitched her, and Walker and I took the mare next door, where an animal hospital just happened to be. Walt hitched Brother, a sorrel "extra" horse that he had, in the mare's place, and he later went back and picked up the mare. She was rested for a few days and then put back in harness.

In Mitchell, Nebraska, at the fairgrounds where we camped, the town folks came with covered dishes! Shades of smorgasbord. After supper, I set up my tent under ominous skies with the air hot and still and heavy. I stripped to the bone to bathe in a bucket of water, and suddenly the wind hit like a cyclone. My tent leaned and whipped, and I had visions of it disintegrating, leaving me exposed to the world in my birthday suit. Huge drops of rain mixed with hail hit like tin saucers, pelting the metal roof of my trailer nearby, and folks scrambled for cars and other shelter. I did a record time redress and put on boots, but the wind died and the hail stopped as suddenly as it had come.

Nebraska was full of surprises and good food. Will and I went to downtown Scotts Bluff one night and had dinner, went shopping, and saw an antique steam engine. We took pictures there. Lon, Will, and I enjoyed dinner there again while we were in Mitchell. I had not been bothered with aches and pain in weeks. I felt great, my skin was the color of alfalfa honey, I had lost my "flab," the country was beautiful, and the people were so wonderful and friendly and proud of their state.

The lawns and gardens, trees, endless farms and countryside were magnificent; a feeling of freedom and joy at being alive seemed to engulf me. One man stopped at the side of the road and walked out to me. I pulled Gus up, and we talked.

"Are you having fun?" he asked. I told him I was having a great time. "Well, as you ride down this road on this beautiful day, with the sky for a roof and the earth beneath you, and never a care of what time of day it is, think of me as I drive in the traffic, to my stuffy office, to hear the constant ring of the telephone for eight hours – think of me and know that I would give anything to be out here with you." He looked up at me with a wistful little boy look in his eyes, and I realized once again, that I was the luckiest woman in the world. . . .

I felt that I had reached a pinnacle in my life. I knew that many people live and die and never realize their dreams, and there I was doing something that I had dreamed of for over fifty years. It was really happening. I had put that dream somewhere in the recesses of my mind long ago when I first met that cowboy, Gene Moore; when my glands started functioning and my childhood flew, then Lea, then Lynda, Sandy, Keely, and Kenny; when I had to become citizen, mother, wife, breadwinner, and so on.

Responsibility has always been mine in huge bundles. Life deals us a hand sometimes different from the one we visualize. My children have been instrumental in molding my life more than any other event, entity, or person. My three marriages, though brief, (ten years with Kenneth being the longest) touched, altered, and influenced, but with much less impact than that of my children. When they came, I wanted to be the best at everything I did. I wanted, and still want, to be their hero, their model, and their star. I never made "the big time" in motherhood, but I received some curtain calls and raves along the way.

My life with my kids has been a magnificent journey down the rough road of learning. I don't know if there were more tears than smiles – I never kept a tally. I know that I would not be the whole person I believe myself to be today had it not been for them. Lea, Sandy, Keely, and Kenny are as close to me as the beat of my heart. Lynda went away many years ago, but that is another story. They are my best friends, and my heroes. When we are together, we re-hash old times, and everyone talks at the same time, telling some forgotten tale about each other, while giggling over the picture albums, and playing scrabble and gin. We respect each other's differences and disagreements on opinions of religion and cultural and moral obligations; of whether I should go to some "home" when I am unable to care for myself, or live with one of them.

Once, when I said that I would probably be a bitch in my old age and should be put away, Keely vehemently exclaimed: "If you think I am going to put my mother in one of those places that smell like pee and disinfectant, you are crazy!" I believe that they have forgiven me for my affairs with married men and my absence from them all the years I worked two jobs, kicked their butts, and withheld the love I felt for them. And I have forgotten the frustrations, fatigue, and futility I felt during the years of raising them alone. But we all remember the good times. Now, I can't imagine my life being anything but what it is and was. Dreams are sometimes best when they are unfulfilled, and life deals some unexpected winning hands. The cowboys in my dreams have always been my heroes. I believe Willie Nelson wrote a song about that same thing.

My love for the wide open spaces, freedom of spirit, and horses, is synonymous with the meaning of "cowboy." I know about cowboys. I have made it my heart's business to know about them.

The word "cowboy," at one time, referred to Texas bandits stealing cattle from Mexicans. Earlier, in Revolutionary War days, the armed Tories who lured farmer patriots with lost cows into the brush with tinkling cowbells and ambushed them were called cowboys. After the Civil War, the term "cowboy" signified anyone working with cows in the West.

The real American cowboy lasted a mere generation – from the end of the Civil War until the mid-1880s. The men who rode the cattle trails across the Great Plains were fewer than 45,000. The average age of these cowboys was twenty-four, and in spite of the guns they carried, their hand-rolled cigarettes, and rugged appearances, they were, for the most part, country bumpkins.

One cowboy in six or seven was Mexican or black or Indian.

They were, many times, drifters, rangeland beggars, saddle bums, former rebels looking for more excitement than the farms could bring, and men on the dodge from the law or some responsibility or discipline. And that might have been why asking a man his name was considered discourteous and sometimes downright detrimental to one's health. Their attire many times was the rags of a Confederate uniform, with floppy woolen hat with brim pinned up by a thorn and army-issue boots.

Possibly the riveting appeal of this untamed, ragged piece of humanity was his unbelievable stamina in crossing the Great Plains with herds of wild cattle, riding half-broken mustangs in terrible weather, while existing on sowbelly, beans, and sourdough. What appealed to me could have been his kinship and his similarity to the very creatures he herded and rode, that free-spirited almost childlike abandonment and rebellion against a more disciplined life; a life like that of the man standing there in the road longing to join me on the drive.

I may have developed a love for that intangible something while following a mule and a plow when I was not much bigger than some of the black clods of dirt kicked up out of the East Texas soil. The smell of horse sweat and the music of leather and chains on harness and the feel of the sun on my back and the dirt under my bare feet may have groomed me for whatever the open road held for me later. The kinship between man and animal that has been fine-tuned by the likes of that dirt farmer who raised me and by the cowboys in American history is a symbol of all that is dear to me. Perhaps that something that I can't quite name is the simple honesty of the animals and those men who live and communicate with them.

Will and Jamie Nail were two throwbacks of the nineteenth century cowboys on the GACD. Jamie was a generation behind Will. He was tall, lean as a whip, daring, perceptive, and free-spirited. His bedroll would sometimes contain a week's supply of worn jeans, shirts, boots, and socks. In the early morning, when all others were getting ready to ride, one could find Jamie easily by the last bedroll still in a tangled mess next to the fire or partially under some trailer, with him still snoring peacefully while horses, cattle, and cowboys walked over him laughing and telling some story of Jamie being up all night into some mischief. One night he had lain too close to the fire, and his bedroll and clothes had scorched and burned right down to his long johns. And even then someone had to wake him to tell him he was on fire.

He went to a horse sale somewhere along the way and bought a scrubby little gray mare, and she was in foal. We all watched her closely because she was making a bag, her teats swelled, and her little belly was sagging and huge with colt. We had a pot, and each of us wrote a date, anteed the pot, and guessed when the colt would make its entrance. Whoever had the correct date would win the pot.

Jamie caught a wild miniature donkey in Wellfleet, Nebraska, and loaded him with the remuda and took him along. That donkey brayed, kicked, and raised hell for days. I heard later that the owner came looking for the little jack. Jamie had orders from Bruce to take the donkey back. I never knew just what happened to that donkey. Jamie did not take Bruce too seriously. As a matter of fact, he never took *life* too seriously.

His little mare threw a colt in Hershey, Nebraska, in the night. The curious geldings surrounded the mare and her foal, and one of them stepped on the colt's leg and broke it, and someone had to put the colt down. I don't know who won the pot, but I do know the mare should have been separated from the geldings, but she wasn't, and the colt was doomed. I cursed those lube-headed men and their lack of responsibility. One of them shrugged and said it wasn't his responsibility because Jamie wasn't there and might get angry if someone interfered. The rest just stood around and waited, some claiming to have tried calling Jamie at the motel in North Platte. They said they couldn't find him. Most of them didn't respond at all. I just cried for the lost colt and saddled up and rode on toward Montana, thoroughly pissed at men in general and their inadequacies and stupidity.

Yeah, even my beloved cowboys.

◆ ◆ ◆ ◆

And speaking of beloved cowboys, this story would not be complete without telling you about "Cowboy." Not just any cowboy, but I am speaking now of *my* Cowboy. Well, I have "owned" him in my heart for thirty years or so, and I have always called him Cowboy. Since names are not always important, I will just leave that as it is. Sometimes he seems to be merely a figment of my imagination, until the phone rings and I hear that voice that sounds as if it comes from deep in the rich earth, then I know that he is indeed real. Strangely enough, my children have accepted the fact that Cowboy and I will always just "be." This is a relationship that has endured, since I finally accepted the fact that Kenneth would not suddenly appear in my world again. He has always been there, even during the seventeen wasted years of my time with another. I wrote an ode about my cowboy:

There are no scars on my heart
for having loved you for almost three decades.
The years have simply enhanced
my ability to conjure up your crooked smile,
with only a thought.
We have ridden down different trails,
left tracks on different mountains,
yet I have always been comfortable
knowing the same sun
spreads its warmth on both of us.
My vagabond heart and restless mind
are content with the memory
of moments spent swaying to music
in some dimly-lit room,
or sitting side by side on hard metal seats
in some old auction barn
rich with the smell of creatures,

black coffee, manure, and hay.
Without thinking,
I can feel your breath on my cheek,
your hands holding and touching me,
mingled with the sound
of your rich laughter.
In a crowd or in my solitude,
because of you,
loneliness is a stranger.
I am smug with knowing
there is a tiny space in your heart
left there for only me.
I am like a child with a secret hideout
known only to one other and shared
with only one other.
You have always been my secret,
my stash, my raincoat, my port, my ace,
You have always been my love. . . .

◆ ◆ ◆ ◆

On the Howard Webster Ranch, thirteen miles out of North Platte, Nebraska, Will, Gloria, Dick, and I sat around the trailer and had a great time bending elbows and swapping tales. It was a beautiful night, the sky clear and black as pitch, and without competition from city lights, the galaxy of stars was as bright as Irish freckles. I awakened in the night to an electrical storm that was so frighteningly beautiful that I was mesmerized watching it until I decided I should get the hell out of the muddy camp with my truck and trailer if I intended getting out at all. On higher ground, I spent the night re-tying the tarp on the trailer, which whipped and beat against the trailer as the hailstones tapped staccato music on the steel top. The wind rocked the trailer in an eighty-mile-an-hour, gusty push and pull. Next morning all was calm and beautiful, and we headed for North Platte.

In our camp at Wellfleet, Nebraska, a lady was seen leading

Stony, our camp dog, away. Stony had joined us at Roaring Springs, Oklahoma, and had just stayed with us. He was akin to the basset family and possessed few brains or common sense about traffic. I just waited for him to be smashed into a sausage by a semi right in front of me one day. He would walk right out in front of oncoming traffic or into the herd, and longhorns are certainly not tolerant of dogs. The cowboys' opinions of Stony were mixed, to say the least. He was both despised and liked. The lady said her little boy's dog had been killed and looked just like Stony, and "your trail boss gave the dog to me for my son." After she left, the cowboys sat around talking and decided that Stony was theirs, and they left camp, found the lady, and brought Stony back.

We were camped on top of the Oregon Trail, on the south side of the South Platte River. The pasture we were in had rich grass with protein content of about fourteen percent, which meant we did not have to feed cake to the steers there. Overlooking camp was a hill the Sioux Indians had used for their lookout point. They could see about thirty miles around from atop that hill.

The Country Bar, in North Platte, had Red Dog Beer Night, and the price was one dollar a bottle. Will won a drawing for Jeff Foxworthy concert tickets and a Foxworthy disc. Vision Quest went home to Arizona for ten days.

"I wish they had taken their tent, mules, and wagon with them when they left and kept going," Will said. Some of the cowboys went home, and several went back to the Pyramid Ranch to help with roundup there while we were down. Dick and Will built bunks in Dick's stock trailer.

North Platte has about 22,000 population. It is clean, rather metropolitan, and boasts a university. We camped at the University Research Center for six days of downtime. Gloria and I found a small room with kitchenette at the Country Inn Motel. We set up housekeeping, and I bought an iron skillet for cornbread, and a small pot for stew, and we had a great respite from yucky camp cooking.

My stew was quite well known in Fort Worth circles. I had given free lunches for seven years in my club there with much success. I learned years before that a pot of stew will open doors to opportunities that are otherwise firmly closed.

Pablo, our cook, was a very nice, genteel man at all times. He was short, a bit chubby, with that hang-dog look that the old, quiet drovers had in John Wayne movies – the look that belonged on the faces of those chivalrous gentlemen of the West. He did not have the fire of "Old Cannonball," the feisty camp cook played by Dub Taylor in many of the old westerns. Pablo was always clean, neatly dressed, with starched jeans, shirt, and colorful vests that his wife made, he told me. He always, without exception, told me I looked beautiful and smelled good, and he was free with his smiles peeking through a full beard.

The food we ate was served out of a window in the trailer, in Styrofoam plates with plastic tableware. We had no place to sit and eat except on the ground. Most of the time the wind would be blowing so hard, that by the time I found a place to park my butt and eat, my food was cold. I thought many times how much fun it would have been had we had a long table where all could sit and eat and visit, just like family. I believe it would have improved morale, brought us closer together, and given us a chance to hear how others felt about camp situations. Food just always tastes better if you have company.

A major portion of the food cooked was loaded with grease and/or cholesterol, with few vegetables or fruit. The scrambled eggs were almost always green and crusty from iron skillets which had been washed in cold water and left to air dry, and the fire under them was much too hot for eggs. The pancakes (which I don't care for anyway because they feel like rocks in my belly) were cold, with cold syrup, and they would not begin to melt the oleo. I was raised on old-fashioned Texas cream gravy, made from scratch, in the same skillet that the meat had been cooked in, and the pasty, ready-mixed gravy we had was difficult to eat, even when I was hungry.

But the cowboys ate heartily and complained little. However, many jokes were voiced about the food, some of which earned no chuckles. When Bud came to camp, we sometimes had lettuce and tomatoes and turkey with our sandwiches. Sometimes we had fruit and packaged dessert. We all laughed when Jim Donaldson called those gut stuffers "gourmet" sandwiches.

Jim had a warm place in my heart. He was thirty, tall and lean like wire, with a ruddy complexion that matched his red hair. His "red hair" temper was roused only under dire circumstances. He was an Oklahoman, cowboy through and through, very male, and might have been born 150 years ago. The girls who came to camp were drawn to Jim like beagles to birds. He sat a saddle better than Bob Steele and had a yellow dun horse who matched him in performance. Ahhh, to have been thirty again.

The Platte River was out of its banks from all the rain and melting Colorado snow. The Nebraska natives talked about it being the wettest year in history. I believed it. We used mink oil and neatsfoot oil on our boots to help ensure some days with dry feet. We had been wet for so long that it had become almost normal to us.

The remuda was full of sore-back horses from wet saddle blankets. I had purchased another blanket to swap on Gus or Red, and they were in good shape, but some of the horses looked like yellow and pink polka-dotted creatures from another planet when they were smeared with ointment. One of the visitors said that he had never seen so many sore-back horses in all his years of ranching. I welcomed our downtime in North Platte to give the horses time to heal.

Some of the pale horses, including Gus, had blisters on their muzzles, and one of the locals said some of the weeds in Nebraska at certain times of the year caused blisters on animals with fair skin. Jim Donaldson said to feed them watermelon to cure the problem. I rubbed Gus's muzzle with pink ointment that I carried for cuts and sores. He was really sensitive about anything touching those blisters. I knew they were painful.

Downtown, next door to the photography studio where Gloria and I took film to be developed, I found *Doris' Bar and Grill*, a little bar about the size of the one I had had in Fort Worth. The drinks were good, and the steak sandwich was next to perfection. Cathy, Doris' chubby, delightful daughter, was tending bar wearing a cap with "Bitch with an Attitude" printed across it. Cathy was Miss Personality and had a knack of remembering everyone's name. I met some great, friendly people, including Doris, and I promised to return the next night and play for them.

I had an SRO crowd who made me feel like home and filled my tip jar. That money was manna from heaven. Funds were getting low by that time because of the extra money I had spent in restaurants and on horse feed, film, stamps, and paper. Gloria and I went shopping too much and bought too many clothes that we had no place to hang. Gloria could afford to buy all that stuff, but this old gal couldn't.

All the businesses in North Platte had inflated prices because of Nebraskaland Days Celebration in its thirtieth year. People came from all over for festivities and the PRCA Rodeo. Gasoline was expensive at $1.24 a gallon, and we usually went in my truck. *What the hell, you can't take it with you.* My daughter, Sandy, always said, "Mother will find a way!" I had called my bank and had them transfer another five hundred out of my house money into checking, and that had to do me until I reached Miles City, where I planned on getting a fortune for Gus and Red and my tack. Yeah, sure.

We left North Platte, traveling down Walker Road on Wednesday, June 6, through the country to Hershey, Nebraska, just down the road from North Platte, where the Union Pacific Railroad has the largest train yards in the world. Each day, 121 trains go through Hershey on double tracks. As I rode along by the side of those tracks, my mind reeled with memories of the old Rock Island yard office where Kenneth had worked until being laid off shortly after Kenny was born. He loved that job and the people he worked with. We always had more bills than we had money to spend, so we cleaned box cars for extra income and picked up wheat on the railroad that sifted out of railroad cars being switched in the yard. The railroad got one third, and we got two thirds.

We had an old'49 Dodge pickup that we had swapped a washing machine and one hundred dollars for. It jumped out of high gear, so we propped a stick against the dash that forked around the gear shift on the floor to keep it in gear when we hauled the wheat to the mill in Dallas. That was money for bills and babies. The tires on that pickup were as slick as a baby's butt (we called them may-pops) and we always had more weight on it than it should have carried. I remember once going to the mill with my pregnant belly touching the steering wheel. When I was weighed in, the old black man at the scales asked, "Miz Smith, did you bring all dis wheat here on dat little biddy ol' pickup?" He had weighed me in with 3,100 pounds net of wheat on that half-ton pickup. And they call modern technology a miracle.

On the cattle drive, we had to contact railroads every time we crossed a track to ensure that we did not get halfway across the track with the steers and get run down by a train. That was one of Bruce's jobs. The railroads were always nice, and the guys handling the signals were always friendly to us. I remember one hot day in Nebraska, when one of the guys waiting by the tracks for us to cross came out and gave us ice-cold bottles of water. It was like your first drink of Scotch on Saturday night.

Hershey was really memorable. We camped in an RV camp ground owned by Mick and Karen Inman. They had a convenience store and the western store next door. They were congenial people who made sure we were happy and comfortable for the two day's downtime there, which turned into three days because of flooding upriver.

We had faucets next to our tents and trailers, showers, green lawns, abundant grass for the stock, and twenty-five-cent coffee and soft-serve ice cream in Mick's store, with an old picnic table where the locals gathered each morning and evening for rap sessions. We discussed and solved world problems, read the paper that Mick brought, and worked crossword puzzles. Across the street was a truck stop with great food. Life was good.

Mick had been a switchman for the railroad for twenty-nine years. His brother and son also worked for the Union Pacific, as did many of the other men in Hershey.

A group of our cowboys went back to North Platte and put on a mock gun battle for the celebration of Nebraskaland Days. "I didn't go, but Dancer fell over when he got shot, and cracked a rib," Will said. A sweet lady named Susan Rainey came to camp the first day and brought sweets she had made for us. She invited me to come to her home on Friday night for sit-down dinner. I could bring four more with me. Susan's late father was a surgeon in North Platte. I invited Walt, Claude, and Gloria. We took the truck and van. When we got to North Platte and drove to this plush neighborhood and into the driveway of a beautiful home, Claude balked, and then Walt. We backed out and took them to the Elk's Lodge, where all the cowboys were being fed prime rib.

We went back to Susan's for lasagna, salad, and garlic bread. Her mom and a cowboy friend ate with us. Her mom was in a wheelchair, and had had open heart surgery and brain surgery both within three years. She was quite an impressive lady who never complained, and she had class and dignity to loan.

Susan gave me a book written by a local author, Nellie Snyder Yost, entitled *Evil Obsession*, the true story of farm wife Annie Cook and her part in the "little Chicago of the west" era of North Platte, Nebraska, history. Keith L. Blackledge, editor, *President Telegraph*, North Platte wrote in his critique of the book: "A fascinating story, Annie Cook is a unique sort of monster – this is the dark side of the 'good old days,' and a reminder that great wrongs can still be committed when respectable people look the other way." I read the book, and it gave me chills and the creeps. Annie was one mean woman, who lived right there in North Platte.

We reluctantly left Mick and Karen's and headed across double Union Pacific tracks in Hershey and up Highway 30 for the Tay Schuff ranch, seven miles west of Sutherland, Nebraska, on the right side of the road. The camp was in a clean oat or wheat stubble pasture. The camp was next to an 11,000-square-foot home with water hoses from the house to water ninety horses, the shires, and the mules. Gloria went to Ogallala and got a room. I went later and took a bath but declined her invitation to stay. I slept in the trailer. Diane and Dick and I went to Ole's for dinner in Paxton. It was a great place with great food, and it was packed. The walls were covered with western artifacts and stuffed animals of all kinds. I took Claude for coffee next day to Sutherlin Quick Stop, and Dick and Diane joined us for a gab fest. Walt had a new tarp made in Sutherlin for his wagon front. It really looked good and much better than the old blue plastic tarp.

Tuesday, June 20, we headed west on 30 to Korty Land and Cattle Co, six and one half miles west of Paxton on the north side of the highway. Bud showed up in camp about dark. I parked the truck almost on the highway. The trains were less than two hundred feet away. I counted eighteen trains before we made camp, one about every eight minutes on the Union Pacific tracks. Two trains met and passed each other many times during the night.

The cattle and horses were on the east side of the road on Graff Land, and camp was on west side on Blackmon land. I met Jenny Blackmon, who owns Country Antiques in Roscoe. We had four great guys from Minnesota who were outriders. Lennie is a deputy sheriff, Tim works for National Security, USA, (earthquakes, terrorists, etc.) Bob, the funny older one, is a builder/developer, and Skip owns a commercial plumbing company. I sang for them, and we drank brandy and laughed and became good pals. The crowds came; the kids stood at the fence and fed Gus and Red through the cracks. Jenny wants me to have a book show in her shop when it is written. She sent her card and a poem next day to camp.

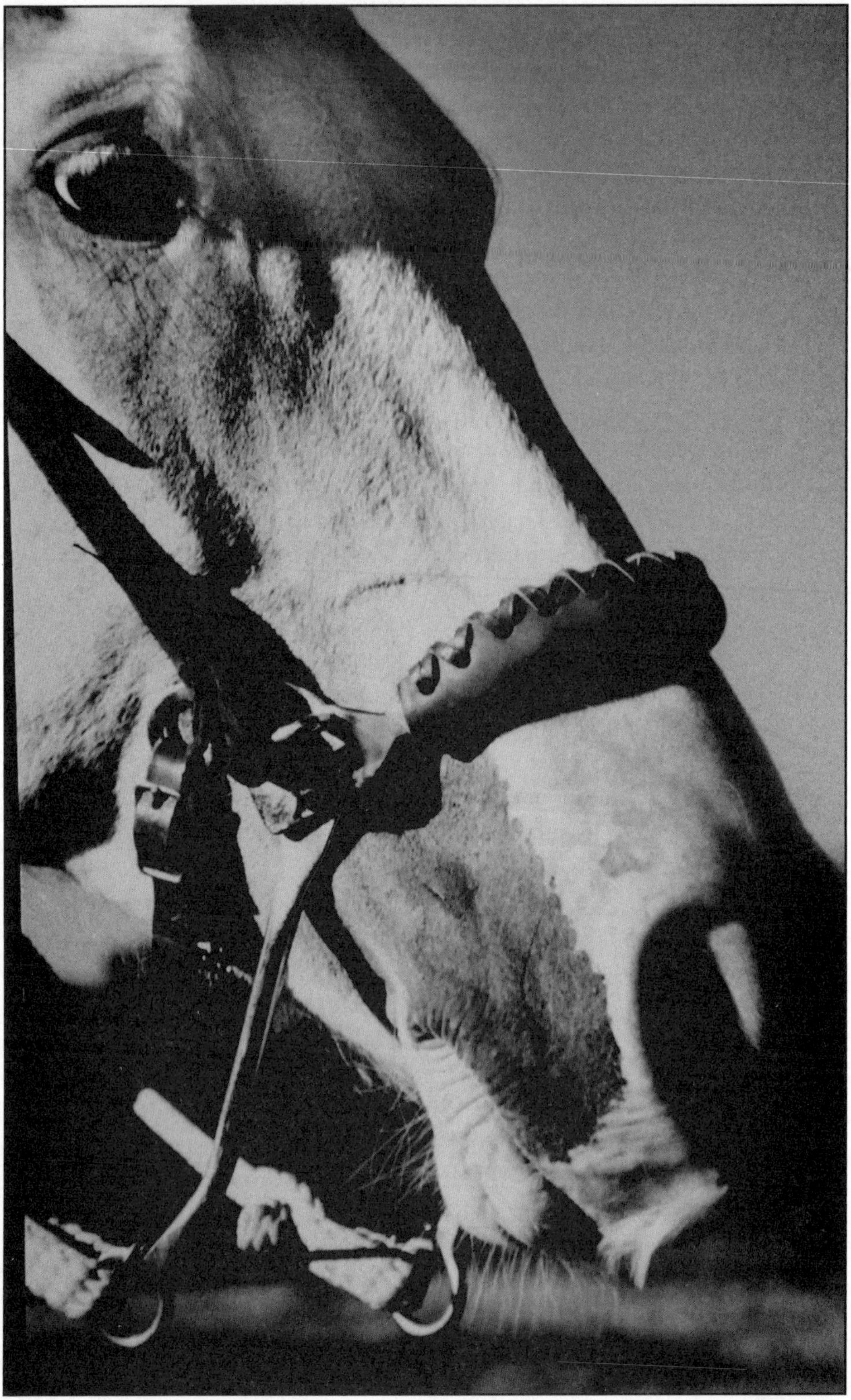

14

OGALALLA, NEBRASKA AND MORE

Thursday, June 22, we all donned our best bib and tuckers for the ride into Ogallala. We had already been to town and seen the stores with signs and hustle and bustle getting ready for us. The reception was unparalleled so far. Ogallala is loaded with history of the West and cattle drives. I rode in front of Jody and Derrick and Juan's wagon down through town. First time I had gotten to be first and it was fun.

Ogallala was warm, friendly, and Western. We camped at the fair grounds by the arena. I found a pen for Gus and Red and fed them. Then we checked in the Elms Motel close by. It was almost dark before we noticed the absence of a phone. Next day we moved to the Days Inn across the band-full river. Thursday night was quiet.

Lenny and Skip and the boys and Susan, a lady with Sherring Plough, one of our sponsors, came to our room and we had Scotches and a gab fest. A good time was had by all. I sang with Steve Schick Friday night in camp in the rain. They loved us.

Saturday morning, I hit the floor at five, dressed, went to camp and fed, groomed, and saddled Gus for the parade. We drove the cattle and wagons downtown in front of hundreds. They had breakfast downtown from nine to eleven and activities all day and rodeos at two and eight. Walker, Jess, and Eldon got thrown but unhurt. I worked on the computer and sent letters to Sandy,

Lea and myself for the GACD stamp (cancelled) on them, an honor the post office there bestowed upon us.

On Sunday, Walt, Jess, Lon, and I went to Indian Hills Manor, a nursing home, and I sang for the old folks – it was such fun, and they loved those cowboys in their boots, hats, and spurs. When someone standing at the back of the room sent word for me to sing "Grandma's Featherbed," I couldn't believe it. That song was a great favorite in my little club in Fort Worth for years. Becky and Bob Davis told me they were old customers who lived in Ogallala, and they had come to the nursing home to say hello. Jimmy and Wanda Bowers showed up back at camp to see me. Jimmy had been Kenny's little league coach in Plano years before.

"We are on vacation and wanted to come and see you," Jimmy said. Ogallala was indeed wonderful as was the rest of that beautiful state. How small and wonderful the world is sometimes.

I spent an hour in the library for some interesting history of that Western town. One old drover from the nineteenth century described Ogallala when he returned to Texas in the late 1870s: "There's gold flowing across the tables, liquor across the bars, and blood across the floors." Is that Western or not!

I loved Nebraska, its people, and the country, and the weather was improving daily. I was as brown as a pecan, lean as a whip, and my jeans actually sagged on me. I loved that! Gus and Red were as fat as town dogs, I had letters from home, and I felt rich and blessed even without any money. I *was* rich.

Seventy-two-year-old Jack Boles fell and broke his hip just outside the souvenir trailer in Ogallala. He was flown back home to Abilene, Texas, for surgery and to recuperate. Jack was the scout for the drive through Texas and other parts along the way. He was a close friend of Bud and worked hard to make the drive a success. He was criticized by some and lauded by others, but I believe he was liked and respected by all. The scrappy old guy mended and rejoined the drive in Montana to finish with us.

The day was hot and long as the thermometer climbed to 104 degrees. It was the hottest day we had had since leaving Fort Worth, and we traveled twenty miles that first day after leaving Ogallala. We traveled down a quiet, sleepy street through Henry, Nebraska, and crossed into Wyoming.

Expressing the feeling I had crossing into Wyoming is difficult. I cannot explain just why it was decidedly more memorable than riding down the streets of Miles City, but it was. When I was a child, going to town on Saturday nights and seeing the picture show (we called the Lyric Theater in Commerce, Texas, the Bloody Bucket because only Westerns were shown), was second only to Christmas. The Lone Ranger, Roy Rogers, Gene Autry, the Cisco Kid, and Lash LaRue roamed the canyons and foothills of Wyoming, chasing the bandits and Indians and all the bad guys. Wyoming was magical, a world away from the cotton fields of East Texas. It was the land of beautiful horses and mountains that reached to the sky, and those exciting creatures who carried six-guns, rode the fastest horses alive on saddles that sparkled with silver conchos, swung wide loops, and always got their man before riding off into a Wyoming sunset. It was a place I could escape to when life was boring or unbearable, and pretend that I, too, was riding with the wind blowing in my face, hair blowing free, my pony's belly low with his feet flying, gaining on and passing those cowboys who rode with me. From topside Gus, I saw the tall sign that read:

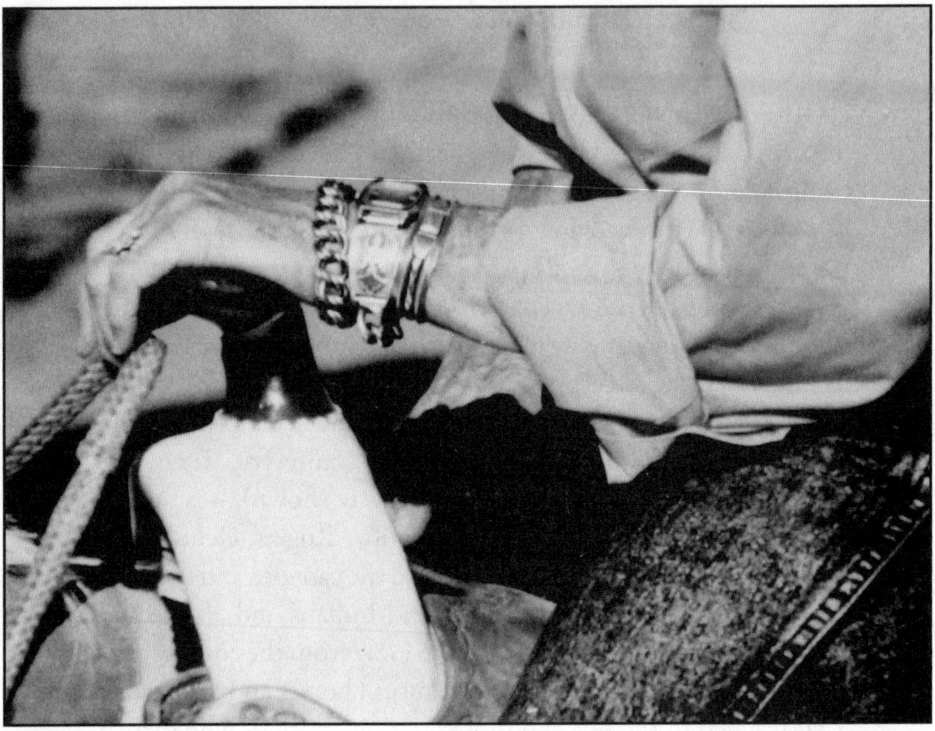

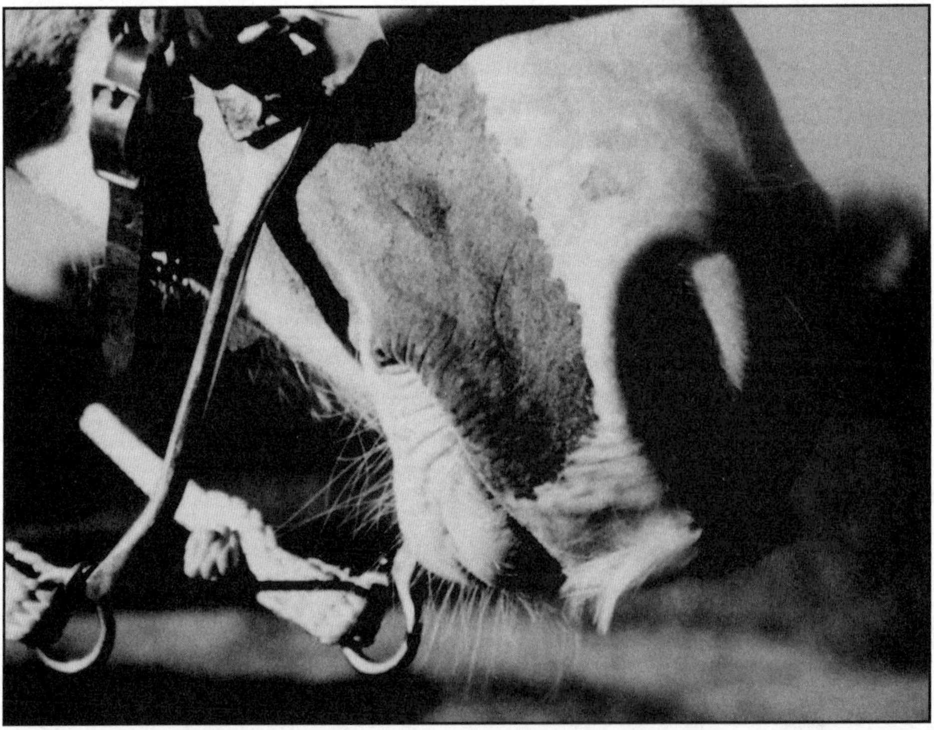

15

WYOMING, LIKE NO PLACE ON EARTH.

It was Sunday morning, a moment before sunrise, July 9, 1995. I could feel my heartbeat without touching my chest. My throat had a lump in it the size of Texas.

Here I am, Wyoming. I have waited all my life to touch you and see you and feel you. Here I am Wyoming! Oh Mack, if you could only be here and see me now! Your little bare-foot shadow, in whose dreams this place has been for fifty-five years. I made it! I made it and what an adventure and experience! We have lived through rain, sleet, hail, high winds, a tornado, extreme heat, and cold. We have struggled with dissension, lack of communication, homesickness, boredom, and frustration with our desires, disappointments, and misunderstandings. We have learned that everything that is different is not necessarily wrong. We have kept going when we really wanted to turn and go home. We have become a unit made up of unusual parts and molded together by adverse conditions, guts, and the determination to succeed. Over one hundred years ago, those whose footsteps we are now walking in experienced the same problems we are having under different conditions. Like them, we will reach our destination. And we will find that we have grown taller, more tolerant, more understanding, older, and much wiser. Hello, Wyoming!

I hugged Gus, laughed, cried, and giggled at the girls at the sign taking pictures. Wyoming made me feel giddy and young and very much alive.

"Please, will you bring me one of those pictures to camp?" I pleaded to the chubby young woman snapping my picture.

"You bet I will," she promised, but she never did.

In Lingle, Wyoming, we camped in an RV park. Word came that one of the horses in the pasture where the steers had been put was suspected of having sleeping sickness, a disease terrifying to a horse owner. The horses were taken back to the last campsite – all but the Shires, Gus and Red, and Gloria's mare. My horses had been vaccinated for the disease.

Will made a casual remark that would later prove to be accurate. "That horse probably just ate some weed that gave him a reaction – something like loco weed." Marijuana and other wild vegetation were called loco weed in the Old West. That old Oklahoma cowboy knew what he was talking about. Next day we heard that the horse had become ill from something he had eaten. The scare was over.

More and more out-of-state cars came by us on the road. Cars from Texas were numerous. We met folks from Arlington and Bluffdale, Texas, a community southwest of Fort Worth, and I realized that many folks from home would meet us in Montana. The mountains were growing taller, the antelope herds larger, and the deer more plentiful. And on occasion, if one were attentive, a bull elk might be spotted, but never close enough for snapshots. The highways were all two-lane with narrow shoulders and a fraction of the traffic that travels Texas highways.

After approximately one thousand miles on the hoof, only twelve of the original 262 longhorns were gimpy or crippled. Those incredible bovines were tough, intelligent, stoic, and strong. They did not waste energy, and they took full advantage of every tender morsel they found. They are as old as time and as modern as tomorrow. How abundant the knowledge available from God's creatures.

With each mile closer to Montana, the anger and dissension simmered and neared the boiling point. Each camp that Walt had scheduled for the drive was changed. Bruce and Jim were the accused culprits. Outside Guernsey, Wyoming, we were stopped and told before we reached camp that it had been changed. Before we reached the new place, we were told to wait where we were for instructions. We were in sight of camp and saw the equipment drivers and Vision Quest, tearing down, making preparations to move.

Bruce said that he had been instructed by the chief of police to set up camp across from where Walt had acquired a camp site. When the owner of the land discovered our camp on his property, he was irate, and the equipment boys had to pick up and move across the street, where we were supposed to be in the first place. *Christ almighty, is this a group of adults or a bunch of dippy twelve-year-olds we have for leaders? Hey, they ought to have a woman running this outfit!*

Something weird happened that has not yet been explained. The souvenir man came over to my truck and trailer, which were parked at the edge of a cemetery next to our camp, and said that someone in town had complained to the police department about my truck being parked "in the cemetery."

"I am not parked in the cemetery, as you can plainly see," I told him.

"I know, Annie, I can see, but they are complaining, and you need to move it to keep peace," he said.

Well, I did move the truck. I unhitched the trailer and went downtown to the police station and asked about the complaint. They said they knew nothing about a complaint. The police suggested I ask the caretaker of the cemetery. I knew just where to go because the caretaker had been talking to me at my trailer only minutes before I had been told of the so-called complaint. I went back to the same spot, parked the truck in the same spot, and found the man I was looking for. He knew nothing about any complaint and assured me that I was not parked on any graves. *I will file this little incident away for future reference. I wonder what the guy's motive was in staging this little farce? He damned well had some reason, I'll bet.*

The cowboys brought the herd into camp in the heat about 2:30. Dick Kennedy had had chest pains about eight that morning on the trail and was taken to the hospital for treatment. He came to camp after we arrived and said he was feeling better, but his nitro pill did not "seem to be helping."

As we moved out the next morning, in sharp contrast to the last couple of days, the weather was a cool fifty degrees, with a north wind that made my goose down feel like Mama's hugs. Grass was lush and still green from an unusually wet year for Wyoming. In the distance I could see Mt. Laramie towering to the clouds with her snow hat gleaming in the morning sun. Because we were traveling north, that would be as close as we would come to it.

We left camp about six and crossed over the viaduct, forty feet above the Union Pacific tracks, across the town of Guernsey and the Platte River again. I saw deer up in the saddlebacks of the mountains and a lone eagle watching us. Buzzards crowded around a deer that had been killed by a motorist.

Dave McCullough, an outrider, was riding Walt's big horse, Brother, that day and Brother got into wire and reared and fell back on Dave, bruising Dave's ribs and body, but fortunately not resulting in anything serious. The horse was cut in several places but not severely. Dave and Lori, his wife, rode with us, I believe, longer than any of the outriders. They grew close to Walt, and Lori rode much of the time on the chuck wagon with Walt. They were neat people, and I still keep in touch with them in Minnesota.

We passed the camp that Walt had scheduled for us – a camp with water, shade trees, and level land – to set up camp where the fence was down and wire was on the ground, a serious hazard for horses, and not a shade tree in sight. No fence meant that the cowboys had to ride night herd. Another camp had been switched, making a change in every camp Walt had scheduled since we had crossed into Wyoming. *Are we having a power struggle here among Walt, Jim, Bud, and Bruce?* I believed that and voiced my feelings to Gloria. She agreed.

From the moment we crossed into Wyoming, Walt seemed different. He no longer teased and bantered with me. He was sullen, quiet, and stayed mostly to himself. He and Dancer had private conversations, and he voiced anger constantly about Jim McElroy and Bruce. He made telephone calls whenever a phone was available. A day out of Glendo, Walt told us, "George Kurkowski, the mayor, is going to declare a Walt Secrest Day in Miles City when we get there." He talked much about people in Montana being miffed at Bud and Jim McElroy and Bruce.

"I may just shut this son of a bitch down," I heard him say more than once.

"If I called the health department, and they came out and checked these steers and horses, they would shut this son of a bitch down in a minute," he raged around the campfire.

Dancer would agree, Lon would agree, and the young cowboys would listen to his every word. He was a very convincing man. He was forceful, his voice was deep and masculine, his size was intimidating, and his charm magnetic. I was sure he could have led those men. I was, however, dubious about his intentions and priorities.

The Indians were conquered, and the West was built and the strong survived the elements led by men like Walt Secrest.

He and Lon Sowers had known each other years before, and Lon had tremendous admiration for Walt. He defended Walt to all who might voice dislike or frustration with the big man. Lon was loyal to a fault. He worked very hard, helping Walt hitch and unhitch and care for the Shires each day, and he stayed close to the chuck wagon at all times. Dancer was Walt's shadow and pep squad, and Johnny-on-the-spot to smooth away wrinkles of doubt in the minds of the thousands who came to see us. The young cowboys were quick to stand up for Walt. The older ones were noncommittal. I said nothing to anyone except Gloria and damned little to her. There were more rumors floating around the camp than in the hallways of a junior high school.

Will coined the phrase, "If I don't hear a rumor this morning, I am going to start one." He was verbal only when he had wrapped himself around a half gallon of bourbon. The rumor around camp was that some of the investors and the souvenir man wanted Walt fired.

Mayor George Kirkowski and his wife, Peg, surprised us in camp just before we reached Glendo, Wyoming. Meeting Peg simply enhanced my admiration for George. She was warm, outgoing, and just a perfect fit for him. I liked her immediately. Gloria and I invited them to dinner at a great steakhouse in Glendo, and we had a wonderful evening. That night cost me one hundred and thirty dollars including tip when I picked up the tab, but I was glad I did. They rode most of the way with us next day, but had to leave for a business meeting and promised to see us in Sheridan.

We camped at the old Glendo airport near a huge lake. When Stasha, one of the counselors with Vision Quest, bathed her Labrador retriever in the horse trough, with the lake in walking distance of camp, I lost my cool completely.

"Stasha, what in hell do you mean bathing that damned dog in the horses' drinking water? Why don't you take him to the lake if you are so set on bathing him?"

"Look, this dog is clean and won't hurt your horses. What do you think the lake has in it?"

"If the dog is so clean, why is it necessary to bathe it?" I stormed off to keep from swatting her in the face, so mad I was choking. I had been feeling tired and a bit under the weather with an earache for two days, and my good nature was somewhere back on the trail – probably stashed in a Scotch bottle. Will picked up where I left off and chewed her out pretty good.

I could not fathom her putting that dog in drinking water for horses that could not be turned out to go to the lake to drink because there was no fence. It was a fight each day just to get water for the horses. Many times we had to wait for hours or ride miles to get water. The damned dog ran free and could go where he pleased. The water situation in each camp was something that I struggled to understand the entire length of the drive.

Bruce and the equipment drivers knew from the beginning that water was the most vital thing on the drive. Yet water was the last thing we got in camp each day. Many times it was simply a matter of making arrangements for the fire department to come fill the tanks we carried with us. Sometimes, it was almost dark before the thirsty horses were watered after a day under saddle.

Something as simple, but nevertheless vital, as having the portable toilet cleaned out was many times put off or just ignored until the thing was impossible to use because it was full and swarming with green flies that were big enough to stand flat-footed and rape a full-grown tarantula. We went long periods of time without toilet tissue. Nobody knew just whose responsibility it was to have those things taken are of.

Bruce's pat answer to almost any question was, "I just don't know" or "Gosh, I haven't the faintest idea," followed by an inane giggle. When Bud was in camp, if one ever had the chance to talk to him, his answer to any question or problem was always the same: "Don't worry, I will take care of that." Just once, I wanted one of them to say to me, "I am trying, but I am having difficulty. Could you help?" or, "We can't do that because there is no money, but let's have a meeting, and maybe someone might have some ideas on what can be done to correct this problem."

My grandmother would have identified the problem as not having "enough gumption to get out of the drip of the house," which comes from the fact that young turkeys are so dumb that they will stand where the rain runs off the edge of the barn, turn their heads toward heaven, and drown.

I was bewildered because the men would not or did not make some sort of move to better the situation in camp. Somewhere along the way, I came to believe that there was not a man in the outfit who was a strong leader or had the courage of his convictions. We just did not have anyone who those involved could respect and follow. I believe that is why we floundered, wandered, and rag-tagged our way across sixteen hundred miles or so, with only blind determination and a warped, but strong sense of closeness to guide us. I now believe that had we had the proper organization and promotion and marketing needed for the drive, that it would probably not have been as similar to the nineteenth-century drives as it was. We were closer to the chaos of those drives than we really knew.

Hell, yes, I wanted very much to make decisions. The common everyday problems, and possibly some of the emotional ones, seemed solvable to me. But to convey my ideas to those men would have been futile. First, I was the only woman actually involved in the working cattle drive. Second, those men were light-years away from accepting a woman as their equal in the saddle, on the range, or in living the adventure we were experiencing. And third, I was old enough to be grandmother to some of them. Their male egos would never have permitted them to listen to the mutterings of an old woman. Lastly, it was a bit late to solve the biggest problem we had – lack of funds and the crisis that was yet to come.

On the morning of July 18, one cowboy's pretty buckskin pony became lethargic, and when it didn't get better, he took it to the vet, where it died with a twisted gut, making five the number of horses we had lost on the drive.

Wyoming's open range reduced Disneyland and technology and the Internet and cyberspace and rocket ships to mere man-made arks that would spring leaks and sink with time and use. I saw miles and miles of open country as it had been for centuries, herds of antelope, mule deer, sage chickens, eagles, and blue skies to infinity. My soul absorbed and relished and basked in that wonderland. I rode out of camp each morning before sunrise, while the rest were eating breakfast, to ride alone in the vastness with my beloved Gus and solitude. I wanted and needed nothing. Time stood still, and I was ageless as I lay nestled in my childhood dream. I heard the hoof beats of the Riders of the Purple Sage, spotted Crazy Horse and his band thundering over a ridge, and raced across the floor of canyons with Flicka and the wild horses. Fences were becoming scarce, and all the highways were two-lane with little traffic as we rode deeper into Wyoming. We saw more and more cars with Texas license plates. People waved and threw smiles and kisses. One lady leaned out the window of a car and yelled, beaming, "Wonderful!" Out there, in that magnificent space, there was no problem bickering, anger, or disillusionment. There were only me, God, and Gus and my dream fulfilled.

The proverbial manure hit the air conditioning in Douglas, Wyoming. We had been moved again. When I got back to camp with my truck and trailer, I was unsaddling Gus when I heard loud voices at the chuck wagon. I turned and saw Jim McElroy walking rather hurriedly with an irate Walt behind him, for all the world looking like a pit bull, spitting froth in an angry tirade.

"You are making a goddamed shambles of this cattle drive. Don't mess around with Montana! They may not let you in Montana! Nobody here likes or respects you. You screw up everything. They will probably run your skinny ass out of this country. You haven't done a damn thing right from the beginning." His face, red as early sunrise, was stark against his black mustache. He stormed toward Jim, and Jim walked away from that formidable presence, looking over his shoulder in obvious fear. He was mumbling something incoherent that was lost in the roar of Walt's voice.

Uh oh, there will be hell to pay now. I wonder if Walt's gonna swat old Jim in the face. Wait until Jim gets to his phone and calls Bud, and then the show will really begin. Unknown to us, a city council member and a representative from the chamber of commerce of Douglas had come to camp to welcome the drive. Both women were witness to that verbal onslaught.

When Bud arrived in camp later that week, he called a meeting and fired Walt. He and Bruce said that much damage had been done to our "image" when the town's leading ladies had witnessed the confrontation and that Bruce had apologized to the ladies. The cowboys rebelled. If Walt had had a run-in with anyone else but McElroy or Bruce, the cowboys would probably have shrugged and told him he was on his own. Not this time. There was absolutely no love in that camp for Jim or Bruce, and when you crossed or had words with one of them, you had to contend with both.

Bud backed down and "reinstated" Walt. I suppose he was afraid that the whole bunch would leave if he didn't. I really didn't care one way or the other. I had begun to watch the power struggles among those men like a spectator who had paid admission to the show. I could speculate and predict and silently bet with my "little inner voice" on who would win any given battle along the way.

"Now that's the damndest deal I ever heard of," Will said later over drinks at my trailer. "When I fired a man, the son of a bitch stayed fired. Bud ain't got no balls atall."

Will was right and this situation was only going to make things worse. Bud was dividing us just as surely as if he had taken a knife and physically cut us apart. *I wish I knew just which way to turn and whom to defend. Hell, I'm going to Montana, with or without all of these damned power-hungry, fighting men. This situation is damned near laughable. So why am I not laughing? Well, at least it makes the time pass faster, and I don't know whether I like that or not. I think that I would like this drive to go on for another six months or maybe even longer. These men are so busy growling at each other, they don't realize that we are making history. I think that we are probably not unlike those before us – just disagreeing under different circumstances. Human beings never cease to be, well, human beings.*

Next morning, I saw one young cowboy climb up onto the chuck wagon wheel and shake Walt's hand and hug him. The young men on the drive were idealists who looked up to Walt. To them, he was a figurehead and a successful force. Good character is a minor ingredient for success in this modern world, I regret to say. Flip the coin and if one reads history, one learns that change, discovery, events that moved the world were many times made to happen by those who dared to challenge right, moral law, and protocol. The doers and shakers in the history of the West were not all saints.

The internal problems we had did not deter the townspeople from welcoming us with food, fun, and friendship. That day and night, about three hundred of them came and ate with us. I sang for a great receptive crowd who loved the old tunes such as "Strawberry Roan" and Jimmie Rodger's classic, "Muleskinner Blues."

I turned in early but did not put the tarp on my trailer because the weather was beautiful. I regretted that decision around midnight when an electrical storm hit with pouring rain. I just grabbed the tarp, pulled it over me, and slept on. Good thing I was parked on a slant so that all the water ran away from me. Next morning, water was about three inches deep in the trailer.

The weather was no big deal. As we rode down Highway 59 toward Gillette with the sun spreading warmth in the early morning chill, I saw a road sign: Bill – 25 miles. I remembered way back in February looking at a Montana map and seeing that little town which then, seemed a lifetime away. Now there I was, riding down a highway on a beautiful morning only twenty-five miles from Bill. The antelope were out in number, curious about the long line of longhorns plodding through their territory. They looked like four-pronged pogo sticks, with wisps of cream and white, bouncing and floating as light as giant snowflakes in a soft breeze.

On the trail that day, two cowboys had words, according to scuttlebutt in camp that night. I was sure they would patch up whatever disagreement they might have had, but it seemed that everyone's tempers were honed sharp, and next day, Dick became agitated with someone over something. I never learned what it was, but I never asked.

"Dick was gonna whip his ass, but that cowboy wouldn't get off his horse," another one said.

Jim Hooks called a meeting in camp that day, and I heard Dick vehemently express his anger, but he also professed his loyalty to the cowboys. I had not been present when he and the other cowboy had words, so the meeting provided little understanding to me, but other things were very clear to me. Like the camp we were in next, which was sagebrush and mounds of other brush, which made driving or walking almost impossible. I had to move my truck and trailer twice before settling down. The second move occurred when I was told by Dancer that I would be in the way of the water truck coming to the water troughs for Walt's team.

Some days when I hurt, when I am tired to the bone, when I have to walk a mile just to water my horses and find panels and put them up, I get damned sick and angry at the way Walt is pampered and assisted with the Shires, and catered to as if he were royalty. Yeah, it's damned sure a man's world, girls!

Few things bothered me about the drive and the little everyday irritations, but some things did. Walt insisted that the portable corral for his horses be set up very close to the chuck wagon. He never had to walk more than a few feet to feed. Hell, he was as able to walk as any of the rest of us. I never said anything about that to anyone, except Gus, but it did bother me a bit.

MINT BAR

16

WYOMING, THE PUBLIC RELATIONS POT STARTS BOILING

Good judgment comes from experience
And a lot of that comes from bad judgment. . . .Will Rogers

On Saturday, July 22, Ron Robertson came to camp. Ron was a big man, towering above Walt. They had been friends for years. Ron had been a range detective for eighteen years, and we were in his territory. He was definitely a talker, but an interesting and informative man. He was an accomplished pianist and a historian who knew the history of the Northwest well. He wanted to go with us on the drive for the rest of the way. He said he could help us with the public relations and setting up camp sites, and he claimed he was an experienced drover, too. *Uh oh! Public relations are Jim McElroy's job. This ought to be interesting. Here is an old friend of Walt's talking to Bud about Jim's job, and Walt hates Jim McElroy and wants him out! May be a connection, and may not. Hey, this place is never dull or lacking in controversy. Let's see, who would I pick to play Walt's role, and who to be Jim McElroy in a movie of this drive? Sam Elliot for sure as Walt. Hey, this is fun.*

Bud talked to Ron in my trailer, out of the wind, while we all squatted down against the sides and shared a drink. Will was there, too. Bud was congenial, willing for Ron to go along, but Bud assured him he would not be paid because there was no money, and we did not need anyone to do public relations. Ron was to go just to see if he would like it. Ron's wife, Patty, said she thought it was great "because he gets restless." So he was going with us.

Bud seemed to make decisions and think later. It was almost as if he suddenly woke up later and realized that Walt and Ron knew each other, and then he put two and two together and came up with what he believed to be four.

"I think I have been set up," he said later. He was furious. I could not see what harm Ron could do. He seemed to be congenial and eager to help, but there was instant dislike and suspicion of him from the other cowboys.

Ron came to camp next morning with two horses, gear, and an aggressive but friendly attitude. Instead of riding with the outriders, he began working as a drover. Perhaps there was resentment toward someone who joined the drive at that late date and was able to ride with us. We all had struggled with the position and the leeway given to the outriders already. That had been a sore spot from the beginning. Now, here was this big guy, taking a position along with the cowboys at the tail end of the drive, sharing in the glory with those of us who had broken our asses in the weather and the crap for four months already. I thought it strange when Ron had told me the night before that he would not ride with Walt or "hang around" with Walt to quell any resentment or suspicion.

That same morning, Bud told Walt to travel behind the herd. This meant that the big draft horses would have to travel at about half the speed that was normal for them. I thought it was a stupid idea, but Walt was strangely quiet and subdued. Dancer was angry and voiced his feelings as we traveled at a snail's pace behind the herd.

"He is just doing this because of his dislike of Walt. He wants to control Walt. I felt like knocking him on his ass." I had never heard Dancer talk so aggressively before. *I think maybe old Dancer might just be right. Changing camps every day and these new orders from Bud are crazy because we can't possibly travel as slow as the herd. I wonder just what will happen next.*

It was like a soap opera. I waited each day for some crisis or confrontation. And I never watched soap operas because they bored me. I was never bored on the drive. I never really took those confrontations on the drive seriously. The men were all under a certain amount of stress, and the weather never seemed to be on our side. But as I rode through that beautiful country, I wondered how any of us could feel bad about anything for very long.

Gene Litton owned the ranch where we camped next door to the home of three thousand buffalo. He was a kind man, and fifteen minutes after he first laid eyes on me, he loaded me in his pickup and carried me fifty-five miles to Gillette, Wyoming, to the emergency room of the hospital. I had been riding point for the chuck wagon and when we turned to enter Gene's ranch, Gus went down on the slick pavement so fast that Walt's lead team almost ran over me. I got up, and Gus was standing over me. Gene Litton took my arm and walked me across the highway and through the gate to his ranch. I do not remember hitting the pavement, but by the time we got to the camp site and I sat down against the chuck wagon wheel, I was blind in one eye, had a goose egg on the back of my head, and felt nauseated. I suspected that I might have a concussion. That is when Gene asked if I felt OK. I told him I was a bit woozy. He asked if I felt that I should go to the hospital, and Walt answered before I could open my mouth.

"Yes, I think she should go to the hospital, and right now." On the way to Gillette, Gene explained to me why the pavement had been so slick. He said that Wyoming was conducting an experiment on forty-five miles of highway by "shaving the pavement" to see if the snow would blow off faster. That same day, six of the horses in the remuda went down on that road.

After one hour of cat scans and examinations by two doctors, I was declared OK (no blood, no crack, and no brain – well, not a big one) and sent back to camp. Gene was waiting in the lobby of the hospital to take me back. I made plans to have Red and Gus re-shod with boron on their shoes. Boron is a hard, rough metal that will not slide on pavement. I would not ride a mile farther without the boron. I had been lucky that neither Gus of I had been hurt seriously in the fall.

When we got back to camp, all the cowboys were there, and several asked if everything was OK. I was thrilled that they were concerned about me. I sometimes felt that they did not know I was even around. I didn't have to drive the cattle because I wasn't getting paid anyway. I decided I could ride anywhere, and that always pleased me. Ace Wright, the tall Montanan, asked about the extent of my injuries. That was nice and made me feel much better. I had much to be thankful for.

I asked Will and Dick to look out for my horses, and I went into the town of Wright with Gloria for a night in a motel and a day on the computer to catch up with my writing. Bud came by on Monday to see about me. He had a long conversation with Gloria. I went into the other bedroom and left them alone because I was not included in the conversation. When I got back to camp next day, Will and I went back to Wright for lunch and a drink. I promised to play that night in the café where we ate. When I went to the souvenir trailer for my equipment, my microphone stand was missing. After much searching, the souvenir man suddenly remembered that he had "loaned" it to a musician in Torrington. I was one mad old woman.

"Well sir, you will buy me another mike stand. One just like the one I had."

Where will I get a mike stand out here?" he asked. I assured him with about $50 (the price of mine) I would be able to find one myself, and I kissed goodbye the money that I would have made for the appearance at the café. *I'd like to ram a mike up his broad ass right now. Damn! I could have used that money.* I went back and apologized to the lady in charge of the café, which by that time was full of cowboys, and we got roaring drunk. About nine o'clock, the cattle boss, Jim Hooks, came in and told us we had to leave camp by six in the morning. We were scheduled to have one more day downtime there, but it seemed that the owner of the land had not been informed that we would be there two days, and he was adamant about our leaving.

Still sore and stiff from my fall, I saddled up and got ready to ride next morning amid hangovers and grouchy cowboys. Some of the cowboys had gone to Cheyenne Frontier Days, and two more had gone home, thinking we would not leave for another day, and we left camp with half a crew and rode to the next camp, alongside the historic Belle Fouche River. Later, over steak and Scotch in Gillette, Will told me about his day on the trail. They had a small stampede; fought the cattle out of alfalfa patches on both sides of the road for eight miles; killed three rattlesnakes, and rode by the Durham buffalo ranch. That ranch has bred and raised buffalo since 1966.

A few days later, we reached Gillette, where we had one week of down time, and all hell came tumbling down on us. The Camplex in Gillette was fabulous. Everything for horses or cattle was there, including pens, stalls, indoor and outdoor arenas, sale barns, and first-class dressing rooms and showers. Each building was designed beautifully, with wide streets and passageways for trailers and pedestrians. Will said it was similar to the Expocenter in Shawnee, except for the pari-mutuel racetrack, which Shawnee does not have. The giant marquee welcomed the GACD. Hardee's had a giant tent set up to feed us that night.

Gillette is surrounded by coal mines. The coal reserve there will last for over five hundred years at the present rate of use. The trains that haul the coal to other parts of the country are loaded at giant silos with conveyors that fill a train at the rate of eleven seconds per boxcar. Each car has a chute underneath that is opened at the destination and unloaded in pits in eleven seconds. Over one hundred trains a day, each with over one hundred cars, are sent out of the mines there.

Gloria and I rented a room with a small kitchen in a family-owned motel. We did laundry, bought film and ate great food in the many restaurants there. I caught up on my writing, and Eldon put new shoes with boron on Gus and Red. I would breathe easier when we got back on the trail.

Bud came to Gillette with two deputies and fired Walt for the second and last time. Walt loaded up his gear, called Renny, and left camp. Gloria and I visited with him and Renny in a motel the next day. We talked little about the situation. I told him I was sorry for the way things turned out, and I meant it. I knew that his absence would affect everybody, including the public. The chuck wagon was always the center of interest to visitors. The campfire drew the masses like light draws moths. Walt was always there, sitting under the chuck wagon tarp talking with everyone, signing autographs, and listening to Dancer tell his tall tales and some of us singing cowboy tunes. Walt was colorful and completely cowboy. He loved talking about his escapades over the years, and everybody loved hearing about them.

When Walt left, he took his Shires, his five steers, Walker, Lon, Dancer, and Robert, another of the cook's helpers. I asked Dancer to stay and go with "the ones who brung him." He told me that I just did not understand – that it was "a personal thing" for him. He was at least partially right. I didn't understand why these men could not drop big egos and false pride for the sake of the drive and the history we were making. I did understand the egos well and believed nothing could have changed the outcome. *What a shame for the sake of the young ones who have looked up to Walt for guidance in this awesome trek.*

Walt said he had talked to Mayor Kurkowski about the firing and that there would be no celebration in Miles City because Walt had been fired. But the mayor talked to us later and told us that he had not talked to Walt and that there was certainly going to be a celebration in Miles City for us and that we would be welcomed there. Lon Sowers remarked later that he "was disappointed in the mayor."

The "Lonesome Drovers," as Dancer named Walt's new crew,

left Gillette two days before the GACD, headed for Miles City, Montana. I believe that Walt was happy to be the *el jefe*, at last. Will Miltimore wrote in his journal:

"Ron, one of the men going with Walt, wanted me to go to the camp where Walt was going and drive his pickup there; then he would bring me back. No way would I do this. Walt talked Dancer Davis, Walker Lawrence, Robert, Lon, and Ron into going with him, I told them to ride for the brand that wrote their checks, as Walt did not pay their wages. I feel like they are making a big mistake. None of the cowboys or wranglers went along with Walt. I told Bud I was proud of him and he should have fired Walt in Fort Worth, as he was always trouble. Walt plans to take his steers and wagons and continue to Miles City. I don't see how he can make this work as it takes money to do these drives, and he has no money. He is not very well liked in Montana and is cutting his own throat, and the men who went with him are stupid to believe anything he says."

We had to have the steers and horses inspected before crossing the border into Montana. It took six days because we had to wait three days for the results after the steers had been tested. All horses and cattle passed all tests. In the meantime, there was much unrest in camp. The young cowboys had not dismissed the idea of joining Walt. Dancer and Lon had urged them to go with someone who "would take care of them." Jess Herbers, for one, was confused and discontented and angry. "I just want Bud to tell me why Walt was fired. Nobody here knows why he was fired. I just want to know." Jess talked to me with a lot of emotion and anger and with a question in his mind rather than on his lips.

I answered that question as well as I could. "Jess, as long as Bud hands you a paycheck each month, you should stay here. You hired out to drive longhorns to Miles City, not play defender for Walt Secrest."

"That is just what my father told me," he said. But his young idealistic heart would not be appeased. Someone told me later that Bud had said that he fired Walt because Walt would not take orders. I recalled the incident in Oberlin, when he refused to pick up the girl downtown as Bud had told him to do.

But for me, the biggest blow of all came from Dick Kennedy. He was angry. He had gone home during downtime and did not know that Walt had been fired until he came back to camp the day before we left. When he learned that Walt was fired, he became almost paranoid.

"Them sons of bitches are going to fire more of us before we get to Montana because then they don't have to pay the bonus they promised when the drive is over." Bud had promised to pay each cowboy who went all the way two months' pay in Miles City.

Something else about Dick was gnawing on me. Somewhere back down the line, he had become cool and distant toward me. He was angry at Will too. He hated Will's drinking. When he came back to the drive in McCook, Nebraska, he had brought his big stock trailer, and Will had moved his belongings into it. He and Dick had built portable bunks in the trailer and slept in it out of the weather. When Will got drunk, he was a problem that Dick could not tolerate.

"He smells like a goddamned whiskey jug and piss," Dick said vehemently.

I never told Will about that remark, but I did talk to him about the change in Dick and his coolness toward me.

"Ah, Dick ain't mad at you, Annie. It's that damned heart medicine he takes that makes him mad all the time." Will did not take Dick's anger seriously. I just knew that Dick had changed toward me and that I did not know why, so I tried to believe that Will was right. Nothing prepared me for Dick's onslaught the morning we left Gillette.

"Did you know that Dick is leaving the drive again and going home?" Gloria asked. She rode Ruby up to me as I mounted Gus, ready to pull out.

"Oh no, I hate to see him go. We are so close to Montana, and he wanted to make it so bad." I told her I was going to his trailer to say goodbye to him.

"I will ride with you and say goodbye, too," she said. We rode down the hill to where he was camped next to the corrals. He was inside the trailer, and Will, still a bit tipsy from the night before, was unloading his bedroll and gear from the trailer. I saw Dick through the slats in his trailer and called to him.

"Hey cowboy, are you gonna come out of there and hug me goodbye or leave without saying anything?" Dick stepped out of the trailer about ten feet from my horse.

"I can't get away from all you lying sons-a-bitches fast enough! I am sick of this lousy outfit, and I am leaving and going where honest people live." He was white around the mouth, and his eyes were fully dilated, his lips pulled in a thin line against clenched teeth. The veins in his neck were bulging to bursting point. I thought he was going to reach up and knock me out of the saddle.

"Dick, why are you so mad at me and saying all these terrible things to me? I have done nothing to you to make you feel this way."

"You are the cause of Walt getting fired. You told Bud that he was no good and that he caused all the trouble in camp." Dick walked out to Gloria, reached up, shook her hand, and told her he appreciated all she had done for the drive. I was speechless for long moments. Here was the man who had been my best buddy – the man who had expressed distrust of Walt and his manipulating; a man who did not trust Gloria and had voiced his suspicions several times that she was going to Bud with information about the cowboys.

"She is a goddamned gossip and a troublemaker," he had said more than once to me and Will. I finally found my voice.

"Dick, I am sorry you feel the way you do. I had absolutely nothing to do with Walt's firing. I have not a shred of clout with Bud, even if I had said anything to him, which I did not."

My words fell on deaf ears. Dick turned from Gloria and

went back inside his trailer and left me slack-jawed and hurt. I cried most of the day along the trail. No one had ever talked to me so terribly and angrily. I could not fathom why he thought that I had anything to do with Walt's firing. I racked my brain, trying to figure who, if anyone, had told him such a lie. Today, it remains a mystery to me. It would be days before I could push it from my mind.

17

FINDING OUR PLACE IN THE SUN

I have lived in a "man's world" the biggest part of my adult life. That is, I was the sole provider for my children after Kenneth was killed, pushing me out into the world dominated by men in the work force. In the sixties, men still held majority in "bringing home the bacon." And before that, in my adolescent years, I preferred the company of boys to that of girls because, being a "tomboy," I spoke their language and found communicating with boys to be much easier and more interesting than with girls. I learned quickly just how important it is to men to dominate. Men are also very territorial, not unlike the tomcat that marks or "sprays" his neck of the woods or yard, as do the male wolf and cougar – a declaration to the world of just where his boundaries are and his dominance within those boundaries. I do not find that trait unpleasant or threatening; however, I don't always understand the methods that some use to acquire dominance over others.

As we rode on northwest without Walt and his followers, I thought of the circumstances leading up to his being fired. When we reached "cowboy country" – Wyoming – I had become aware of a manifest change in Walt Secrest. I had chalked it up as reaction to hostile feelings for the management of the drive. That may have been a part of the change, but he became much more aggressive and decisive the closer we got to Montana. I remembered his earlier words during the meeting in Texas when he had told Bud and the investors that the drive would not cross Montana if he left. Walt had clout in Montana. The Northwest was his territory. Cowboy country was where he lived and worked and established boundaries. Walt was the kind of man whom women like my sister would have latched onto in an instant; the kind of man that physical men admire and follow - strong-willed, macho, aggressive, and ruthless with his ambitions. This kind of man, in many instances and through the ages, has changed the world.

I had no doubt that Walt could have made waves and gotten things done. Hell, I believe a *lot* of people could have done better, and a lot of people probably would have known that by the time we reached Wyoming, it was a bit late for confrontations and the firing of a man with so strong an influence as Walt Secrest. To have waited until we reached the country where his name was known well was foolish and tremendously damaging to the morale and unity of the other members of the drive, not to mention the impact his firing had on those who had known him and were fellow citizens of Montana.

On a flip of the coin, it is always easy for one to stand on the outside and look inside and see the mistakes of others when none of the responsibility rides on one's shoulders. What did I know about driving a herd of cattle to Montana? I had never done it before, but then, neither had anyone else with me.

Not that there was great love and respect for Walt in his country. He evoked various emotions from those who knew him. In Buffalo, Wyoming, the man who worked the front desk of a motel there grinned and shook his head when he learned that I was on the cattle drive.

"Well, I know old Walt Secrest on that drive. His brother and I are good friends, and we have laughed and said it was some sort of a miracle he is still on it. Walt can't take orders. He is used to running the show himself." One cowboy who wants to remain anonymous remembered that Walt was "trouble back in Fort Worth."

"Bud should have fired old Walt before we even got started. I could see he was gonna be trouble right off. Bud just ain't got no balls, and he don't know 'come here from sic 'em' about a cattle drive anyway." That same cowboy thought Walt could do more harm after being fired than he could have done had he been allowed to continue on with the drive.

In camp, I visited with two residents from Miles City who said that Walt wanted very much to be governor of Montana. These same men said that Walt was an opportunist with only self-interest in the success or failure of the drive. I know he loved attention from the media and was quick to promote Brother, his sorrel horse, whom he ponied with the chuck wagon when someone wasn't renting and riding him.

"This is the only horse with the drive that has walked all the way from Texas," Walt would say of Brother. "I am going to give him to my granddaughter when we get home." Walt called Brother his "spare tire." If anything happened to one of the Shires, he could and did hitch Brother to take the sick or lame Shire's place. Brother was ridden a big part of the way by Dancer when Dancer's horse went lame, and Dave McCullough rode the horse whenever he and his wife, Lori, were in camp for a few days. Walt did not wait for someone to ask for his autograph. He wrote his name everywhere, and he would walk up to people and ask if they wanted him to autograph whatever they had bought at the souvenir trailer or simply a piece of paper they might be holding or their shirt or cap. He wasn't shy about being a celebrity. He loved recognition and attention. He was a born politician.

Many of the cowboys were shocked that Bud went through with firing Walt. They were disenchanted with Bud and needed very little provocation to resent his actions. They despised Bruce and Jim and believed them to be the catalysts for Walt's dismissal. The general feeling was that Walt was "kinda pushy" and, yes, he did keep trouble stirred up in camp, but he shouldn't have been fired just before we finished the drive. Some believed that Bud fired Walt just to keep from paying him what was owed him.

Many believed any day Bud would fire the whole or part of the rest for that same reason. The relationship between Bud and the men was as fragile as spun glass. It was interesting but a bit scary to stand back and observe the different reactions to Walt's dismissal from the remaining cowboys.

Eldon Winn was noncommittal to most. He worked hard, stayed pretty close to his wife, Bobby (she had joined the drive after she got laid off from her job), and had little to say publicly about any situation. Eldon felt Walt wanted to be boss of the drive – to be hero and the main character in our drama.

Ace Wright thought it had been stupid to fire Walt. The tall Montanan was all cowboy and all business concerning the drive. He had absolutely no use for Bruce or Jim. Always one of the first up each morning, he looked out for the younger cowboys, did his job efficiently, and led me to believe he really cared about the success of the drive, in spite of his many conflicts with the outriders. He voiced concern about the safety of outriders and especially the danger of their causing injuries to the cowboys. He and Walt were friendly, and I believe the two of them could have managed the cattle and men with financial help from Bud and the investors. But I also believe firmly that had those two been in charge from the first, I would never have been allowed to go on the drive.

Ace was terse and quick to comment when asked a question. However, he usually listened with little comment in group discussions that I heard. He was astute, respected, and liked by most of the crew. He enjoyed driving the cattle, visiting with the crowds, and eating candy bars and clowning with Dick Kennedy. He was an avid reader, he liked music, and I believe that Ace also kept a journal. I would have liked to share the information in our journals, but I never felt comfortable enough to suggest such a thing. Ace joined the cowboys at dance halls or clubs in the small towns, but he never drank alcohol and was usually the designated driver back to camp. He loved the attention he got along the streets and highways, flirted with girls, and talked with the elderly and children. In sharp contrast, he paid scant attention to me or Gloria in camp. He was distant but polite. Ace also wanted to be a movie star.

Claude Voiles had helped with the harnessing of Walt's teams from the beginning. Claude helped anyone in need. He did a huge hunk of Walt's work in morning and evening preparations for camps and moving. He kept his gear in Walt's trailer until he moved it to Dick's trailer somewhere along the way. He and Walt were close, and Claude disliked Bruce and Jim intensely. I believed when Walt was fired if any of the drivers left with him it would be Claude, and I was worried. Claude was one of the best cowboys on the drive. He talked very little, did not gossip, did his job each day, and complained little about anything. As I expected, he was furious about Walt's firing and laid most of the blame on Bruce and Jim. He contemplated leaving with Walt, and Gloria pleaded with him not to go, but I believe he may have been influenced most by Miss Jayne, his boss and the lady who owned the ranch in Wyoming where he had worked for eleven years. She was also his best buddy, and I am sure her opinion was important to Claude. I was relieved when he opted to stay.

Jim Hooks, Jim Donaldson, and most of the crew, stayed busy getting the cattle ready for inspections. Jim Donaldson visited with me, curious about my reaction to the firing. I told him I regretted the firing but that I believed Walt was a big boy and could take care of himself. All the conflict and hostility between Walt and the management, the firing might be better for all concerned, including Walt. Jim listened and expressed his feelings in his slow Oklahoma drawl. "Well, I am staying here. I hired out to drive cattle to Montana. As long as I get my check, I will work, but I wonder just how many more checks we will get. I bet we never get that bonus Bud promised us." That was a long speech for Jim. He was a quiet young man and listened more than he talked. He worked cattle like a veteran, loved pretty women and beer, and was usually the last one home from nights on the town. He was pure cowboy, and everybody liked the redhead.

Jackie Joe, the youngest drover and Jim's nephew, also talked to me about what had happened. "Annie, do you think he will fire any more of us? I bet he fires us all before we get to Montana. I can't believe he fired Walt now, just when we are nearly there, and for no reason I can see." He asked and answered his own questions, expressing frustrations and fear of what was to come. Rumors had flown like blackbirds through camp. The same rumor ran rampant – that Bud was going to fire more of the cowboys at any time. Dick Kennedy and some of the others even came up with the figure of six cowboys, no names mentioned, who were destined to be fired soon. No one ever knew just where such rumors started – they just seemed to start.

When Walt and his crew departed the Camplex in Gillette, Wyoming, the last day of July, they left a confused and disgruntled group of cowboys and a gaping hole in the core of the GACD.

A man named Larry Clyde came to camp the day before we left Gillette. We were told he would be the new chuck wagon driver. He was polite, talked nonstop, and was ecstatic about going. He brought a team of quarter-bred mares and hitched them to the chuck wagon. I thought the mares were small to pull that heavy wagon up and down Wyoming foothills, but Larry assured all that "these mares can handle it. They just have to get used to the traffic and all." He was working without pay, someone said. He said someone else had let his team run away making them spooky and likely to run away again.

"I've been working with them since that happened, and I have got them calmed down and doing well," he said.

The sorrel mare was quiet, but the bay was fractious and nervous. They were both eighteen years old - too old, I feared, but I thought that maybe their age would slow down the skittish bay after a few hours pulling that heavy wagon. I figured that she was like all us old folks – we all slow down after we reach a certain age, especially when we are pulling heavy loads. I couldn't have been more wrong.

In the nineteenth century, when hundreds of thousands of

longhorns were driven north to markets, the chuck wagon was the heart and soul of those drives. It was always driven ahead of the herds to give the cook time to prepare his sourdough and beans and coffee for the hungry wranglers and drivers. I am sure that wagon was a welcome sight for the cowboys at the end of the day after they had been eating dust or fighting bitter cold or Indians or stampedes.

Bud changed that tradition and moved Clyde and the chuck wagon behind the herd, carrying jugs of water or lemonade and snacks for the outriders and cowboys. I thought it was silly. Each of us could simply carry a bottle of water and snacks in our saddlebags. I believed that Bud's system was disruptive and slowed everything, but Bud never asked my opinion, and I never offered it. The wagon may have helped to alleviate some of the boredom of driving the slow-moving herd. A steady stream of riders traipsed back and forth to the wagon for water and snacks.

One boy from Vision Quest made a trip to the wagon about every fifteen minutes. Each time someone wanted a drink or something to eat, the wagon had to stop. I was riding point for the wagon the day that same VQ boy had stopped the wagon for one of his many trips, and I was about fifty feet in front of the wagon. I turned to wait for the move ahead. I saw the bay mare turn her head, and in one movement, she rubbed her head under her mate's neck, her bridle slipped off, and the mare lunged forward – all in less than two seconds. Pandora's Box was sprung open.

Larry had no control over the speeding team. He could not pull the line controlling the sorrel for that would have caused her to turn sharply and would have caused the wagon to turn over. He screamed over and over for someone to stop the runaway mares. The wagon tore through the herd, stampeding the longhorns, causing them to scatter right, left, and forward behind the team. The wagon flew down the pavement, swaying side to side, reeling like a crazy drunk. Darik and Jim Donaldson, Jackie

Joe, and others I could not identify, raced after the team of mares. Somewhere along the three or four miles they ran, the sorrel's traces came loose, which left only the breast yoke and the bay's traces attaching the mares to the plunging wagon.

I was riding in a short lope behind the runaway team and wagon, silently praying for the lives of Larry and Evan Owens, Jerry's little boy, who was riding in the wagon that day because he did not feel like riding horseback. The wagon was still on the pavement, and I feared that if it turned over Larry and Evan could not get out without suffering serious injury or even losing their lives.

I believe that Darik's loop was the one that finally settled around the bay mare's neck and brought the bleeding, lathered mares and the wagon to a halt. Their feet were torn to bloody shreds. The sorrel's back hocks or knees, if you prefer, were bloody and battered where the surging wagon had repeatedly lunged against her. Both mares' back shoes had come loose, and the nails in them had been driven into their hooves.

My heart sank, and my stomach churned like an unruly sea. Larry had stark terror painted on his face. Little Evan got up off the floor of the wagon, his tiny face ashen but a wide, uncertain grin on his face.

When a trailer moving to the next camp was flagged down and the mares finally loaded and carted away, I did not believe they would ever recover. Larry laughed a shaky, nervous laugh and said they would be ready for work the next day. *Mister, you are either in shock from fear or you know not a damned thing about livestock. Those mares are probably ready for the killer pens.*

The cattle had been quieted, the mares were gone, and I rode ahead of everyone, needing to be alone to collect myself. I felt empty, homesick, heartsick, angry and disgusted. So many emotions, and all negative – stirred by the heart-stopping minutes of the runaway - came rushing to the surface of my mind like logs over the falls in a raging river.

Damn these men and their funky hang-ups, stupid decisions, and male egos the size of football fields. We are caught in between, as we flounder, stumble, stagger, fuss, and fight. We grumble, complain, and most of all, we struggle with our own pride and the burning desire to reach Montana with this herd for the satisfaction and glory; for the delight and wonder of the thousands who have followed us for hundreds of miles, while boosting our self-confidence and praying for our success.

Tears ran down my face and spilled onto Gus's neck as I raged inside until another voice within purged the anger, and I felt drained and tired and limp with fatigue and spent emotion. Then, my sense of fairness broke through, and I felt that I could be all wrong about our so-called leaders and thought of the plaque hanging on my wall that reads: "Grant I never judge my neighbor until I have walked a mile in his shoes. . . ."

Yeah, and on the other hand, we have seen the West between a horse's ears. We have been hugged, fed, prayed for, and greeted by thousands; we are traveling on a journey the world would give anything to experience; we are learning the meaning of living with others, and how to do without the everyday luxuries we take for granted in our sheltered lives. We are facing defeat daily and staggering on with renewed hope with the dawn and bright sun and rolling green hills, snow-capped mountains, bounding antelope and the sense of total freedom we feel. We stand a good chance of becoming better human beings when we ride down the streets of Miles City. Yeah, and I wouldn't trade a single one of these cowboys, or their oversized egos. Hell, I ain't no trip to Hollywood myself. I am just a scared old broad who hates ever seeing an animal hurt, like those mares were.

My thoughts lurched between the good and bad issues of the drive. It was a beautiful day, and the Wyoming countryside was better therapy than anything that could have been found in a psychiatrist's office. I spat my words out into the clean Wyoming air, and hearing them made me feel better and cleaned the rubble out of my mind for awhile. I wasn't sure what I had said was correct, but at least I had had my say, even though Gus's and

God's were the only ears that heard, and I am sure that neither of them was seriously concerned with such trifles. And being the extrovert that I am, I soon became content just to be where I was with my horse and my freedom of thought and Wyoming's space.

Spotted Horse, Wyoming, sat smug atop a hill, conspicuous in the vastness of wide open country. No town, church, store, cross streets, or houses – just a ramshackle building housing Spotted Horse Tavern. Outside, a wooden black-and-white rearing horse held up the small sign announcing Spotted Horse. Through the sagging screen door, one observed a pool table, tall tables with bar stools, a couch, an old piano, and a short L-shaped bar and kitchen. An old pot-bellied stove dominated the small alcove where the couch sat. High shelves around the rooms held antique churns, bikes, tack, and bric-a-brac. Paintings, covered with dust and brands around their frames, decorated the walls. The air conditioning consisted of a fan in the kitchen, and the rest of the tavern was on its own. The single toilet sported fixtures that had not been cleaned for quite some time, and the water that came back into the yellow-ringed commode looked like it might have been rerun. But the cold water from the sink felt wonderful on my face, and the tiny, dirty bar of soap lathered enough to cut some of the grime from my gritty-feeling hands. I had not the nerve to dry them on the towel, which matched the floor and surroundings, and chose instead my shirt sleeves and pants legs. The owner of the establishment had opened the tavern just for us because it had been closed, period. Its owner was a skinny, gray-headed guy with an effeminate voice and a haughty attitude. His smile was fake, greedy, and seldom, and his mama was his partner in the tavern.

The beer was cold and expensive, but it soothed my dry throat and felt cool and lively in my empty belly. Beer was two bucks a can, and whiskey was three bucks a shot. I went to the bar for two bags of ice for my cooler and paid $5.

◆ ◆ ◆ ◆

For years – forty or so – I have earned a living in the food and beverage business, in just about every position needed to run a bar or restaurant from dishwasher to cook to barmaid, waitress, and entertainer. I have met the greatest, worst, weirdest, most eccentric, and the most congenial people of those frequenting the pubs, cafés, elite restaurants, hotels, and nightclubs across America. All of these people and establishments have their own personalities, idiosyncrasies, and messages to the world. The things one remembers most are courtesy and congeniality. Those two commodities make up for high prices every time.

◆ ◆ ◆ ◆

I should have told old ugly to take his ice and stick it. I said nothing, but instead paid and walked out with a better education than when I had entered. Not exactly a place to buy ice or for unemployed drunks to go for a night out.

Spotted Horse was the closest inhabited spot to the Harris Ranch, where Claude Voiles lived and worked. Several pictures of Claude hung on the walls there in the tavern, and signs welcomed him back.

Saturday night, hundreds, yes hundreds, came from the hills and mountains and valleys and canyons, with great food, song, and frolicking to honor Claude, and that cowboy beamed and said more than I had heard him say since leaving Texas. Miss Jayne Harris, owner of Harris ranch, came and celebrated with her friend and employee. Her affection and pride in Claude was obvious.

Motorcycle riders were there also. In Sturgis, South Dakota, a bikers' convention is held annually. Some 100,000 gather on bikes for the convention, which did not start until the following Monday, but they were already gathering, and some stopped for all the festivity and food and to see the cowboys and longhorns. I am sure that was the biggest crowd gathered there since the opening of Spotted Horse in 1928.

Will said that one man drove an old ice truck into camp. It was a Graham Brothers truck – a 1928 model – and "the only one I have ever seen." On one wall of the tavern was a sign that had been recently painted. It read: Lonesome Drovers were here first! August 1st 1995. All the way to Miles City, Montana.

Walt and Dancer and the rest had signed their names under and around the sign. The separation was complete, the "peaceful" war had been declared, and the unexpressed or suppressed emotions could be heard loud and clear in the deafening silence.

I could not find Skip Nelson in Spotted Horse after we set up camp. The man worked no less than fourteen hours a day. He climbed hills, rocks, trees, and the top of his Suburban, and behind camera and tripod, he took thousands of pictures and miles of videotape of the drive. He was first up in the morning and the last to bed at night. His limitless energy and brilliant smile were constant, and he always seemed to drive by with a cold soda or water or ice-cold raw carrots just when I needed something for a parched throat. He was a joy and an upper for me always. He was conspicuously absent, and I worried, fearful that he had fallen into a canyon or off a rock while taking pictures of the cattle in some secluded spot, where he would die in the heat. (Well, I have a vivid imagination). Skip told me later that he had been in Walt's camp, down the trail ahead of us. He feared that our cowboys might resent his being there instead of in our camp.

"I am taking pictures of this cattle drive, and Walt and his bunch were a part of it, and I must get the entire story," he told me. Our cowboys did not resent Skip's going to Walt's camp. Many of them secretly did the same thing. Their camp was lively and filled with the music of Big Ron playing an old piano he had brought to their camp from home. It was carried on the big lowboy trailer, and each night he would play, and those people visiting Walt's camp would sing around the campfire, with Dancer directing, I am sure.

Skip told me about Robert, the cook's helper who had gone with Walt, falling into one of the irrigation ditches on his horse while chasing a steer and almost drowning. Walt picked up more steers and bulls from people he knew along the way to take to Montana. He also had more horses, but only a handful of inexperienced "volunteers" to help drive them.

In Leiter, over coffee in the one and only business – a small restaurant and log cabins for rent – Skip and Gloria and I discussed the situation between Bud and Walt and the drive in general.

Skip said, "I believe it is too late for any money to be made on this drive. I think it is terrible that Walt and the rest are separated from you and the cowboys at this late date, no matter what Walt did, if anything." Skip expressed sincere regret and cited the lack of media coverage and proper management as primary causes of the anger and separation and financial failure of the drive. We talked about the fact that Paul Harvey had given us a real boost when he talked frequently about the drive, but it was for naught because he was the only "biggie" who did. I had written him a thank-you letter on behalf of the drive. I listened to his broadcast in the truck whenever the chance presented itself, which was seldom, and he mentioned the drive many times. I was proud of that because we got little publicity from the big media.

Afterwards I shrugged off our conversation, knowing Skip had voiced my thoughts, and opted for the positive side. *Hell, I am going to wait for my kids to come join me in the finish, see the country, meet the people, and ride to Miles City with Keely and Kenny and Gus and Red and see the culmination of my dream. To hell with those who are determined to make things miserable for the rest of us in their struggle for power and supremacy.*

Gloria and I turned our horses out and went to Buffalo for fun and sightseeing. The town was teeming with celebration, bikers, and people. Two conventions were there. In Buffalo, the triker convention and the Basques. The trikers were not a part of the convention in Sturgis. I was amused and fascinated, watching those people (mostly middle-aged) on those three-wheeled motorcycles of unbelievable description. They paraded through

Buffalo on trikes re-built to look like Model T's to Corvettes to race cars or sporting homemade frames; all had three wheels, brightly painted in purples and red and yellows, with grandpas and grandmas, young and old and in between, riding topside.

One female senior citizen sat prim and proud on her trike, clad in black leather jacket, pants, and boots, while her companion in the buddy seat was a huge stuffed gorilla. I loved it!

◆ ◆ ◆ ◆

I remembered almost fifty years earlier when I had ridden a 1946 Indian Chief motorcycle down North Hill in Commerce, Texas, on a bitter cold night with a thin sheet of ice lying in wait on the Middle Sulphur River bridge. Headlights behind me told me I had an audience. When I crossed the icy bridge, I rocked the cycle and touched the bridge with the chrome crash bars to make sparks fly. My performance was complete perfection without mishap (probably because God watches over idiots, drunks, and old people), and I was on a natural high until I discovered that the headlights behind were on Mack's truck and that performance was the end of my career as an amateur daredevil cyclist. Who knows – had he not been there, I might have grown up to become a female Evel Knievel.

Next day in Buffalo, descendants of the Basques of Spain's Pyrenees Mountains celebrated their heritage. Their magnificent draft horse hitches, in festive and elaborate harness, pulled the traditional sheep wagons, some complete with shepherd and unbelievably brilliant sheep dogs that gently and deftly guided the sheep down through Buffalo as thousands lined the streets, cheering them on.

Every day I encountered new adventures and creatures along the trail. One morning between camps, Gloria and I were riding ahead of the herd and wagon when we saw ten or twelve sage hens alongside the road – brown fluffs of feathers looking similar to little fat pheasants, only smaller. Will told me the Indians killed them with sticks because "they were too dumb to hide or run." Like doves, the sage chickens might have been too trusting of humanity.

On August 6, the Wyoming sun beat down, and the hot winds blew up a 105-degree day. The fourteen miles we rode that day took us east of the Powder River to a valley ranch of four thousand acres. We saw three cowboys herding Angus cattle out of a pasture making ready for the longhorn.

Gloria and I went into Leiter, got one of the small log cabins with a kitchenette, and I set up the computer and wrote stories for *Trails* magazine and brought my journal up to date. The cabin had no air conditioner, and neither did the restaurant. The two ladies who owned the cabins and restaurant were congenial and hard working. Martha cooked, and her very pregnant daughter, Jill, waited tables. The food was tasty, and the red wine was excellent. There was a full-size stove in the cabin. I borrowed a big pot from the restaurant and bought dried beans, green peppers, onions, and ham and soaked the beans overnight. I borrowed spices from Martha, cooked the beans, and made a cake for the camp in celebration of Jess Herber's birthday. The cowboys really liked the beans.

That night Nan Creel came to camp with a letter to Walt from her husband, Ed Creel, a lawyer representing Bud. I was not aware of the letter until she and Gloria and I were in the car on the way to Walt's camp, which was ahead of us several miles. Nan and Gloria had asked me to go, and I joined them in what I thought was just a friendly visit to Walt's camp to see everybody. When I learned what the trip was for, I made some flimsy excuse about being thirsty and asked to be let out in Clearmont at the local bar and restaurant, where I caught a ride back to camp. I just did not want to be a part of the discourse.

The letter warned Walt not to sell souvenirs with anything resembling the GACD logos under threat of lawsuit. *Oh please, don't let it destroy our chances of getting there. We are so close, just leave us alone with your private war and let us get these steers and horses safely to Miles City and the good people waiting for us there.*

God, I want this to happen so much. My kids are coming, and the small world that knows about this undertaking is waiting with bated breath for us to succeed.

I sat in that tavern, hugging a Scotch, beating myself to death trying to figure out how to make that damned drive reach Montana. I wanted it to succeed for me – me and my vagabond heart and desire to succeed in everything I attempted, and that bunch of cowboys. I was on stage. The world was watching me and "those cowboys." I remembered that man's prediction so many weeks back on that bitter cold day as we went down the streets of Boyd, Texas – he said we would never make it. He was wrong. We *would* make it. I was sure of it. We were not going to let the many down who had been supporting us all the way. The Scotch and my blind and deaf determination seemed to ease my stiff spine and feelings of foreboding.

When I left camp next morning, there was frost on the meadows. I added a T-shirt under my shirt, pulled on the goose down, and Gus and I headed out about one hour after dawn. I knew that when the sun was high, it would be hot again, but right then it was a beautiful day with the air crisp and clean. I smelled new-mown hay, which left a rich sweet taste in my mouth. The shadows in the early morning sun painted smoky patchwork quilts on the faces of the foothills. Rounding a switchback, I saw the majestic Bighorns reaching skyward through the early morning mist, and the ribbons of snow looked silvery soft and cool as they streamed downward. I saw mares and new colts romping in green pastures with mule deer fawns and antelope. The Powder River meandered by on its way to somewhere, and rattlesnakes were out in number. One unfortunate porcupine had met his fate on the asphalt. Had we been in Texas, the road kills would have been armadillos, but in the Northwest, I saw plenty of porcupine. They all decorated the highways with quills scattered to the four winds, but I never saw a live one the entire drive.

On the ninth of August, we were one mile east of Ucross, Wyoming, on the John Campbell property. The steers were getting slower and harder to move faster than about two miles per hour. We went through Clearmont, which had a few stores and a post office, but Ucross had only a beer and liquor store with sandwiches and groceries. Across the road from camp, nestled in beautiful landscaped acres was a writers' and artists' retreat sponsored by a foundation. The foundation decides on the time of the stay, and one is accepted on letters of recommendation from folks who know the applicant and his or her work. With Skip Nelson, I visited the place and got an application. I thought how great it would be to go there to live for awhile in that awesome country.

In camp, the pasture had strips of fence down, so I set up a trap in a corner with my trailer and rope for Gus and Red. I went to Ucross and got a six-pack and built sandwiches for Will and me just as the cattle came in. It was hot again, and the trailer made a cool shade. Skip joined us for a cool one and talk. Gus and Red were nearby waiting for apples, and I basked in my contentment and pleasure at being with my friends and my beloved horses.

18

THE HOME STRETCH

August 20, I talked to my son, Kenny, by phone, and he told me that he and Keely, my baby daughter, would find me, wherever we were camped, on the 28th. I could hardly wait to see them. They had been so supportive and excited about my making the drive. I knew it would be a great break for them both. Kenny was in radio in Tyler, Texas, and Keely was wife and mother of two and worked on a ranch in Mississippi. I chuckled to myself, thinking about Keely riding with the cowboys. She "sits deep and throws a wide loop," as a cowhand would say. I knew she would not have any problems riding with the herd. She would be a match for any cowboy on that cattle drive. My kid, all female, was tougher than a woodhauler, but she was happy being married, I believed.

Keely and I were much alike in many ways. I loved men, too, and yet you could not get one thin dime from either one of us for the so-called liberation of women. Hell! Women run the world already as far as I am concerned. I was content and happy being a woman and living in the man's world I was in. Women have been making history since time began. They figured heavily in the nineteenth-century cattle drive era. But one must search to find stories of female involvement to the physical aspects of history.

J. Marvin Hunter's great book, *The Trail Drivers of Texas*, has an interesting account of one happening along the trail. In 1886, Samuel Dunn Houston of San Antonio, Texas, went to work for

Holt Livestock Company of New Mexico, as trail foreman, and drove his first herd for that company in the spring of that year. He had trouble finding cowboys because the population was sparse in that part of the country. At Seven Rivers, he found four men who had come up from Texas and hired them, completing his outfit. He was driving 2,500 head three years or older. Sam discovered later that the four men from Texas were outlaws, fired them, took away their guns, and left them sitting in their saddles on the prairie.

He went into Clayton, New Mexico, a small railroad town ahead, to hire more men. Sam tells the story like this:

When I got there I found there were no men in town, but I met an old friend of mine and he told me that there was a kid of a boy around town that wanted to get with a herd and go up the trail. His name was Willie Matthews. He was nineteen years old and weighed one hundred and twenty-five pounds. His home was in Caldwell, Kansas. I was so pleased with him that I wished many times that I could find two or three more like him. We were on our way to Hugo, Colorado, a little town on the old K.P. Railroad, near the Colorado and Wyoming line. After dinner that night, the kid asked me if he could quit. He insisted, said he was homesick, and I had to let him go. About sundown, we were all sitting around camp, and the old herd was coming in on the bed ground. I looked up toward town and saw a lady all dressed up, coming toward camp, walking. I told the boys we were going to have company. I couldn't imagine why a woman would be coming on foot to a cow camp, but she kept right on coming, and when she got within fifty feet, I got up to receive my guest. Our eyes were all set on her, every man holding his breath. When she got up within about twenty feet of me, she began to laugh, and said, 'Mr. Houston, you don't know me, do you?

Well, for one minute I couldn't speak. She reached her hand out to me, to shake hands, and I said, Kid, is it possible that you are a lady? That was one time that I could not think of anything to say, for everything that had been said on the old cow trail in the last three or four days entered my mind at that moment. In a little while we all crowded around the girl and shook her hand, but we were so dumbfounded we could hardly think of anything to say. I told the cook to get one of the tomato boxes for a chair. The kid sat down and I said, now, I want you to explain yourself."

"My papa is an old-time trail driver from Southern Texas. He drove from Texas to Caldwell, Kansas, in the '70's. He liked the country around Caldwell very much, so the last trip he made he went to work on a ranch up there and never returned to Texas anymore. In two or three years, he and my mother were married. After I was ten or twelve years old, I used to hear papa talk so much about the old cow trail, I made up my mind that when I was grown I was going up the trail if I had to run off. I had a pony of my own and read in the paper of the big herds passing Clayton, New Mexico, so I said, now is my chance to get on the trail. I saddled my pony and told brother I was going out in the country, and I might be gone for a week, but for him to tell papa not to worry about me, I would be back. I had on a suit of brother's clothes and a pair of his boots. In three or four days I was in Clayton looking for a job and I found one."

After Samuel Dunn Houston got through and returned to the ranch on the Pecos River, he received many letters from the little girl and her father, thanking him for the kindness toward Willie and begging Sam to visit them.

◆ ◆ ◆ ◆

I felt a kinship with Willie for her daring. Our motives were different, our situations worlds apart, but our desires for adventure through uncharted waters (or prairies) paralleled. The call of the out-of-doors and daring feats rang loud and clear in both our hearts.

I thought of that young woman when I met another woman from a local newspaper. Will and I were sitting by the trailer bending our elbows and wagging tongues when the newspaper woman came by and asked if I was the "lady who is writing a book about the drive." I told her that I was keeping a journal and planned to write a book when the drive was ended.

Cynthia Rhodes, a reporter with the *Sheridan Press*, was excited that she had found me. "I can't believe that you are the only woman on the drive and that I haven't heard of you until today, and that was quite by accident. You are the *real* story on this drive!" I was pleased and laughingly told her that I was also the best-kept secret.

"She not only keeps a journal about the drive – she works as a drover and she makes a hand. She can ride with the best and does as good a job as any on the drive," Will said, plugging me as eloquently as any press agent could have. Cynthia's story about me was interesting, complimentary, and informative, complete with my picture on the front page, and a great boost for me. It came when any positive press about the drive was scarce.

The day following the interview, Will saddled up in spite of my begging him not to. He was running a fever, pale as a ghost, and really sick.

"We are gonna have to do night herding, and Jim Hooks will think I am faking sickness to keep from having to work tonight," Will said. I thought his feeling that way was ridiculous, but I knew it was senseless to argue with Will. A loud silence existed between Will and Jim. Jim hated Will's booze, and I believed that Will resented the younger and less experienced man being in charge. That old Oklahoma cowboy could have been Sam Houston reincarnated. He could have stepped from the pages of history of a century ago. He could think like a horse or cow. He was like sagebrush and prickly pear and dust storm and mountain. There was no gray in Will's life - just black and white. He understood the longhorns probably better than anyone there. He believed that Jim was secretly afraid of them.

"Them damned steers lead us; we don't drive them," he would lament often. "Jim's so afraid they are gonna stampede that we fart around all day waiting for them to move when we should be pushing them to camp before it gets so damned hot we fry our brains, and they balk on us because of the heat and no water out there." I was oft times amused at the unspoken feuds between the cowboys in general. That is, feuds without serious confrontations. Those riding drag would come into camp bitching about those riding point.

"If the point men would move on out instead of riding in front of the lead steer, we could have gotten into camp two hours ago," they would complain.

"If I had been riding back there, I could have gotten those sons-a-bitches to move on out instead of jawing with the outriders, and we could have made camp hours ago," someone else on the other end would echo. When Will rode drag, he would chase the steers with wild hoots and yelling, and Jim, who was always on point, would ride back and sometimes voice his disapproval with anybody pushing the steers too hard. Many days, Will would still be high from swimming around in his bourbon bottle the night before - a constant irritation to the sober, docile Jim. Jim wanted to be the good guy who made everything run smoothly, and Will wanted to show the steers who was in charge. He didn't give a damn whether anybody liked him or not. He figured that people could take him as he was. It was their choice.

Ace Wright voiced his disgust because the steers were not being moved fast enough. Claude also realized our shortcomings with control of the herd, but he was usually silent and did his job. The younger cowboys were usually bored and were constantly throwing ropes, riding back and forth visiting with each other, and flirting with any young outrider girls who might be riding for the day. Everyone complained because the outriders constantly intermingled with the herd, cutting it in half, getting in the way, and causing problems each day. Without exception, they all believed themselves to be expert trail men. But that "belief in self," or being unaware of ignorance of the massive undertaking that we were attempting, may have helped us get to Montana as much, or more than anything else. Obviously, we all were lacking in one manner or the other.

We were doing something that had not been done in over one

hundred years under unique and much different circumstances. I couldn't help admiring those men. They ran on guts and braggadocio and suppressed any fear they might have had by strutting and stumbling on toward our goal and glory. Just believing in oneself will get one halfway there. We all were sometimes stumbling around in the dark.

I am sure that Goodnight and Loving and other nineteenth-century drovers would have said: "To hell with this damned asphalt, these thousands of automobiles, trains, trucks, and infernal paid-to-ride dudes; regulations, tests, laws, and people lining the roads, getting in the way and asking thousands of stupid questions." I believe they would have just ridden off into the sunset, never to be seen again.

The complaints were justified, but there were no quick solutions to our problems. In truth, we had done an impossible job quite well without killing the outriders or each other, or even crippling one of our peers. Threats of fights and "settling up" in Montana were made, but we continued on our way together.

We had no campfires anymore. That could have been because of the heat, but I felt that no one was interested enough to find wood and start a fire. The campfire had always brought people together, if only temporarily. We had not had a campfire since Dancer and Walt had split. On the other hand, perhaps that lack of organization and control at the top was the irony that drove us closer together. Whatever the reason, we kept going – stumbling north and west toward our destination – as a unit; a lumpy oneness; a melting pot of humanity, all heading for Miles City.

The mountains were getting taller, the hills steeper, the view more spectacular, and the antelope herds larger. My friend, David, an outrider and upstate New Yorker, and I rode ahead of the herd and wagon to suck up the early-morning coolness before the sun peeked over the mountains warming the winds that sent waves of heat into our faces.

Will and I drove up into the Big Horns and took pictures

and gazed in awe at the splendor of Wyoming. Our camp was in a small valley, and I parked my trailer and truck on a hill overlooking that serene valley. One of the small investors was back in camp for the first time in weeks.

Dave McCullough and Walker Lawrence came from Walt's camp to ours to see everyone and say hello. Dave and Lori had gone with Walt to ride with his group when the split occurred in Gillette. Dave and Walker walked into an unfriendly wall.

Will and I were up on the hill and did not know they were in camp until the confrontation was over. One of the cowboys told us the small investor ordered them off our camp grounds. I couldn't believe that Dave and Walker had been run out of camp, and I felt guilt as strong as if I had been a party to the gauche, insensitive encounter. *Christ almighty, whatever happened to the tradition of the West – the hospitality to strangers or friends along the trail, when a spot close to the campfire, a hot cup of coffee, and a bowl of beans were offered?* Because I had not been present to say hi and let them know that I did not feel any hostility toward them, I was sure they would believe that the investor mirrored the feelings of the camp in general.

A few days later, I accompanied Derk Hansen to Walt's camp for steaks that Derk was going to cook that night. Dave and Lori hugged me tight and laughed and assured me they knew the investor did not speak for the rest of us. Walker did not speak to me at all. Lon was aloof and polite, and Ron was nice and friendly as if nothing had happened. Walt was terse and icy cool but polite. And Dancer was his usual ersatz self. I was extremely uncomfortable, stayed only a short while, said goodbye to Derk, who was insisting that I stay for steaks, slunk to my truck, and went back to camp feeling emptiness, anger, and sadness.

I wonder just what old Walt is feeling? Dave and Lori have chipped in several thousand dollars to help him; he has Dancer, who is a capable press agent; and Lon and Ron lend friendly warmth and sincerity to his entourage. I am at a loss at why he has turned hostile toward me – he and Dick Kennedy, too. I wonder what the connection is, if any, between the two.

Over pie and coffee in town, Skip told me that he and Derk had not been paid a cent for their work so far and for the two hundred copies of the first video they had produced and brought to the souvenir trailer.

"We have not been paid for the tapes of the first segment of the drive. They are selling them out of the trailer, but not paying us. They are selling all three of the tapes with the last two not even produced. Those people are not going to get those other tapes until we have been paid. We can't afford to produce the other two if we can't get paid for the first one. We will not make another tape until Bud has brought the money due us up to date."

Damn! Why doesn't Bud square with these two wonderful hard-working guys? They have brought so much class, professionalism, and integrity to this trip. If Bud doesn't have the money, then why in hell don't he just say so? They might have some ideas on a solution to his problem.

I did not get to sleep until early morning. When I awakened, camp was as still as death, and it was late. A north wind had come up in the night, and the tarp on the trailer was whipping like the flag on the capitol building. I found out that we weren't leaving until later, but no one else had known either. The coffee had been made at 3:30 a.m. as usual, and it was cold as Alaska. The investor was going to hold Sunday services that morning before we left. Well, I felt that I couldn't handle that, so I headed to the top of the hill for Gus and Red's company.

From camp, just two miles outside of Sheridan, some of the men had gone to town, and a fight broke out in a bar. Jim and Jackie Donaldson were put in the pokey. I went into town later to the police station to see if I could help get them out, but the dispatcher told me they were already out. Rumor later was that Stasha, the Vision Quest counselor, had been part of it and had been insulted in the bar and that the men had somehow become involved. I never talked to either one of them about it. One came to me later and thanked me for "caring," but I never asked for details.

Those two young Oklahoma cowboys came from the old school that taught that a man protects a woman's virtue. Sound corny? Well, those old beliefs still exist and were strong on that cattle drive made up of men who still believed women to be the weaker sex and in need of protection - possibly from themselves. I did not know if that was the cause of the situation at the fight, but it did cross my mind.

My favorite philosopher, Will Rogers, once said: "Give a woman her way, and she will defeat herself in the end." Yep, you said it, Mr. Rogers.

XXL

19

SHERIDAN, WYOMING

I drove Skip's Suburban down the streets of Sheridan, Wyoming, for our parade there so that he could ride on the top with his tripod and camera for great pictures. I did not mind missing the glory of riding on horseback down the streets of the biggest town we went through on the drive. The reception was wonderful. Not a gap in the hundreds lining the streets, welcoming the GACD.

There was an aloofness ringed with friendly smiles, on the faces of the people of Wyoming. It was an expression that said to us: welcome, but don't get too close. They are an independent, earthy, tough people who love their land, environment, and strength. And strength is what it takes to live in that country. Mother Nature is harsh and has no sympathy for the weak and foolhardy. The winters have left those people scarred but stronger and more proud and sure that they are able to overcome any hardships. Wyoming (just as I had envisioned in my childhood) is Western to the bone, as exemplified by its instantly-recognizable logo, the bucking horse. We brought momentary prosperity to the businesses there and left the city a hot check for rent on the fair grounds where we camped.

King's Saddlery there has a museum, second to very few, displaying possibly every piece of tack that belonged to legends of the Old West. Will and I spent one whole day there before crossing the street to imbibe at the Mint Bar. We met two locals in the bar and discussed world problems and decided that we could run the government, clean up Washington, and eliminate a large portion of crime on the streets if only someone would ask us. Ain't it funny how two or four old drunks become extremely sage and discerning after ingesting a generous amount of alcohol? My tongue becomes free and agile, my brain shifts into overdrive, my waist becomes smaller, and my topside larger after several Scotches. I could tell right away that the two we had the powwow with were politically affiliated with the parties Will and I belonged to (either Republican or Democratic, I don't recall) and shared our views on many social and political matters. The afternoon raced by and fun was had by all, including those within earshot of us.

After only the first drink, I learned by accident that the Mint had given free drink tickets for each of us to "one of the guys with the drive."

"I don't understand why you guys don't use them. Nobody used a single one last night, and there was a gang of cowboys in here," the barmaid told us. I asked her if she remembered to whom she had given the tickets. She said that "Roger" had passed them out and that he would be there when she got off.

When Roger, the night bartender, came to work, the four of us were still warming stools. I asked to whom he had given the tickets. "Some skinny older guy named Jim. He said he was the boss of the drive."

Will hissed like a water moccasin about to strike, and I spat forth a bit of East Texas profanity. Every day, it seemed, Bruce and Jim dug their graves of alienation a bit deeper and grew further away from the rest of us. All along the trail, when I went to places like cleaners and laundromats, camera shops, and such, I was told that my "bosses" had already been there and brought clothes to be cleaned and so forth. Jim and Bruce told the merchants that they were the big bosses on the drive. After awhile, it grated even on my ego. It made the cowboys furious. Those two men, except for about one week's ride along with Bud, never saddled a horse nor entered into any camp conversations, festivities, or events with the rest of us. They rode in air-conditioned cars and trucks in starched clean clothes, with phones hanging off their ears. Many of the articles that came out in local newspapers displayed their pictures and always depicted them as the big bosses.

I knew that Jim had not given those tickets to the cowboys, because neither Will nor I had seen one, and I knew that if the cowboys had any tickets they would have spent them the night before. We all were broke almost to the point of panhandling. However, that episode did not dampen our spirits. It was no match for bourbon and Scotch camaraderie.

Next day, I confronted Jim, and he said the Mint had given him orders not to give the tickets to us until the last day we were in Sheridan. Pattie, the barmaid, and Roger denied giving any such orders and said their boss had told them to give the tickets to the cowboys with no strings attached.

"We wanted you to have them immediately. I didn't tell them anything except welcome," Roger told me later.

Will carried a big bag of resentment toward Bud and the leaders, and when he got a snoot full of alcohol his anger poured forth. He still smarted from finding out that the jackets that one of the western clothing companies had given to the cowboys had been sold in the souvenir trailer.

"We were given two jackets, one winter and one lightweight one. We got the lightweight, and they sold the heavy, expensive one for $125," Will lamented. "They just cheated us out of one of our jackets." *Hell, Will, I didn't get even one jacket, and Jamie McCain promised me the same benefits as the cowboys in the beginning, and Bud later echoed Jamie.* I had quit worrying about material benefits miles ago. Hell, most of the time, we didn't even have toilet paper. In Sheridan, Bud told the men that the payroll would be a few days late.

"The cowboys are plenty pissed over the payroll," Will said. He told me that he had caught a ride to town with Jim Peck to do his laundry and had to catch a cab back to camp because Peck never came back for him. It seemed to me that someone was always leaving Will somewhere. It made me angry. There was little respect between those men.

A letter began forming in my head – a letter I was going to write to the cowboys. I wanted to bring unity back. I put on paper what I felt in my heart.

Dear Cowboys,

In the beautiful cool Wyoming morning, riding through the foothills, I could not help wondering how we could be angry, restless, resentful, and alienated, as we all have felt at one time or the other lately. We have come so far, we have done so much with so little leadership, under so many adverse conditions with so much doubt from so many, that I am convinced we could do anything. We have made uncountable mistakes, we have blundered and stumbled close to fifteen hundred miles and done what everyone said we could not do. If our mistakes were weighed, perhaps the heaviest one would be our sense of pride, fading in these last few days before trail's end.

Let's don't lose sight of our original goal of writing a brand new chapter in American Western history. We are putting our petty complaints before bigger and greater achievements and goals. We are a group of people from across the United States with different lifestyles, tastes, ages, and cultures who have been thrown together between God's sky and earth to handle and care for some of His creatures while we work together toward a common goal. We must not forget what we set out to do.

I read the letter several times, pictured what effect it would have on the cowboys, if any, and then chickened out and never gave it to them. I was not able to convince myself that they would even read it. Maybe it was really my faith that had weakened and faltered.

Will failed to get a ride downtown, got restless, and saddled up his gelding and headed for the Mint. I passed there and saw the horse tied to the light pole on the sidewalk. The Mint was in the heart of downtown Sheridan. *Oh, hell, the cops will put that old gray coyote in jail sure as manure stinks.* I parked the truck and went in.

"Will, why did you ride down here? I would have brought you anytime. You know that."

"Yeah, I know. No problem. I just ran out of cigarettes and decided I'd saddle the old gelding. Hell, he needs the exercise. I'm going back to camp in a minute." I knew that he would be there until he was totally snockered, but I was helpless to do anything because he was already on his way. Skip came along later and found the gelding wandering up the alley with a broken bridle. He caught him and tied him and took his picture, which came out on the front page of the next day's paper. The cops had already been there and made Will move the gelding to the alley off the main sidewalk. There will never be another Will Miltimore. The world can handle only one at a time. He didn't get put in jail, and he made it back to camp. I am sure the gelding brought him back without much help. They were two of a rare kind.

Many of the horses were coughing, with snotty noses, and feeling lethargic. I suspected that they had contacted shipping fever from being near the racetrack in Gillette. It is common for that to happen. I asked Jamie Nail to give Red and Gus another round of shots. The dust, too, might have had a lot to do with their conditions.

I left the motel and moved into my trailer. I built pens from some of the portable panels for Gus and Red so they could have more room and get out of the dusty stall they were in. My trailer was parked next to the stalls. There was something reassuring and analeptic about the sound of my horses snoring in the night. Gus could saw logs with the best of men. He was such a trusting and sweet-tempered creature that he slept like a baby with no worries. The two of them were like kids waiting for their grain each morning, and I loved them dearly, but Gus will forever live in my dreams.

I strolled by the souvenir trailer next morning and saw a painting on display by another artist with the words, "Commemorative painting of the Cattle Drive 95" over it. That was a direct breach of Derk's contract, which had made him the official commemorative artist on the drive. I was once more dismayed at the way things happened and at the blatant discourtesy and disregard for contracts and commitments that Bud seemed to display. It happened almost everyday.

Skip had told me of an incident that happened in Gillette. A woman had walked up to him, indignant, demanding her money back for "this tape which is defective." She showed Skip a tape in a white cover, and he told her that he had not produced any tapes with a white cover. The tape was a copy of the first of the three videos that he and Derk were producing of the drive. Skip borrowed the defective tape, and when he confronted Susan McCasland with it, she told him that she had, indeed, had copies of the tape made and had sold them.

"They only cost me four dollars each, which was a lot cheaper than yours," she told him. When Skip told her that she was in serious trouble for copying his tape, she assured him that she had talked to her lawyer, and "he said it was no problem at all and perfectly legal." Skip and Derk had copyrighted all videos sold of the cattle drive. It appeared that they were being slowly squeezed out of the drive altogether.

Derk was angry and said that the display of that painting at the souvenir trailer made his contract null and void and opened the door for a lawsuit by him against Bud McCasland. He took pictures of the display for any decisions he would make about bringing charges. I sat mute in a coffee shop while Skip talked, not knowing what to say or do about our situation in general. Each day brought one more surprise that left me dumbfounded and wondering what was to come next.

I had asked Bud several times about the catalog to be printed for the sale in Miles City. Each time he had said he was working on it. In Gillette, I backed him into a corner and almost demanded to know about the catalog.

"Bud, we should have that catalog in the mail ahead of time." He told me that the catalog had already been done and that the Texas longhorn people were distributing it for the drive. "Whoa! You never asked for the description of my horses that will be sold in Miles City," I exclaimed.

"Oh, we just listed it as the horses and steers from the GACD," he laid on my incredulous ears.

For many years I had sung for exotic cow sales all over Texas, and I was familiar with the preparation of the catalogs mailed to prospective buyers. Those catalogs were cardinal to the success of the sales. They had to be distributed far enough ahead of sale time to give the buyers time to make plans to attend. I also knew that a description, bloodline, age, and condition of each animal to be sold were provided in such catalogs. Our sale was doomed from the onset, and I knew it. I was heartsick, disgusted, angry, and helpless to do a damned thing about it. I never asked if the catalog was printed, and I never saw a single one at the ill-fated sale.

Fewer than fifty people attended the afternoon performance of the ranch rodeo and state celebration in Sheridan. But a good crowd came that night. Will and I went to the Cattleman's Steakhouse and wrapped ourselves around rib-eyes and red wine, and I got to bed about 10 p.m. As I crawled into my sleeping bag, I saw a line of cars leaving the grounds. The take from that ranch rodeo would not make a dimple in the GACD debt.

Some of the wranglers, including Larry Orrell, Jess Herbers, and Jeff Christenson, did not leave Sheridan with us because they had not been paid. No one had been paid, but only those three remained behind. They said they would not ride until they were paid. They were promised that they would be paid the following Monday or Tuesday. The men were getting even more cynical about Bud's promises.

When we left Sheridan, the rumor floated through camp that President Clinton was going to meet us at the Montana border and ride with us on that day. And what effect did it have on the cowboys and me? Well, right after the subjects of water for the horses, what was for supper, where and how far to the next camp, and what were we going to have for snacks along the way, we vaguely wondered if we would have to put up with eleventy-seven Secret Service guys and a ton of press if the prez showed up and if it might bring us more publicity and a bit of financial help, too.

We watched for helicopters when it crossed our minds. I wondered if he could ride a horse any better than he could play golf or the sax. Beyond that, it just wasn't important. Nothing was crucial or momentous or compelling. We did not need the presence of the president. We bitched and moaned, because we were mere Homo sapiens who had lived the material life so long that we automatically wanted material and man-made things and thus believed that we needed them. But had we been forced to choose between having all the material things we had had all our lives or living the life we were living. I, for one, would have had no problem making a choice, and I believed that the cowboys felt as I did. We had something out there – an entity so wondrous and magical that nothing could compete or compare. We did not need the president to find water or a good camp or to guarantee lettuce and tomatoes on our bologna sandwiches or soft ground for sore hooves – we could handle all that ourselves. Nothing was important beyond those things – certainly not President Clinton or his press or security or helicopters and man-made noise.

Being outside, in God's living room, surrounded by His partner, Mother Nature, is an experience existing both inside and outside the human mind. The exhilarating feeling of aliveness, of tasting sweet freedom of the soul and body, of living in total abandonment, is in unequivocal contrast to our programmed, disciplined, and predictable lives. Watching those ridgebacks stoically plodding down miles and miles of earth and asphalt, feeling and smelling the hairy beauty of a horse underneath, and not caring if it was Sunday or February or the year 2000, made my heart swell with new life and the sheer joy of living. It was so easy to change my priorities. Levels of importance were drastically different out there. So we rode twenty-one miles into warm sunshine, stopped at the Tongue River for great sandwiches (with lettuce, tomatoes, onion, and tons of mustard and mayo), played in the shallow, rocky, river, relaxed, visited, and took great pictures.

When we got back onto the trail, I rode swing between Claude and J W Beeson. Claude and I talked some, and he told me that Miss Jayne was going to bid on Gus at the sale. I had mixed feelings about that bit of news. I was happy that Jayne would maybe own Gus and felt that he would have a good home on her ranch with Claude there, but I also felt a chill at the thought of never waking up again to his sweet, gentle snore and feeling the touch of his velvet muzzle, nudging for some favor or tidbit to eat.

When we crossed into majestic Montana, we were met by the warm, friendly citizens of Miles City and welcomed by my soon-to-be friend, Kelly Reed, and his entourage of businessmen, best buddies, and friends. Mayor George Kurkowski had ridden with me part of the day but had gone on ahead to be there for us when we arrived. We unsaddled, fed, and headed for Kelly's beer wagon. There, we gulped down $2 beer and swapped lies and tall tales, and I played the guitar and sang and finally lay down my exhausted body to sleep around 10 p.m.

No sleep came because the hired musicians had set up their stage and "entertained" us until 1 a.m. They were loud and close to my trailer. I finally got up and looked out to an empty camp while their music continued without an audience. I was pissed and tired and sleepy. I walked over and asked why they were still playing. In a grumpy voice, I explained to the young lady that we got up at four in the morning and that we had ridden twenty-one miles that day and why in hell did they not call it a night and go home while we still had three hours to collapse in.

"We were hired to play, and we just want to earn our money and not cheat those who are paying us," the girl said in a small voice. She couldn't understand why I was angry. That music was so loud that it could have blown the lid off a water tower at five hundred yards. Next morning, I was still wondering just who in hell they thought they were playing to after everybody had gone to bed. Well everybody, that is, but Jim Donaldson and Aaron Payne and the little young things who had come to welcome them to Montana. Yeah, I am a grouch-ass when I am tired.

"Few things keep me awake, but that damned band sure did," I heard Will say next morning.

The weather was hot, the trail was dry, and the roads were gravel and treacherous on the steers' hooves. The dust was constant like the wind that blew it on, around, and through us. Each day I would catch a ride with one of the equipment trucks back to camp for my truck and trailer, which were covered inside and out with a thick layer of dust. Driving slowly did not prevent that infernal stuff because I would inevitably meet the boys in the trucks again on the way to the new camp and eat their dust again. My bedroll was gritty, my socks were gritty, and I didn't bother trying to keep dust out of my food because it was useless. And anyway, I couldn't tell any difference in the taste.

I rode ahead of the herd and camp, alone, across the foothills. At the base of the mountains, in the silence of the infinite capaciousness of wild and desolate Montana, it was just me and Gus and my thoughts. The Tongue River meandered cross the country between and beneath sheer cliffs and mammoth boulders, its clear, sparkling water inviting and cold.

At one camp, two ladies, Misty and Sherri, cooked great lasagna for us with awesome homemade brownies for dessert. One night we camped on the ranch of Sherri's in-laws, Bill and Ann McKinsie. Ann invited me to come to the house and shower. I washed my hair and basked in the luxury of all that water and a fan blowing on my naked body. It was the first time I had been cool for some time. I parked the trailer under giant cottonwoods in Ann's front pasture in weeds six feet tall and as thick as jungle. It gave cool respite from the hot sun. Will came over and pitched his bedroll nearby under the shade of one of those giants.

The cowboys were angry because they still had not been paid. Miles City residents sent $2,500 for them (that amounted to $100 for each of them), and Will was sitting in our camp sippin' and did not get his share. I believe he got it only after demanding it from Bruce later on. Bud had come to camp, stayed only for a short time, and had gone back to Fort Worth. The cowboys said he made no explanation about the money due them.

I don't believe Bud has a dime, but why doesn't he just tell us that and let us share his frustrations? I racked my dusty brain for any explanation to the situation and its possible outcome. I made excuses to myself for Bud one minute and cussed him for his stupidity or lack of communication with the men the next. I believed that every man there would have understood if Bud had told them he was out of money and asked them to keep going and help him make it to Miles City. He just would not talk to or believe in those men, or he did not give a damn about them – it had to be one or the other. The situation had been a struggle inside of me since the beginning, and the few times I had talked to him, I had found him to be a master of evasion.

Ashland, Montana, was a small, scrappy town filled with Indian shanties, standing stark in bare yards that were littered with plastic toys, sagging fences, and trucks and cars sitting on jacks or blocks, with goats and horses grazing around them. The people were friendly at the Stop and Go, where Will and I went for dinner one night. We all delighted in finding our bodies under layers of dust in the showers at the local school. The one café in town served decent food and had a back room filled with gambling machines, including a nickel machine similar to a slot. The pie and the coffee were good, and it was cool inside.

Jim Peck took a load of steers on to Miles City. I believe they were crippled and couldn't handle any more of the continuous gravel roads. Jack Boles had joined us again, looking hale and hearty. Bruce, Jack, and the souvenir man all had separate rooms in the motel there, which was full. The owner was quick to stop anyone from taking a shower in a friend's room. When I could not get a shower elsewhere, I bathed in a bucket at camp when water was available.

Gus, Red, and many of the other horses were coughing almost constantly. It was either because of dust or because they were still suffering with shipping fever. I gave Gus and Red shots again, in case it was a virus. Jamie Nail was threatening to sue Bud for the money owed him. *You will have to get in line, Jamie.*

I was counting the days until Keely and Kenny would arrive in camp, and I was down to three. I could not stay mad or unhappy for long with those thoughts rambling around in my mind.

Something so funny happened outside of Ashland, I still laugh each time I think of it. We had to cross the Tongue River with the cattle and ride across an Indian reservation. The Indians were not friendly and had told our "bosses" that we were not going to cross over the reservation with the cattle unless we paid $1,000 per mile. The distance across the reservation was about four miles with no other way to go. We had camped on a ranch owned by Mark Bloxum just outside of Ashland. The Indians proposed that if Mark Bloxum would lead us across the reservation, they would permit us free passage.

Mark went to our souvenir trailer the night before we left and wanted to buy a commemorative buckle from the souvenir man. The word came back that the souvenir man was "extremely rude" to Mark, so he left the trailer angry and did not buy the high-dollar buckle. Next day, when the cowboys reached the boundary where Mark was to meet them to lead them across the reservation, Mark was waiting at the fence and shouted to Ace Wright and whoever else was riding point that day to "stop right there!"

"Who the hell are you? Get out of our way!" Ace was terse and abrupt with his demand.

"I own this land, mister. Who the hell are you?" Mark told them that he had gone home the night before and "just got madder and madder as the night wore on at the arrogance of "that son of a bitch running that souvenir trailer. "Now, before you cross this land with those cattle, I want two of those buckles from that trailer, and I may go back there and whip his ass yet."

Someone had to ride back to camp and get the buckles for Mark before we could continue. How I would like to have been there and seen the look on the souvenir man's face when the cowboy came for those buckles. And I believe I could have sold tickets to all to watch that ranch owner whip his ass. That could have been a money-raiser for the drive.

The tires on the Ford trucks were as slick as a baby's butt, and those gravel roads were eating them alive. Bud's son, one of the drivers, had a flat almost everyday. The others complained that they did not have money to have the flats fixed and certainly not to buy new tires. It had come to that. I heard some of the cowboys and drivers had used their own money for gasoline several times. They tried to talk me out of my spare tire. I declined. Will had not been paid in two months. That was one month more than the rest because Bud had carried Will's check home to Fort Worth on the visor of the van. When Bruce called Bud and told him that he had not paid Will, Bud promised to mail the check to camp immediately. Will never received that check.

Ed and Nan Creel told me that in a magazine or weekly newspaper in Montana, they had seen a copy of the letter I had written for the cowboys back in Oberlin, Kansas. I wondered if Walt Secrest or Dancer Davis had been the one who saw to it that the Montana publication received a copy of the controversial letter.

Legendary singer, Hank Thompson, came to one of our camps and set up a portable stage with his band and performed. Walt and his crew, minus Lon Sowers, were there, sitting near the front in folding chairs. The band fronting the star called Walt and Renny up to the bandstand for a tribute to the drive and lauded them for their contribution to its success. No one else was recognized. Walt was far from humble, and Dancer was talking to all who would listen.

The man running the concession stand spoke out in an unusually loud voice: "All drinks and food is free to Walt Secrest and his group. Everybody else pays." I considered the grandstanding and loud announcement to be rude and discomforting and totally uncalled for.

The GACD cowboys stood around silent and subdued, and my heart was heavy for them. Some of the cowboys were not so subdued and talked of revenge in Miles City in the form of an "ass-whipping" for Bruce and Jim and Bud. No blame was placed on Walt or Dancer by the younger cowboys, but some of the more mature men believed that things had really become "hostile and warlike" between the two groups. That hostility became more apparent the next day when we found padlocks on our next campsite.

Hell, I think, it would be fun just to see them get into a brawl in the middle of this dusty gravel road. I could sell tickets, and the Montana boys could sell beer off the beer truck.

Parts of the Tongue River cut through tall mountains with sheer cliffs dropping down on the narrow gravel roads that we had to drive the sore-footed steers along. It was pure agony for them. The sun was hot, the dust almost unbearable, and the days were long. The river meandered like a silvery ribbon, cold, shallow, and beautiful with its sharp rock bottom. I bathed in that river several times and was torn between the enjoyment of a clean body and suffering the bone-chilling cold. At least it wasn't as muddy as Willow Oak Creek, in Texas, where Sidney and I used to swim, and there were no water moccasins to deal with.

Along the river one day, Sonya, a young outrider, had a wreck on her horse and broke her arm. Her horse bolted through the herd, causing a near-stampede. The cowboys held them, and then one old steer stopped under a tall cedar tree to scratch. The tree had squatters. A swarm of angry bees in a cluster the size of a quart jar covered the steer, causing him to shake his head vigorously and switch his tail, but other than that, he handled the onslaught without much ado.

After that extremely long and eventful day, a meeting was scheduled in camp because the men were waiting for the late payroll. Rumors had been flying that some were going to quit if they did not get paid. No checks were forthcoming. Will said later that some of the men were paid part of their money and that he was supposed to see Jim and Bruce about his "part" of that money. He did not attend the meeting and failed to get his part. He knew no further details. The money that Bud had promised on the twenty-first had not materialized for the last payroll, and Jess Herbers, Jeff Christenson, and Larry Orrell had called Bud's office in Fort Worth. We all wondered if they had been fired, because they had not been in camp since we had departed Sheridan.

Will said, "I talked to Bruce today, and he said Bud would send my check directly from Fort Worth to Diana (Will's wife) in Ardmore. Bruce said Bud would be in camp tonight and give me a partial cash payment on my check. The men in camp are beginning to talk money and how to get it legally."

In one camp, Jackie Donaldson dived into the Tongue River and cut his side open. It had to be sewed up inside and out. He had hit a rock, and some of it had to be removed from his side. That was not the only wreck that week. One of the outriders crossed an irrigation ditch, and his horse bucked him off. Will went to rescue him and found him unconscious. He was taken to the hospital twenty miles away, and for hours he did not know what had happened or where he was. He had a bruised hip and a concussion. The number of outriders increased each day that we got closer to Miles City.

I savored the wonderful feeling inside, in spite of the hot sun, on Sunday, Aug 27, counting the hours until Kenny and Keely would arrive the next day. The dust was unbearable, and the gravel roads reminded me of the old washboard that Ma used to scrub the soil out of dirty overalls. Roads shook every bolt loose on a vehicle, and they were wearing out the hooves on the steers and the dust was causing the horses to cough constantly.

We rode a hot, dry eighteen miles only to find padlocks on the gates and then rode on to the other camp, which was on wheat stubble with lots of room. I found a distant spot for some privacy and pitched my tent. Down the hill from me, the Miles City boys (Zane, Kelly, Ron, and Johnny) came with the beer wagon, and we had a blast. Nan and Ed Creel showed up, and we played and sang at the beer wagon and consumed generous amounts of wine, beer, and trusty old J&B. Life was good.

An eighty-four-old man pitched his tent almost on top of mine, and I cursed generously but silently. *Damn! There ain't no privacy anywhere around here. Here I've got Methuselah on one side and Will on the other, I will have to walk nine miles just to pee.*

In the night a hell-bound wind came up with some rain, and I heard Will and the old man scrambling for tarps to cover themselves and their bedrolls. We were camped on a hill overlooking the pasture where the horses and steers were. The camp was loaded with outriders in fancy motor homes and trailers. Will and I were near the back part of the camp, and the cook trailer was at the foot of the hill, about a quarter of a mile from my trailer.

One of the young cowboys came looking for Will. "Will's gelding is sick. I can't get him to move. He just stands like he was glued to the ground, and I can't tell what is wrong with him."

I did not know where Will was. In a little while, I wandered out into the pasture where the gelding was standing. I ran my hand over his body, feeling for something – I didn't know just what. He wouldn't move, in spite of my tugging on his halter. Under his throat, I found a hard knot. No wonder he could not or would not move – he was having difficulty breathing. It looked like distemper or strangles, as distemper was sometimes called, a deadly disease. Distemper is akin to pneumonia in human beings. The gelding's throat was full of mucus that was slowly closing his windpipe.

When Will showed up, he couldn't get one of the trucks to haul the gelding to a vet somewhere. He was furious at first but then resigned himself to wait. I believe that the gelding survived only because he was tough. He did have distemper and was not able to finish the drive. Will went back to Montana and got the gelding after the drive was over.

Next day, I heard Keely before I saw her, squealing, "Mama, Mama!" She came running up that steep hill to the top where I was camped, and what a delicious feeling to hold her and hug her and be smothered with her kisses and joy. Kenny and his girlfriend were behind, and what a day we had. That was the first time I had met Myra. She was beautiful and gregarious, and she had a genuine, sweet, smile. It seemed that my son had found someone special. We talked and laughed, played with Gus and Red, and Keely bunked in the trailer with me. The world was great, and life was indeed good.

Myra and Kenny went sightseeing, and Keely rode with me on the trail. We talked about her life with her children and husband and our closeness and how our lives had paralleled. She has always been special to me. She is tough as nails; she can work rings around any two you can pick, but she brought many hardships upon herself with her idealistic and loyal heart. Not prone to heed advice from anyone, especially family, she takes life in stride and fights the self-imposed adversity she faces almost daily. I am proud of her for overcoming so many obstacles – two divorces, husband abuse, and ill health, and just as her daddy fought with no chance of winning, she fights an addiction to cigarettes. We have always been comfortable with each other's company, but with her, I fought the hardest and made up the quickest of any of my children. When she was born, her daddy looked down at her little skinny red and wrinkled body and said: "Now, I have two Annies!" It was only fitting that she should be with me in the home stretch of one of the great moments of my life.

We rode toward Miles City, with Keely topside Red, to his and Gus's joy. Those two horses were best buddies and always content just to be together. We were going to complete the drive; we were going to be successful in spite of all the snags, upsets, and bad weather. I had ridden from Texas to Montana, across my wonderful Wyoming, just like in my childhood dreams. I looked over at my beautiful baby daughter, lost in her own thoughts. I thought of my Kenneth, her father, dead for twenty-eight years.

I know he must be proud. Hell! He was proud of everything I ever did and usually built things up to be greater than they really were. This would make him bust the buttons off his shirts – the same shirts that he went around bragging that his wife had made. Oh, and how he would love to see Keely and Kenny, all grown up, both lean as whips and looking just like him. Hey, they did good in spite of their mother, who ran blind through their growing up. I wish my brother and sister could see me now, with my two babies. Maybe they, too, would be proud of me.

My son is head and shoulders taller than his father was. He is a gentle giant who was a Little League coach at the age of sixteen, worked as a caddy at the country club, paid for his first car when he was fifteen, and has grown into a wonderful man who is loved by all who know him.

I felt like I might just burst with the dozens of thoughts tumbling around in my head. I was on parade for all those whose praise was manna for my very being. I thought of my brother – my stoic, undemonstrative Dale, who made such a great name for himself, first in television, and then in Congress. Dale, who never seemed to know that I existed except when I embarrassed him with my impetuosity, my profanity, or dirty jokes. He was always a bit afraid of me and Sidney and of our antics when we were growing up. But I cried with joy and awe at the letter he wrote to me at my graduation from the university. I framed it and it hangs beside my degree on my wall.

Dear Ann,

In the 60's I disapproved your plan to become a professional singer. With 4 young children, it was obviously impractical. In the 80's I discouraged you from opening a business. Later when it produced wall-to-wall customers, I encouraged you to open a larger place. In the 90's I branded your plan to enter college as unrealistic. Even though you spurned my sage advice, I must admit you are the only member of our immediate family or our predecessors, to hold a college degree. I love you and I am proud of you. Dale. p.s. In the future, if you should have a yen to move a battleship to Jackson Hole, Wyoming, let me know! I will run up there and find a place for you to park it!

He told me how proud he was of me – and I believed it for the first time in my life. Riding down Montana highways, I could just picture him, sitting in his chair at home watching television and seeing me profiled on Channel 4. I have been little more than a stranger to my sister, who lives so far away, and the chances of our ever healing all the scars are minimal.

Somehow, in some strange way, I felt I had reached a milestone in my life and had atoned for whatever stupid blunders I had made in the past. I suddenly knew that it was not important to impress my siblings. I just had to be happy with myself. I was. I shook the past memories out of my head and came back to the present in the Land of the Big Sky, with my baby girl.

But I could not face the sale and the idea of parting with Red and Gus just yet. I did not permit myself to think about it. I could not conjure any thought of any future event or plan beyond Miles City. I was totally exhausted, broke, excited, anxious, and glad to be alive and with two of my children.

Welcome Great American Cattle Drive AUG. 30-Sep. 3
J. C. PENNEY CO.

KANSAS

20

THE TRAIL'S END

In the predawn hours of Friday, September 1, 1995, I dressed and stepped outside, where trucks, cars, and trailers were arriving in long lines, bringing outriders for the final day with the GACD. Cowboys with hangovers began to crawl out of bedrolls, and the camp was suddenly buzzing like a beehive. Everything was chaotic. George Kurkowski was nervous as a pregnant hooker in a Primitive Baptist Church because he had told the television people we would arrive at the city limits at 10 a. m. sharp. Will and Diana arrived, and Will was still tipsy but happy and laidback and smug as a well-paid lawyer with an acquittal for his client. Will handled his whiskey quite well when Diane was with him. He was clean shaven and rather handsome and quite drunk.

There weren't enough horses to rent to the outriders. People were complaining that they had come from far off and had been promised horses and could not get one. An older man was thrown twice from his rented horse (no fault of a horse that could not buck worth a damn). When he was thrown for the third time, someone persuaded him to ride in a car the rest of the way. Others who had taken a chance and come without making reservations for horses were disappointed at not being able to ride into Miles City with us.

Jim McElroy's wife would be at the city limits with the flags for us to carry down the streets in our end-of-the-trail parade.

George had brought me a boot for my flag. I visited with members of the Fort Worth Sheriff's Posse who were there to police the parade. One posse member, my old friend and customer, Bobby Cloud, would be carrying the Texas Flag, and I would carry the GACD flag, to be second in the parade behind the man carrying Old Glory, and leading the parade along with George. Keely was about twenty-five feet behind me on Red.

Gus looked beautiful, and I had donned my old chaps and favorite boots and my worn old Stetson with a starched shirt and jeans. I looked up to see if I could spot Kenneth, or Mack, or my brother, Dale. I felt like they were somewhere near me. I wanted to shout loud enough to reach that guy in Boyd, Texas who said we would never make it to Miles City.

I looked around at the hundreds of people dressed in their best Western outfits, and I could feel their sheer joy in the moment. The horses sensed the excitement and danced and pranced with impatience to move on down the road.

How does one prepare for a parade over six miles long? A parade going ahead to announce the arrival of 262 head of longhorns, driven from the heart of Texas, across six states, for the first time in 109 years. The Fort Worth Sheriff's Posse took their places at the head and along the way to keep order. I was so proud they were there.

We were late leaving camp, but we arrived at the city limits of Miles City right on time. The trip into town seemed short because of the constant lines of cars and people and the happenings along the way, cameras clicking, friends and relatives of those in the parade waving and shouting, and the excitement of knowing that we were at last reaching the end of the trail. It is all a blur of heart-stopping anxiety, anticipation, and wonder at just what we had done. For six months I had watched the faces of those along the highways and roads. I had felt the hope and hunger and deep wishes of the onlookers to be with us and to experience the feeling of freedom and fulfillment and accomplishment.

Someone said that Walt and his crew had arrived before us

and were camped somewhere on the outskirts, waiting until the next day to parade down the streets. They had promised back down the trail that they would not go into Miles City ahead of us. In spite of the excitement of the moment, I felt melancholy for Walt and Dancer and Walker and the rest – like a part of us was missing – a hole in the whole of us. We had made it, but we had arrived in shards. *Why do you always have to have everything perfect? Hell, we are here. We are all in one piece and still on our feet – or with butts in the saddle. Be happy with what you got, old woman, and enjoy the moment.*

I reached down and hugged Gus and smiled at the people lining the streets of Miles City. They were there to see us as well as a group of wagon trains from across the nation that was scheduled to come through Miles City that same day. The city had asked Walt to wait until the next day for his entrance. Walt paid no attention and brought his crew down the streets shortly after we arrived. George told me later that he had given in and let Walt parade that day, too. George was a kind gentleman, and Walt was determined. That combination proved to be successful for Walt and the Lonesome Drovers.

I did not watch them when they came into town. I was thinking about my horses and the auction. I was worried about how much money my equipment and horses would bring. I knew that no catalog had been printed and that with no catalog there would be few, if any, buyers. I was torn between the anguish of leaving my two old friends behind and going back to Texas without them, and facing the fact that I would not only leave them but also come out with the short stick on what they would bring in the auction. *Damn! How I wish I could take you home with me, old pal. You are going to freeze your white ass off in the harsh winters here. God, I hope whoever buys you will learn to love and appreciate you as I do.* I hugged Gus and patted his silky hide and fought back tears. There would be time for them later, when I was alone.

Something else blew my dress up. I had heard that Bud was going to charge everyone $10 to come to the auction. I was astounded. I considered that to be just one more stupid decision. To charge people to come spend money seemed to be the icing on that collapsed cake that he had baked. I did not think about that for long.

For the first time, I had done something just to satisfy myself and not merely to impress someone. It no longer mattered what *others* thought. I had arrived! I was no longer listening for the applause – just enjoying the warm and fuzzy feeling, and *they* no longer existed.

I glanced back to the years and realized I had been on stage every moment of my life – spending each waking hour performing, striving to please, but never quite perfecting my performance. *I feel light as a feather, almost transparent, giddy, and happy to be alive, and I forgot for a moment about my horses. I have great kids, great friends, family, and good health. I have survived not only these six months of my life, but also financial and personal loss, heartache, and years of loneliness, and hey, I am OK. I don't have to impress anyone – just me – wonder why it has taken me so long to feel this way? Why did I always need assurance and recognition? Why did it take a damned cattle drive for me to win an Oscar for self-esteem?* My hand tightened around the GACD flag, I sat taller in the saddle, touched Gus with the other hand, and my grin was pure Texas.

Miles City was bursting at the seams. Cowboys were everywhere, the streets were lined with traffic, laughter, and the feeling of celebration had consumed everyone.

Frank and Marie Putt had been unable to get a room anywhere within one hundred miles of Miles City, even though they had called months before. Frank bought a thirty-five-foot motor home, and they were there for me and the six-mile-long parade. I looked for them in the crowd but never saw them. Kenny and Myra yelled from in front of Kelly Reed's Log Cabin Bar, and I spit out a blood-curdling Texas yell, and the quiet, subdued crowd came to life.

Gus seemed to step higher, his ears were forward, and he fairly glistened in the morning sun. I glanced back and saw Keely and Red, and she was sitting tall in the saddle and echoing my Texas yells.

Through the main drag lined with the natives and with those who had driven for hundreds of miles to see us finish, we rode out to the fair grounds to celebrate and let the realization of what we had done soak in, and to wait for the auction scheduled for the third of September.

I was thirsty, and after finding stall for Gus and Red, I gathered Keely and headed for the Log Cabin Bar. My heart was heavy with thoughts of leaving those two behind, but I really needed the money. I had no place to go myself, without considering where to put two horses and then caring for them while writing a book with scant income. My common sense assured me that I was making the right decision, but my heart was lower than seaweed.

They danced in the streets, and the bars blossomed with bubbly festivity, music, bent elbows, and celebration. We had dinner at a café downtown after a long wait. Everybody was congenial and congratulatory. Marie and Frank were parked at an RV park just off the main drag and insisted on my staying in the bus with them. I declined, and Keely and I bunked in my old trailer at the fair grounds close to Gus and Red. It would be two days before the auction.

Frank cooked steaks for us at the trailer one evening, and we sipped wine and enjoyed each other under the tall trees in the park. The kids visited the museums, went shopping, and watched the people who gathered there.

Next night Marie, Frank, Keely, and I followed George and Peg, winding through the dusty night to the wagon train for a party there in a pasture in the dark. Everybody was drunk and rowdy and loud. On the trip out there, we ate a zillion pounds of dust following behind the string of cars. It was laughable next morning, but that night was a bitch.

We had a barbecue at the John Deere House, and the awards

were given out. The town of Miles City gave us each a bronze bust of a Cowboy, and George made a sweet and warm speech, congratulating us for what we had done. Bud handed out the silver and gold buckles and told us what a great job we had done, and then he also gave buckles to his son and to others who had not been on the drive all the way. As with the drovers and wranglers, my buckle was engraved with the words, "Official Cowboy." Those buckles were supposed to be for those of us who worked as cowboys all the way from Texas to Montana, and giving them to those who had not, took away some of the magic.

I felt the magnitude of the moment anyway. We ate barbecue and beans and the trimmings and said goodbye to each other. I hugged those I could find in the big crowd, gathered some addresses, and drove back to the fair grounds. I felt strange. I wanted that feeling of accomplishment to run through my body, leaving me with a high better than Scotch. I wanted us all to hug and kiss and cry together for the thing we had achieved. We had met for the first time in our lives and lived together for six months under the most trying of circumstances. But we all went our separate ways, doing whatever we did for those two days before it was finally over in Miles City. So why was I waiting for something else? That warm "together" feeling just wasn't there for me. I have often wondered if any of the others felt as I did. Maybe I did not feel as close to those cowboys as I wanted to believe I was. And perhaps we all were just so tired and glad it was over that we had no adrenaline left.

I found Skip out behind the arena where Gus and Red were stabled, and he filmed me saying goodbye to the longhorns in a poem I had written at his request. The words came easy for me. They were from my heart. . .

Longhorns, longhorns
from beneath the Lone Star,
majestic, mighty bovines
indelible in this heart of mine,

may the grass be rich and green
wherever you are. . . .

Old doggies, old ridgebacks,
my buddies, my friends
I'm sad but proud
as we come to the end
of the trail where you led us
to worldly acclaim.
As we walked in the hoof prints
of your ancestors once again.

With quiet purpose you plodded
up to the Northwest,
through hail storm and bitter cold.
You've proven you're the best
of the breed that made history,
brought cowboys into the world,
and you've left a warm feeling
in the heart of this old girl.

Longhorns, longhorns
beneath the Lone Star,
in the land of the Big Sky
We will part by and by.
May the grass be rich and green
wherever you are. . . .

Skip and I talked about how things had turned out and speculated on his chances of ever getting back his investment and the money owed him.

"I don't believe we will ever get our money. I don't think Bud will ever be able to pay us because he isn't going to make what he thinks on this auction, but I still have the copyrights to over 4000 still life pictures and 50 hours of video." *What a magnificent motion picture those videos would make and the pictures are priceless and one-of-a-kind that this gentle man owns. I hope some day the world will be able to see them.*

Sadly, I had to agree with him. Things looked bleak for the auction, but I went to the table that had been set up and registered my horses for sale. I took Gus's registration papers and the application for registration on Red and his family registrations to the people at the table.

I was way down on the list posted next day for running Gus and Red through the auction. That was not good. Those at the top in an auction usually bring the most money. I noticed that the Herbers were near the top of the list with all their horses. It seemed odd that all their horses' numbers were drawn close to first. That was good luck for them. I later heard some of the cowboys grumbling about "favoritism" concerning the Herbers' luck in the draw.

I did not have time to think about that long. There were other things to take care of. I pulled my trailer into the line with the equipment to be sold and took my tack to the space allotted for it. I looked at my beautiful saddle with my name embossed on it, and it seemed a lifetime since I had picked it out back in Fort Worth. That was only the third saddle I had ever owned solely mine.

◆ ◆ ◆ ◆

I remembered the first saddle I ever had, and chuckled. It was given to me by an old man in Greenville, Texas. I was working in a small café there, and he used to come in for coffee, and I would sing with the jukebox for him and tell him about riding horses and learning how to rope and run barrels. He said that I should have a saddle of my own. He took me close to Rockwall, Texas, and introduced me to a man who made saddles and I told him what I wanted, and he made it for me. It was plain rawhide with a roping seat, narrow swell, and low cantle, and very well made. That was the most beautiful saddle in the world to me. I was about twenty years old. A young man who was that saddle maker's apprentice helped to make that saddle. His name was Billy Cook.

There were light, funny moments in Miles City. Keely and I had spotted an old Dodge truck driving down the street with a Texas license plate during the parade. The mustached cowboy driving looked very Texan, and we laughed and talked about him. Later, in the Log Cabin Bar, Keely found that cowboy and brought him over to our table.

"Mama, this guy is from Graham, Texas. He is here to try and collect money that Bud owes him for T-shirts that were sold to Bud back in Texas before the drive started."

"Yeah," he drawled, "he owes me eight grand that he has promised to pay about ten times."

I looked with amusement and doubt at that man with his handlebar mustache and generous beer belly and laid-back countenance. *This guy will have to get in line, and I doubt he will make it out of this bar in time to collect any money from Bud.*

Wrong!

On the first performance of the championship ranch rodeo that night, that Graham cowboy sauntered to the ticket booth with the deputy sheriff and collected the night's take. Along with the take in the next performance, he got the remainder of his eight thousand. We heard about it next day in the bar. That shows how little I know about Graham cowboys, beer bellies, and ingenuity. He may be the only soul who ever gets his money owed by the Great American Cattle Drive.

The auction was a complete disaster. Many of the steers did not bring market price, and many of the horses were pulled out and taken home. I saddled Gus to show in the ring. I had a lump in my throat the size of a bowling ball, and my chest felt like a loaded dump truck was sitting on it. I remembered fifty-five years before when Mack traded our plow animals for his first John Deere tractor and how he kept two mares in spite of Lettie's disapproval, because I cried so hard and begged him to.

There was no Mack in Miles City to rescue me from the pain

of leaving my horses behind. Stark reality told me I would indeed have to go through with it.

Without my knowing it, Carolyn Hunter, editor of *Trails* magazine, took my picture crying behind the bleachers and she published it with my September story for the publication. Skip caught me in my agony with his camera. Everybody identifies with sadness, I suppose.

I sat in the saddle on that faithful horse for the last time and thought of the tears I had shed over animals in all of my idealistic, sentimental years. I thought of all the joy and companionship those creatures had brought, of the knowledge and wisdom and understanding they possessed, of their total honesty, and of how they accept one for whatever one happens to be at any given moment.

Gus performed like a champ in the sale ring, always ready and eager to please me. When the auctioneer looked at me for the final nod, confirming that I would accept the price bid, I felt like Brutus must have felt when he betrayed Caesar. The mallet fell, and I rode out of the show ring limp with the emptiness in my gut. I unsaddled Gus, carried the saddle to the tack tables, hugged him for the last time, and never looked back again. I could not face him and see his trusting eyes asking why I was leaving him.

Horses forget quickly, but that horse will be in my heart until they strew my ashes in Buck Creek, in Palo Pinto County Texas. I walked away, to begin the first day of the rest of my life. . . .

EPILOGUE

BACK UP THE TRAIL

I give thanks to a higher power responsible for the many gifts bestowed upon me. My family, my friends, the joys of learning through adversity, discovery, and temporary freedom from modern society; and the wonder of wide open spaces, creatures, and nature that has filled my life with great meaning.

The six-month journey with those cowboys was a revelation. I grew younger in the joy of companionship with the generation behind me, and I met and touched great people who go about their lives quietly, creating, giving, making tracks, raising families, and never making waves. I saw the world between a horse's ears, came to understand the huge impact animals have on our lives, and how that helps us to better understand humanity with all its warts and blemishes. The cattle drive was a stepping stone to understanding the heart and soul of Annie Golightly.

We lost five horses on the drive. The steers arrived in Montana in better shape than when they left Fort Worth. We had arguments, disagreements, harsh words, disappointments, hideous weather, lousy food, and those little street urchins that we could have done without much of the time. But those kids did cleanup and setting up of camp that none of us wanted to do. I give thanks for that.

We formed new friendships, overcame obstacles and sickness, witnessed nature at her finest, escaped the hum-drum of everyday life, while finding and discovering our inner strengths and limits.

Bud McCasland had a dream of driving cattle over the trails of the nineteenth century trail blazers, who left a legacy of courage, determination, and tenacity, along with new roads for those who followed. Nobody believed we could do what we did. Bud had the guts and chutzpah to organize us and send us on the trail to Montana. In an article for the *Fort Worth Star Telegram*, September 4, 1995, Art Chapman summed up the outcome of the cattle drive: Bud had hoped to raise $3 million for his budget, but when the cattle and cowboys left Fort Worth, there was $36 in the bank account. Steers that Bud thought would bring $3,000 each at the auction in Miles City, brought less than market price. The cattle drive was $200,000 in debt, and the equipment turned out to be the most active sale of the day bringing in about $70,000. Many cowboys were also disappointed with the money bid on their horses. The crowd was not interested in the smaller, cutting-bred Texas horses. Gus and Red brought a bit more than I had paid for them, which did little to dissolve the lump in my throat at the auction.

Today, I think back over the trail and give thanks for one of the great events of my life. I don't know where they all are; those young cowboys who carved a niche for themselves in modern history; while paying tribute to the cowboys before them, and proved wrong all who did not believe they could do it. They each hold a spot in my heart from our experience together. Jim and Jodie Hooks live not far from me in Parker County. My buddy and friend who lives on in memory in my heart, is gone. Will Miltimore died after losing his battle with cancer. Diana, his wife, also lost her life to cancer several years before Will. That Oklahoma red head, Jim Donaldson went home and married the sweet girl who waited for him. Jamie Nail is now the *el hefe* on the famous Nail Ranch in West Texas.

Skip Nelson, that delightful Minnesotan and hall of fame photographer who captured my admiration and love of humanity, keeps in touch and of course, furnished the photographs in this book. Derk Hansen, our commemorative artist still resides in St

Paul Minnesota near Skip. A print of his painting of the drive hangs over my bed.

I have tried unsuccessfully to find Gloria Shaefer again. She no longer lives in Toole, Texas. Ed and Nan Creel, owners of a Longhorn ranch in Trinidad, Texas, and among the private sponsors of the drive, believe that Gloria is now in Dallas. I understand Bud is here in Fort Worth, but I have only an email address and have been unsuccessful in making contact with him.

Someone once said, "How do I know what I think until I see what I write?" Now, as I read the words between these covers, I realize they are tonic, psychiatrist, counselor, and healer for me. I learned many things about Annie Golightly in these pages. I discovered myself and found out that I like myself much more than I ever deemed possible. I forgave myself for being an impetuous kid, a hard and tough mother, a foolish lover, and most of all, for being so damned hard on myself. I have stopped believing I have to be perfect, and I now know that not being perfect is damned well OK. I discovered that being a bit "weird" ain't too shabby either. I also came to know what a great life I have had, with tremendous opportunities to meet unforgettable people. I have lived close to my family much of the time and been loved by them deeply. I have fans that are loyal and true no matter what.

I am learning to be more tolerant of the frailties of other people. So I feel that Walt was pushy and overbearing and an egomaniac – and Bud made stupid mistakes and decisions – and the young cowboys stumbled along blindly, faking knowledge of how to drive cattle, handle horses and people – so what? Those men are part of a breed that conquered the West. They are among the "mavericks" who blundered over uncharted lands to "cut trail" for the less-daring, and for the doubters.

I have been called a maverick, a weirdo, and a rebel, but I've never been accused of being doubtful or shy about my ventures. I was never "one of the gang." You can take that and a dollar and buy a cup of coffee, but there isn't enough money to buy the feeling of accomplishment I have about that cattle drive. My relationship with those men is of little importance but my understanding of self is the "fat hog that I cut in the butt" (as Ma would say when someone did something outstanding). The cattle drive was one more chapter in a charmed life of joy, accomplishment, love, and unbelievable fun. It was a stepping stone to greater things in the future. Most of all, it was the key that unlocked the door to a new and wondrous self-esteem.

To all of the cowboys, young and older, I salute you. I would not have missed that experience for an added ten years on my life.

The human spirit is a light that shines over the world, disputing the words of cynics, proving to naysayers that anything worth dreaming is worth doing. . .

Annie Golightly Fall of 2006

Today we are but silt that drifted down
into the sea of humdrum. . .
No more do we soar with the eagle
or ride the White Horse, racing across prairies
with the ghosts of Goodnight, Loving, and Chisum. . .
No more do we smell the breath
of vast fields of alfalfa and the shimmering wheat
or chase the wild *cimmarone*
listening to the click click of his mighty horns
and tasting the hot fear of his thundering hooves
in stampede!
We dance no more with butterflies
through blankets of wild flowers,
sing songs around a campfire, or
awaken to morning's dew
bathing bedroll, boots, and Stetsons. . .

We have returned, our wings once more clipped,

our traces hooked, our backs bent in civilization
in the here, the now, the todays
The White Horse is gone,
But the dreams live on. . . .